£16.01

GCSE Health & Social Care

for EDEXCEL

Double Award Student's Book

Angela Fisher, Stephen Seamons
and Mike Ancil

endorsed by
edexcel

Acknowledgements

Photos:

p.iv 2009 © elenathewise. Image from BigStockPhoto.com; p.v © Andrey Mirzoyants/Fotolia; p.2 © iStockphoto.com/Damir Cudic; p.3 © Galina Barskaya/Fotolia; p.4 © erwinova/Fotolia; p.8 © Vladimir Mucibabic/Fotolia; p.10 © Adam Przezak/Fotolia; p.12 © Kurhan/Fotolia; p.14 © moodboard/Fotolia; p.15 © PCmi/Fotolia; p.18 © iStockphoto.com/Mara Radeva; p.19 © ACE STOCK LIMITED/Alamy; p.20 © Monkey Business/Fotolia; p.24 2009 © endomotion. Image from BigStockPhoto.com; p.26 © iStockphoto.com/Frances Twitty; p.28 © iStockphoto.com/Tomaz Levstek; p.31 © Yuri Arcurs/Fotolia; p.34 © iStockphoto.com/Stephanie Horrocks; p.36 © Diana Lundin/Fotolia; p.39 © Monkey Business/Fotolia; p.42 (top left) © Monkey Business/Fotolia, (top right) © Renata Osinska/Fotolia, (bottom) © iStockphoto.com/Manuela Krause; p.44 © Eddie Mulholland/Rex Features; p.46 © Joe Gough/Fotolia; p.51 (left) © iStockphoto.com/fotoVoyager, (right) © Stephen Finn/Fotolia; p.58 © Kristian Sekulic/Fotolia; p.59 © iStockphoto.com/Karen Town; p.67 © iStockphoto.com/Joey Nelson; p.71 © Thomas Perkins/Fotolia; p.72 © Monkey Business/Fotolia; p.73 © iStockphoto.com/Jennifer Trenchard; p.75 © endostock/Fotolia; p.82 © iStockphoto.com/James Pauls; p.84 © iStockphoto.com/Yarinca; p.87 © Rex Features; p.92 © iStockphoto.com/Rich Legg; p.95 © photoconcepts1/Fotolia; p.96 © iStockphoto.com/Winston Davidian; p.97 © deanm1974/Fotolia; p.100 © Monika Adamczyk/Fotolia; p101 © David Büttner/Fotolia; p.102 © moodboard/Fotolia; p.106 © iStockphoto.com/Sean Locke; p.107 © Natalia Romanova/Fotolia; p.108 © iStockphoto.com/Sean Locke; p.111 © Pavel Losevsky/Fotolia; p.120 © John Edward Linden/archaid.co.uk; p.122 © John Birdsall/John Birdsall/PA Photos; p.125 (top) © Jonathan Hordle/Rex Features, (bottom) © David Hoffman www.hoffmanphotos.com; p.131 2009 © vgstudio. Image from BigStockPhoto.com; p.133 © Roman Milert/Fotolia; p.137 © Imagenatural/Fotolia; p.141 © photoconcepts1/Fotolia; p.144 © Paula Solloway/Photofusion; p.146 © Monkey Business/Fotolia; p.147 © Monkey Business/Fotolia; p.157 © deanm1974/Fotolia; p.159 © Carsten Reisinger/Fotolia; p.160 © Roman Milert/Fotolia; p.168 © Fotolia IV/Fotolia; p.169 2009 © andres. Image from BigStockPhoto.com; p.177 © Allstar Picture Library/Alamy; p.179 © iStockphoto.com/lillisphotography; p.180 (top) © iStockphoto.com/fotoVoyager, (bottom) © foto.fred/Fotolia; p.182 © Denis Pepin/Fotolia; p.183 © iStockphoto.com/technotr; p.185 © ITV/Rex Features; p.187 Reproduced with permission of the Department of Health; p.188 © iStockphoto.com/Joseph C. Justice Jr.; p.193 © Janine Wiedel Photolibrary/Alamy; p.196 © iStockphoto.com/Catherine Yeulet; p.199 2009 © danabeth555. Image from BigStockPhoto.com; p.200 © Burger/Phanie/Rex Features; p.204 © iStockphoto.com/Jim DeLillo; p.206 © iStockphoto.com/Joseph Abbott; p.207 © iStockphoto.com/Christopher O Driscoll; p.208 © Fotolia V/Fotolia; p.214 © iStockphoto.com/Ernesto Solla; p.226 © John Birdsall/John Birdsall/PA Photos; p.228 © Monkey Business/Fotolia; p.229 (top) © Artyom Yefimov/Fotolia, (bottom) © iStockphoto.com/Mark Papas; p.235 (top) © ITV/Rex Features, (bottom) © David/Rupert Hartley/Rex Features; p.237 © Rex Features; p.240 © Rex Features; p.241 © Richard Saker/Rex Features; p.247 © Dragan Trifunovic/Fotolia; p.250 © Steve Maisey/Rex Features; p.252 © Lisa F. Young/Fotolia; p.253 © iStockphoto.com/Jonathan Hill; p.255 © iStockphoto.com/Loic Bernard; p.259 © iStockphoto.com/Vinko Murko; p.261 © Chris Pizzello/AP/Press Association Images; p.262 © iStockphoto.com/Sean Locke; p.263 (top) © Rex Features, (bottom) © Leo/Fotolia; p.264 © iStockphoto.com/Juan Herrera; p.265 © Damian Dovarganes/AP/Press Association Images; p.274 © Monkey Business/Fotolia; p.278 © iStockphoto.com/Aldo Murillo; p.280 © Ray Tang/Rex Features; p.282 © iStockphoto.com/philpell; p.284 (top) © tohengchai/Fotolia, (bottom) © John Birdsall/John Birdsall/Press Association Images; p.286 © Joanne O'Brien/Photofusion

Other:

p.138/139 *New hope for Alzheimer's sufferers after new treatment 'restores memory in minutes'*, by Jenny Hope: Reproduced with permission of the Daily Mail/Mail Online. p.172 World Health Organization logo: Reproduced with permission of the World Health Organization.

United Kingdom: Folens Publishers, Waterslade House, Thame Road, Haddenham, Bucks, HP17 8NT.
Email: folens@folens.com

Ireland: Folens Publishers, Greenhills Road, Tallaght, Dublin 24.
Email: info@folens.ie

Editor: Geoff Tuttle
Editorial advisor: Sue Morris
Text design and page layout: Neil Sutton at Pumpkin House (studio@pumpkinhouse.demon.co.uk)
Cover design: Jump To!
Cover images: (left) © Monkey Business/Fotolia; (centre left) © Monkey Business/Fotolia; (centre right) Marzanna Syncerz/Fotolia; (right) © moodboard/Fotolia
Illustrations: Debbie Hinks and Tony Randell

First published 2009 by Folens Limited.

British Library Cataloguing in Publication Data. A catalogue record for this publication is available from the British Library.

ISBN 978-1-85008-437-2

Contents

Introduction to the course

You will need to decide whether to follow the Single Award (2HS01) or the Double Award (2HS02) in Health and Social Care. If following the Single Award you will be learning about personal development and relationships, and about the health, social care and early years sectors. When moving to the Double Award, the two additional units will focus on making sure that you understand how to maintain health and well-being, and further developing your knowledge and understanding of some of the key aspects of learning already covered.

The Single Award is made up of **two** units. These are:

Unit	Title	Type of assessment
1 (5HS01)	Understanding Personal Development and Relationships	Externally tested
2 (5HS02)	Health, Social Care and Early Years Provision	Controlled assignment

If you are following the Double Award the additional units will be:

Unit	Title	Type of assessment
3 (5HS03)	Promoting Health and Well-being	Controlled assignment
4 (5HS04)	Health, Social Care and Early Years in Practice	Externally tested

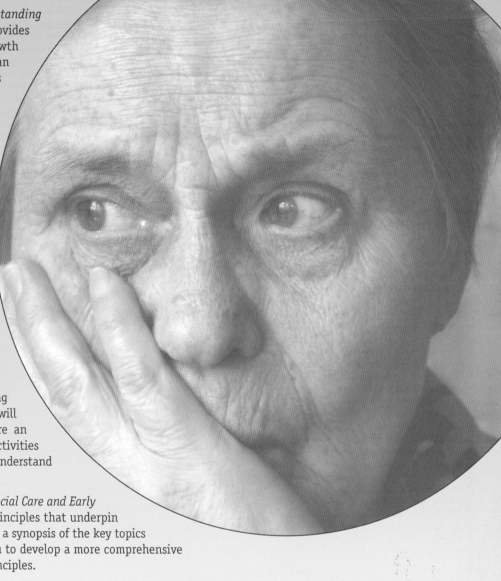

In this book, *Unit 1 (5HS01): Understanding Personal Development and Relationships* provides information about characteristics of growth and development, the factors that can influence the development of individuals and major life changes, showing how individuals can be supported and how such support will help them to cope.

Unit 2 (5HS02): Health, Social Care and Early Years Provision considers the different types of services available to individuals and how these are organized. Some of the job roles available in the sector, and the skills and qualifications needed to do these jobs will be considered. You will also find out about the different types of clients who use the services and the barriers that can prevent people from accessing the services.

When looking at *Unit 3 (5HS03): Promoting Health and Well-Being* you will give consideration to factors that can affect health and well-being, and ways of promoting and supporting health improvements. You will also be asked to use methods to measure an individual's health status. Some practical activities will be incorporated which will help you understand the topics in your student book.

The topics within *Unit 4 (5HS04): Health, Social Care and Early Years in Practice* reflect some of the core principles that underpin any work in these sectors. The unit provides a synopsis of the key topics from the previous three units, allowing you to develop a more comprehensive knowledge and understanding of these principles.

You may, as part of your course, be asked to visit health, social care and early years settings, or you may have visits from specialists from the care sector. Such visits will be very useful for your coursework but you must remember that confidentiality will be very important. For example, you must change the names of the people and the care setting so that they cannot be recognized.

Working through the topics within each unit will help you to gain knowledge, skills and understanding, as well as helping you to prepare for the controlled assignments and external tests.

It will be important to follow the specifications for each of the units, the grading requirements and the guidance given in order to achieve successful outcomes.

We hope you will enjoy using this book and that it helps you to have a broad knowledge of the care sector, as well as being successful in achieving the qualification.

How to use this book

The book is divided into units. These are shown in the contents.

Each unit has sections. These are shown in the contents.

At the beginning of each section is a Getting started page. This shows you what you will know when you have completed the section.

1 Understanding Personal Development and Relationships
Human growth and development

Human growth and development

▶ Getting started

Students will gain an understanding of:

a the different life stages:
  i infancy (0–2 years)
  ii early childhood (3–8 years)
  iii adolescence (9–18 years)
  iv early adulthood (19–45 years)
  v middle adulthood (46–65 years)
  vi later adulthood (65+ years)

b physical growth and development across the life stages, including gross and fine motor skills

c intellectual/cognitive development across the life stages, including language

Key words are shown in bold type. The word check boxes tell you what they mean.

Answering these questions will check your understanding of what you have read.

Extra material for those working at a higher level is shown with a yellow tint behind it.

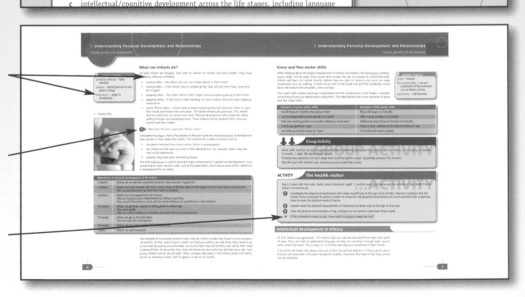

ACTIVITY   Information for new parents

1. Cut out a picture of an infant and paste it onto the centre of a page of A4 plain paper. Draw a line out toward the four corners and write on each physical, intellectual, emotional and social characteristics. For each area of P.I.E.S. give **five** physical, **five** intellectual, **five** emotional and **five** social characteristics.

2. Produce **four** handouts to explain the terms physical, intellectual, emotional and social development, giving **three** examples for each of the P.I.E.S.

3. Draw a timeline and mark in the life stages and the age span for each.

4. Arrange to interview a parent who has a child between 0 and 2 years. Find out how they helped to develop their child's self-esteem.

Doing these activities will help you to develop knowledge, skills and understanding.

CASE STUDY   Fion

Fion, who is four years old, attends playgroup three times each week. The assistant at the playgroup becomes very worried as Fion has bruises on her legs and on her tummy. She notices these when she takes Fion to the toilet. The assistant reports the bruising to the 'named person' at the playgroup.

Two weeks later, Fion is found to have more bruises and she seems to be very sad and cries a lot. The named person at the playgroup telephones social services to report their concerns.

1. Why did the assistant report to the 'named person'?
2. Why do settings that provide care and education for children have a 'named' person?
3. Produce your own short case study to include a different third-party referral.
4. Exchange your scenario with another group and check whether it is a third-party referral.

This is a 'third-party' referral because the playgroup named person has telephoned the social worker. It is not a self-referral because the child or her parent has not done the referring. It is not a professional referral because a professional care worker has not referred the child. Instead, another adult has done the referring and so this is a 'third-party referral'.

Case studies show different health and social care situations. Some show people working in health and social care. Others show clients with health and social care needs.

Group Activity

Try to visit a nursery and a residential home or day-care centre to find out the different methods of referral that have been used. You may wish to do this during work experience. Alternatively your tutor may arrange for two professional care workers to visit your centre

The third way in which clients can be referred to health, social care or early years services is called 'third-party referral'. This is when another person, who is not a professional care worker, refers or draws attention to an individual. The person who makes the referral could be a relative, another professional, a neighbour, an employer or a friend.

In all educational and care settings for children and young people, there has to be a 'named person' who will take responsibility for reporting suspected cases of child abuse. This is a legal requirement and the instructions given within the legislation state that a 'named person' must be in place and should have undertaken the required training. Any suspicions by staff must be reported to the named person, who, after considering the facts, will probably contact a social worker or key worker, who will investigate the concerns further.

Other examples of third-party referral could include:

- a teacher telephoning a social worker because they have concerns about a child

Group activities are for more than one person or the whole class to join in with.

Human growth and development

▶ ▶ ▶ ▶   ASSESSMENT PRACTICE

Section One

1. Which is one of the first physical characteristics of a three-month-old infant?
   - ☐ **A** standing by holding furniture
   - ☐ **B** walking
   - ☐ **C** crawling
   - ☐ **D** moving head from side to side [1]

2. Which is an emotional characteristic of an infant?
   - ☐ **A** listening to a story
   - ☐ **B** cuddling their mother
   - ☐ **C** learning to speak
   - ☐ **D** feeding themselves [1]

Section Two

Megan is one year old and she lives with both her parents in a comfortable three-bedroomed house.

1. Which life stage is she in? Give the age span for this life stage. [2]
2. Describe **two** intellectual characteristics for a one year old. [2]
3. Describe **two** emotional characteristics for a one year old. [2]

Assessment Practices allow you to prepare for your exam or portfolio assignment.

1 Understanding Personal Development and Relationships

Contents

About this unit

The focus of this unit is to develop an awareness of the norms of development and to apply and compare these to the development of individuals in the different life stages. You will need to understand how factors can influence growth and development and contribute to the development of self-concept. At the end of this unit you will be asked to complete a test that is externally assessed to make sure that you have understood the content of the unit:

- the stages and patterns of human growth and development
- the different factors that can affect human growth and development
- the development of self-concept and personal relationships
- major life changes and how people manage their effects
- the role of relationships in personal development.

This unit is tested through a 1 hour and 15 minute written exam with 70 marks available. The paper will contain multiple-choice questions and longer questions based on the case studies and shorter scenarios provided.

The examination paper will test knowledge and understanding and the ability to apply it to a range of contexts. You will need to analyse and evaluate the issues and problems presented. In addition, you will be expected to present conclusions and draw reasoned judgements from the material presented in the short scenarios and case studies. Quality of written communication will be assessed in this unit.

▸ Introducing this unit

Individuals develop at different rates. The rate at which an individual develops is measured against 'the norms' of development. An individual's development is compared to these norms or averages to make a judgement about whether their development matches, is ahead of or behind the 'norm'. In this unit, understanding how individuals who are in different life stages compare with the 'norm' in their physical, intellectual, emotional and social development will be one of the main focus points.

> **To Do...**
> Work with another person to find out when you each learnt:
> * to crawl
> * to stand up
> * to walk.
> Find out how this compared with the norm.

Various factors influence development. Human development is affected by many factors that may have a positive or negative influence on our lives. Understanding the factors that influence human behaviour means that the 'nature versus nurture' debate must be considered. For example, which has the stronger influence – nature or nurture? Is it inherited factors, such as inherited disability, known as the 'nature' factor, or the experiences an individual has, for example, education, known as the 'nurture' factor? In other words are the skills that we possess inherited or are they learnt from social experience? An individual will be influenced by these factors and will behave in a particular way because of such influences.

> **To Do...**
> Draw a picture of 'you' in the middle of the page (a rough outline will be sufficient). Around the picture write words to show what has influenced your development, for example, family.
> Now share the results with another person.
> Which factors are similar? Which are different?
> What do you think has made you different from the other person?

Why do researchers study the behaviour of people? The answer is that if a person intends to work in health and social care settings, they will be very close to people who need to feel respected. Individuals will also need to understand their own feelings and attitudes to make sure that they do not treat others with disrespect or prejudice. When people feel 'at risk' they often become aggressive or defensive, behaving in a way that is threatening to the professional care worker. This is because they do not feel in control of their lives. Not all people will want to be happy, but they will want to have a positive emotional feeling about themselves and to feel satisfied with their lives.

The behaviour of individuals is not constant but is forever changing as a result of environmental, social, economic or cultural issues.

> ✓ **...WORD CHECK**
> **nature versus nurture** – the qualities we are born with that make us what we are, versus how we are influenced when we are young and by our environment.
> **constant** – always the same.
> **environmental** – to do with the surroundings.

Human behaviour is very complex, and to understand why people behave in a particular way, it is necessary to study the influences that have affected the development of an individual such as inherited, social, economic, environmental and psychological influences. It is these influences that will help us to form our 'self-concept'. That is the image that we have of ourselves.

Work with another person. One of you should, in three minutes, tell the other 'how you see yourself', for example, independent, confident, happy, shy. Say 'why' you think you have the characteristics. Then change roles and for three minutes your partner should tell you about themselves.

The whole group should then sit in a circle and one person should stand behind their chair. They should say, 'I would like to introduce X. S/he is ... .' This person will then sit down and the next person will stand behind their chair and say, 'I would like to introduce X ... .'

As a whole group, discuss what makes us see ourselves as we do.

Throughout life individuals will experience change. Some changes will be for the better, while others may be unexpected and upsetting. Life events can have a major impact on an individual's personal development. Some life events are predictable, for instance everybody starts school at the same age, everybody goes through physical changes such as puberty around the same age and all women go through the menopause at some time in their life. Other life events, such as serious road accidents, are completely unpredictable. A certain number of people will be killed or seriously injured on the roads each year, but there is no way of telling who it will happen to, or when.

Other major life events include settling down with a partner, having children, getting a divorce and being made redundant. These may or may not happen in an individual's life.

All life events cause stress, which may cause feelings such as anxiety and depression. This is a sign that the individual has to adapt to the life event in some way so that they can live with it comfortably. Adapting to change promotes personal development. During times of serious change we may need support to help us through. The source of support could be through family, friends, professional care workers or from voluntary organizations.

...WORD CHECK

menopause – the age when females stop menstruation or having their periods.

Work with another person to find a newspaper article about a major life event or change, for example, an accident, a fire or a disaster. Read the article and then write down the effects such an event may have on the lives of the individuals. Who could offer them support? How could the support help?

Share the newspaper article with the whole group, stating what changes the event is likely to have caused for those concerned, who could provide support and how the support would help.

Human growth and development

▸ Getting started

You will gain an understanding of:

a   the different life stages:
   i   infancy (0–2 years)
   ii early childhood (3–8 years)
   iii adolescence (9–18 years)
   iv early adulthood (19–45 years)
   v middle adulthood (46–65 years)
   vi later adulthood (65+ years)

b   physical growth and development across the life stages, including gross and fine motor skills

c   intellectual/cognitive development across the life stages, including language development

d   emotional maturity across the life stages, including bonding and attachment, self-image, self-esteem and self-concept

e   self-concept across the life stages and how it is affected by factors such as gender and appearance

f   social development across the life stages including the formation of relationships with others and the socialization process.

LIFE STAGES

During periods of our life we are said to be in a particular 'life stage'. These are periods of time, for example infancy or adolescence, that are recognized as a normal stage of development for human beings. Because we all develop at approximately the same rate and do the same things at around the same time, scientists have called these '**norms**' of development. This means that if we compare our development with that of others of the same age and they are very approximately the same, it is considered that we have developed according to the 'norm' or expected rate of development.

Within each of the life stages, specific development **characteristics** occur. Some of these are physical, some intellectual, some emotional and others are social characteristics. These are often referred to as P.I.E.S.

...WORD CHECK

norms – that which is considered normal for the majority of the population.

characteristics – a feature; a trait.

We experience growth and development during each life stage. Growth is increase of **size** and **mass**. Development includes the **skills**, **intellectual ability** and **emotional responses** that a person gains at each stage of development.

- Physical development is about growth or changes in our bodies. It is also about how people gain more control over their bodies and become able to look after themselves and others.

- **Intellectual** development is about being able to recognize and remember things, and to think about them. Thinking about our views and opinions and sharing them with others is something that most adolescents, adults and older adults like to do. Problem solving is a challenge and stimulates the mind.

- **Emotional** development is about feelings and how we behave when we have them. Love, hate, fear, anger, disgust, curiosity, surprise and guilt are all emotions. There are two aspects to emotional development. As people **mature**, they experience a wider range of emotions, get better at understanding the feelings of other people, and develop beliefs about themselves, their **self-image** and **self-esteem**. Emotional development is also about how a person learns to control their behaviour when they are experiencing emotions.

- **Social** development is about relationships, how a person learns to understand others and develops the skills to get on with them. It is also about how a person learns how others expect them to behave in certain situations. This is called **socialization**.

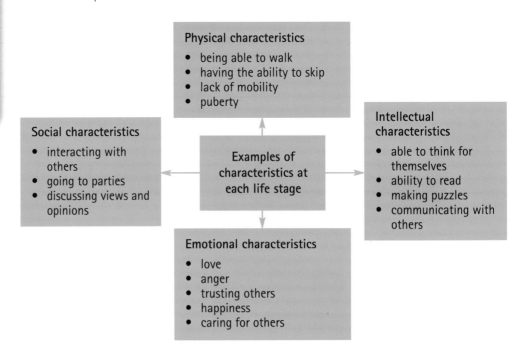

Physical characteristics
- being able to walk
- having the ability to skip
- lack of mobility
- puberty

Social characteristics
- interacting with others
- going to parties
- discussing views and opinions

Examples of characteristics at each life stage

Intellectual characteristics
- able to think for themselves
- ability to read
- making puzzles
- communicating with others

Emotional characteristics
- love
- anger
- trusting others
- happiness
- caring for others

WHAT ARE THE KEY FEATURES OF GROWTH AND DEVELOPMENT IN INFANCY (0–2 YEARS)?

At the beginning of infancy the individual is completely helpless and dependent on their parents or main carers. By the end of the infancy life stage, the infant is beginning to be able to do things for themselves. They also learn to communicate with, and relate to, others.

Physical growth and development in infancy

Infancy is a period of very fast physical growth where infants double their birth weight in their first six months. They double it again by the time they are three years old. Health visitors record infant weights on **centile charts** to monitor their development. Centile charts show the normal range of weight or height for boys and girls at different ages. There are different centile charts for boys and girls because boys are usually heavier at birth, and grow taller. It is important that you understand how to use these charts.

✓ **...WORD CHECK**

centile charts – records that show development.

Group Activity

With your teacher's permission, invite a midwife or other professional to your centre to show you how to read a centile chart to find out whether a child is meeting the 'norm', or is ahead or behind the norm.

Length-for-age and weight-for-age percentiles (girls)

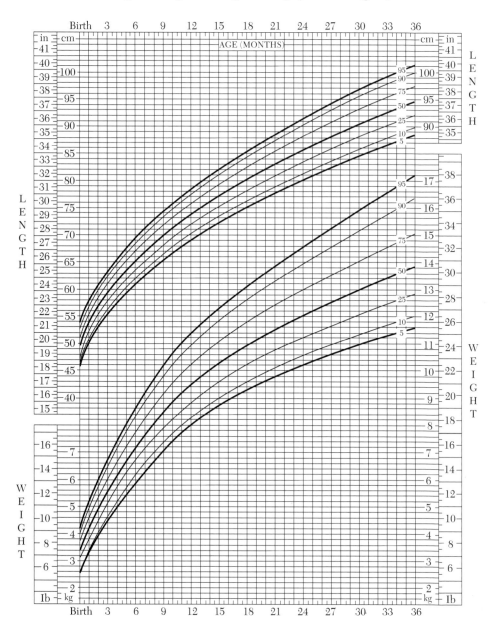

What can infants do?

At birth infants are helpless, with little or almost no control over their bodies. They have **primitive reflexes** including:

- sucking reflex – the infant will suck on a finger placed in their mouth
- rooting reflex – if the infant's face is stroked gently, they will turn their head, searching for a nipple
- grasping reflex – the infant will curl their fingers around anything placed in their hand
- stepping reflex – if the infant is held standing on a firm surface, they will make stepping movements
- startle (Moro) reflex – a loud noise or being moved quickly will cause the infant to open their hands and throw their arms back. The startle reflexes are automatic. This means that the infant has no control over them. Physical development will include the infant getting stronger and developing skills. These reflexes will be replaced with conscious control over their bodies.

▼ Grasping reflex.

1 ➤ What does the term 'automatic reflexes' mean?

Every person is **unique**, that is, they develop at their own pace and reach **milestones** of development more quickly or more slowly than others. This could be for a variety of reasons such as:

- the genes inherited from their mother, father or grandparents
- the influences that have occurred in their development, for example, where they live, their social experiences
- whether they have been affected by illness.

The term **milestones** is used to describe major achievements in growth and development, such as learning to crawl, stand or walk. Look at the table below, which shows some of the milestones in development for an infant.

Milestones of physical development of the infant	
3 months	Infants can sit with their head held steady for a few seconds, if supported.
6 months	Infants have more strength and muscle control. They can lift their head, sit with support and turn their head to look around. They can pull themselves up when their hands are grasped.
9 months	Infants can sit unsupported for ten minutes. They are starting to move independently by rolling or squirming. They can pull themselves to stand, and can stand holding on to something for a few moments.
12 months	Infants can get from a laying to a sitting position without help. They crawl rapidly. They can walk by holding on to furniture and stand alone for a few moments.
15 months	Infants can get to their feet alone. They can walk and crawl upstairs.
18 months	Infants can run, walk upstairs and crawl downstairs.
2 years	Infants can walk downstairs.

One example of increasing control is toilet training. Infants usually have bowel control by about 18 months. At first, carers have to watch out because infants can only show they need to go to the toilet by looking uncomfortable. Six months later they will tell their carer about their need in plenty of time. At about this time, they will also be dry during the day. By three years old, most young children will be dry all night. Other changes take place in the infant's body. First teeth, known as deciduous teeth, start to appear at about six months.

Gross and fine motor skills

When thinking about the physical development of infants and children, the terms **gross** and **fine motor skills** will be used. Gross motor skills involve the use of muscles to control the body. Infants will learn to control muscles before they are able to balance and carry out large movements such as walking. Control occurs first at the head end and then gradually moves down the body to the shoulders, arms and legs.

Fine motor skills involve hand–eye coordination and the coordination of the fingers. Examples are learning to pick up objects and to drop them. The table below gives some examples of gross and fine motor skills.

...WORD CHECK

gross motor skills – having the ability to use and coordinate the larger muscle groups.

fine motor skills – use and coordination of fine movement, for example, use fingers correctly.

egocentric – self-important.

Examples of gross motor skills	Examples of fine motor skills
Can lift head at 3 months when lying on front	Plays with fingers at 3 months
Can sit unsupported for short periods at 6 months	Able to grasp an object at 6 months
Pulls into standing position at 8 months, holding on to furniture	Deliberately drops things on the floor at 9 months
Crawls very quickly at 1 year	Starts to show a preference for using one hand at 1 year
Can walk up and down stairs at 2 years	Can hold small crayons properly

Group Activity

Work with another person to produce handouts showing gross and fine motor skills for infants at 3 months, 6 months, 9 months, 1 year, 18 months and 2 years.

Produce two questions for each stage that could be used in a quiz. Separately, produce the answers.

Play the quiz with another pair, making sure you record the scores.

ACTIVITY   The health visitor

Ray is two years old. His mum, Sonia, meets Desmond, aged one, and his mum, and Jackie and her mother at the Health Centre. Jackie is six months old.

1. Investigate the physical characteristics that Jackie would have at the age of six months. Prepare a handout that the health visitor could give to Jackie's mother to show her the physical characteristics of a one-year-old child, explaining how to meet the physical needs of Jackie.

2. Explain what the physical characteristics of Desmond are likely to be at the age of one year.

3. Give the physical characteristics of Ray, stating how his mother could meet these needs.

4. If Ray attended nursery school, how could his physical needs be met?

Intellectual development in infancy

At first, infants are **egocentric**. This means they can only see the world from their own point of view. They can't talk or understand language, so they can only learn through sight, sound, taste, smell and touch. This is why a 6–12-month-old baby puts everything in their mouth.

A 6-month-old infant who drops a toy out of their cot will not look for it. If they cannot see it, they do not know that it still exists. By about 9 months, they learn that objects that they cannot see are still there.

As infants learn to talk, talking and listening become more important ways of learning. They begin to ask questions and put their thoughts into words. Infants, when they have learnt to talk, are always asking 'why' questions. Learning to talk is an important intellectual development in infancy. Communication is part of an infant's development but learning to speak depends on the opportunities an infant has to practise and use language. Infants learn to smile and use their eyes to make contact with people. Frustration is common in infants and before they learn to talk, they often find it hard to get their message across.

The chart below gives some examples of the milestones of intellectual development for an infant.

Milestones in intellectual development of the infant	
3 months	Infants make noises when they are spoken to.
9 months	Infants practise making sounds, repeating syllables like 'mum-mum' and 'dad-dad'. They begin to learn that the sounds their carers make mean something. They understand a couple of words, like 'no' and 'bye-bye'.
12 months	Infants know their own name and understand several words. They understand simple commands with gestures, like 'Give it to mummy'.
15 months	Infants understand and obey simple commands, like 'Bring it here'. They can say a few words and understand many more.
18 months	Infants will try to join in with nursery rhymes. Soon after this they can put a few words together to make simple sentences.
2 years	Infants can use around 50 words and understand many more. They ask questions all the time, like 'What's that?'

Group Activity

Work with another person and try to work out at least **three** different ways in which an infant will learn to communicate.

How does an infant show frustration?

How does an infant show that they are happy?

ACTIVITY   At the playgroup

Bethany aged one year and William aged two years attend Bowleze Cove playgroup.

1. Draw up a table to show the milestones in intellectual development that Bethany and William should have reached.

2. Explain how the playgroup could meet the intellectual needs of Bethany and William.

3. Explain why it is important to meet the intellectual needs of infants.

Emotional development in infancy

▲ Showing our emotions.

Emotional development is about the way a person feels about themselves and how they feel about others. During their first year an infant will develop a strong emotional bond with their parent or main carer. Have you ever heard a young baby crying because they were hungry or uncomfortable? If you have, you will know how simple their emotions are. Because they have little control over their bodies, they do not have a wide range of responses to their emotions. As they get older they develop a wider range of emotions. These are connected with other forms of development. For example:

- They have to bond with somebody and experience attachment before they can feel jealous.
- They must be able to tell the difference between strangers and people they know before they can feel shy.
- If bonding does not occur, the infant can become disruptive and may feel unloved and unwanted.

An infant can experience a wider range of emotions by the time they are two years old. You may have seen a six-month-old infant beginning to be shy of strangers. It is common to see a two-year-old infant showing how jealous they are of a new brother or sister.

At two years old, an infant still can't control how they respond to their emotions. You have probably heard mothers talking about the 'terrible twos'. A two year old will often have tantrums when frustrated. An infant lying screaming on the floor in the supermarket because they are refused sweets is not doing it to embarrass their mother. They have no idea how their mother feels. They only know they aren't getting something they want, and they can't control their feelings about it. Tantrums are less frequent when infants become young children and can control their emotions better.

Self-concept

The way infants are treated by carers affects their developing self-concept. If they are encouraged and treated kindly, they will feel better about themselves than if they are criticized and shouted at.

Age	Milestones in emotional development of the infant
Newborn	• Enjoys having a cuddle from parent or main carer. • Gazes into parent's eyes. • Moves whole body to express enjoyment. • Smiles at parent.
3 months	• Recognizes familiar people and smiles. • Shows enjoyment at bath time. • Enjoys being talked to.
6 months	• Afraid of strangers. • Cries and laughs when others do this, so recognizing the emotions of others. • Laughs when enjoying activities.
9 months	• Expresses fear of strangers by crying. • Dislikes going to bed and will express their feelings. • Likes comfort objects, for example, teddy bear or comfort blanket. • Likes being noisy.
1 year	• Very affectionate towards family. • Enjoys playing games. • Shy towards strangers.
2 years	• Able to express their feelings. • Gets angry if they cannot express themselves. • Likes to try out new activities. • Can be confident and independent, or clingy and dependent on parent or main carer.

CASE STUDY   Kelly's family

Kelly is married to Tony and they have two young children, Alicia, aged two, and Mark, who is nine months. Alicia attends nursery for three mornings each week.

1. Produce handouts to show the milestones in development for a two-year-old infant and a nine-month-old infant for emotional and intellectual development.

2. Explain how Kelly and Tony could provide intellectual stimulation for both children when they are at home.

3. Explain how Kelly and Tony could meet the emotional needs of the children when they are at home.

4. How could the nursery school meet Alicia's emotional needs?

Social development in infancy

▲ Bonding between mother and infant is important.

Newborn babies have no sense of personal identity but they do like company. They know nothing about the world, and don't understand that there are other people in it. They are very interested in faces and soon get to recognize their main carer. They get to know their carer's face, voice, smell and touch. This is called **bonding**. The way an infant is cared for affects their social development. The better they feel about themselves, the easier they will find it to make friends.

By the time an infant is six weeks old they will smile at their carer. This is a infant's first social action. The infant soon learns to enjoy being played with by people. By the time they are six months old they can tell people they know from strangers. They become shy with people they don't know.

They still don't understand that other people have thoughts and feelings. Because of this, they will not be interested in playing with other children for a long time yet:

- up to the age of two, infants will play alone (solitary play)
- by two years, infants will play near other children but do not know how to play with them (parallel play)
- by two years, infants are interested in other children playing but still have no idea how to share play things.

Infants begin to develop their self-esteem, which helps them to cope with any situation and to develop independence. Parents and main carers should try to be positive at this time by giving praise, providing older infants with choice, allowing them to express their opinions and to gain independence.

The development of infants is a continuous process and 'milestones' are not achieved on one particular day or time.

> ⊘ **...WORD CHECK**
>
> **bonding** – forming an emotional tie.

ACTIVITY — Information for new parents

1. Cut out a picture of an infant and paste it onto the centre of a page of A4 plain paper. Draw a line out toward the four corners and write on each physical, intellectual, emotional and social characteristics. For each area of P.I.E.S. give **five** physical, **five** intellectual, **five** emotional and **five** social characteristics.

2. Produce **four** handouts to explain the terms physical, intellectual, emotional and social development, giving **three** examples for each of the P.I.E.S.

3. Draw a timeline and mark in the life stages and the age span for each.

4. Arrange to interview a parent who has a child between 0 and 2 years. Find out how they helped to develop their child's self-esteem.

▶ ▶ ▶ ▶

ASSESSMENT PRACTICE

Section One

1 Which is one of the first physical characteristics of a three-month-old infant?

  ☐ **A** standing by holding furniture   ☐ **B** walking

  ☐ **C** crawling   ☐ **D** moving head from side to side [1]

2 Which is an emotional characteristic of an infant?

  ☐ **A** listening to a story   ☐ **B** cuddling their mother

  ☐ **C** learning to speak   ☐ **D** feeding themselves [1]

Section Two

Megan is one year old and she lives with both her parents in a comfortable three-bedroomed house.

3 Which life stage is she in? Give the age span for this life stage. [2]

4 Describe **two** intellectual characteristics for a one year old. [2]

5 Describe **two** emotional characteristics for a one year old. [2]

6 Describe **two** social characteristics for a one year old. [2]

7 Describe **two** physical characteristics for a one year old. [2]

8 Some milestones in development are:

can smile   can walk   can stand   can skip   can roll over from back to front

Identify the order in which these milestones of development would usually occur. [5]

9 Emma is two years old and she lives with her mother in a small bedsit. Her mother needs to work but she is having difficulty finding a playgroup in the area. Describe **three** ways in which positive emotional relationships could be promoted in Emma's life. [3]

10 Explain how a playgroup could promote Emma's intellectual relationships. [5]

11 Explain how attending playgroup could promote Emma's social development. [5]

12 What is meant by the term 'self-esteem'? How could Emma's mother promote Emma's self-esteem? [10]

WHAT ARE THE KEY FEATURES OF GROWTH AND DEVELOPMENT IN EARLY CHILDHOOD (3–8 YEARS)?

Childhood is considered to be from the age of three to eight years. In this life stage children develop much more control over their bodies, and their emotions become more complex. Children develop more communication skills and learn to relate and to interact with others.

Physical growth and development in early childhood

Some milestones of physical growth and development for a child

A child can run, skip and hop between the ages of four and six years

A child will become stronger and taller during this life stage

A child enjoys playing ball games

Muscle tissue will increase and 'baby' fat will be lost

A child will develop distinct features

A child's head is larger but is smaller in proportion to the rest of the body

The second or permanent teeth grow

Facial features will change very little after this period of growth

...WORD CHECK

features – an aspect or characteristic.

permanent – for ever.

growth spurt – to grow quickly; to develop at a fast rate.

proportions – the size of different parts of a child in relation to other parts.

Physical growth in childhood is more gradual than in infancy, although there is a **growth spurt** between five and seven years. Throughout this period, the **proportions** of the child's body change. A child's head is larger than an infant's, but is smaller in proportion to the rest of the body. Fine motor skills are developed further and the sense of balance improves. It is very important that children make time for physical activity in order to help the body to function normally and to improve motor skills.

Intellectual development in early childhood

During childhood, children learn to talk and develop a much wider vocabulary. By the end of this stage, they begin to understand concepts. These are ways in which we use our minds to organize thoughts and information. Concepts include colour, number, size and symbols. A child understands that a number of different red objects are all the same colour, and that ten beans is the same number as ten buttons. The child now has a simple understanding of right and wrong.

2 ▶ What are concepts?

When a child starts school at around five, they begin to learn how to organize their thoughts. They are helped to do this through the various activities provided by the teacher. The child also begins to learn new vocabulary as they listen to other children within their class and the new words introduced by their teacher. These new abilities are then applied to activities that occur outside of school.

◄ Children enjoy the challenge of learning new things.

CASE STUDY **Thelma**

Thelma is six years old. She attends the local primary school where she has lots of friends and enjoys doing different activities. She learns how to read, how to form letters and to write and count. Thelma also enjoys making things, particularly making cakes, and also painting and building objects.

1. How has attending school helped Thelma's language development?

2. Explain how making cakes and painting are helping with Thelma's intellectual development.

At this stage the child is no longer egocentric. This means that they can now see things from someone else's point of view. They are beginning to be able to work things out, but need to see and touch things to understand and solve problems.

What do theorists think about the intellectual development of children?

Piaget is a theorist who wrote about child development. He was a Swiss scientist who thought that children were born with some basic abilities and that a person's intellectual potential gradually developed as a result of their experiences. Piaget thought that children would try to draw conclusions from their experiences.

Piaget studied the development of children very carefully. He thought that there were several stages in the intellectual development of the child. Some of these were:

- the sensory motor stage, which occurs between 0 and 2 years. This is where babies find out about the things around them and what they do

- the pre-operational stage, which occurs between the ages of 2 and 7 years. This is where thought processes are developing. At this stage, children need to see and feel things in order to learn

- the concrete operational stage, which occurs between 8 and 11. At this stage of development, children can think more logically and follow rules.

Group Activity

Work with another person and find out about either Erikson's theory or Carl Rogers' theory.

Produce a handout to help parents understand one of these theories for the childhood life stage.

Emotional development in early childhood

Children can experience a wider range of emotions than infants. This is because more complicated emotions depend on other learning and development. At the beginning of childhood a child will base their judgement on the rights or wrongs taught to them by other people. But as they progress through the life stage, things become more complex. They learn that they should express their emotions differently in different situations. For example, a child might lash out if they were angry with another child, but would not do so if they were angry with a teacher. The behaviour of the child in lashing out at another child is wrong. The child will need help to understand why this type of behaviour is unacceptable.

Children still depend on their carers and close family members, but now there are other influences as well. As children get older they meet more people outside their family. Their development will be affected by their relationships with others, for example school friends and

▲ Feeling happy and secure.

teachers. If they are popular in school, and have lots of friends, it will have a positive effect on their self-esteem, they will feel secure and will probably be full of energy and enthusiasm about the things they are asked to do. On the other hand, a child who is bullied at school is likely to have a negative self-image. They could become withdrawn or they too could become aggressive and bully other children.

Some milestones of emotional development for a child

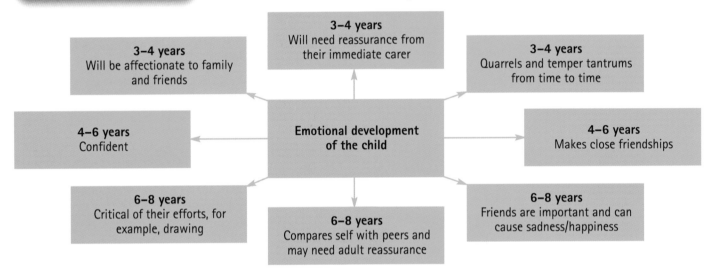

3–4 years
Will be affectionate to family and friends

3–4 years
Will need reassurance from their immediate carer

3–4 years
Quarrels and temper tantrums from time to time

4–6 years
Confident

Emotional development of the child

4–6 years
Makes close friendships

6–8 years
Critical of their efforts, for example, drawing

6–8 years
Compares self with peers and may need adult reassurance

6–8 years
Friends are important and can cause sadness/happiness

Having emotional **stability** is important in the development of the child, as it is likely to influence their actions and attitudes throughout their lives.

Social development in early childhood

Some milestones of social development for a child

By the age of four, children need other children to play with. They are much better at understanding the feelings of others.

By five years old children are attending school, meeting lots of new children and choosing their own friends.

Children understand how to take turns. They can be separated from their main carer without distress.

At five they cooperate with others in their peer group in games, and understand rules and fairness.

At five years because children understand more about how others are feeling, it becomes more important to have the approval of the other children.

By the age of seven years children are aware of sexual differences and prefer to play with children of the same sex.

By the age of seven children are usually quite independent.

By the age of eight some children may be self-conscious and may need encouragement to join in activities.

Social development for children between the ages of three and eight years alters dramatically. They may have younger **siblings** to cope with, who require more of their parents' or carers' time, so they have to learn to share. Also, the number of people with whom they meet will expand to include not only their extended family but also teachers, new friends and their parents' wider circle of friends.

Attending school will mean that the child will extend their vocabulary by talking and listening with others, and through learning new skills. Good **role models** are essential at this time as the child will start to compare themselves with others at a very simple level and will either admire or dislike people. Parents, teachers and others whom they meet will influence their actions and beliefs.

Self-concept

Self-concept begins to develop in childhood. This is because as children get older they come into contact with a much wider range of people. All of those individuals will start to influence the way the child sees themselves – their self-portrait. This portrait will be influenced by gender. Girls will begin to see themselves as different to boys and will begin to realize that the people they are in contact with will often expect them to behave as 'a girl'. This is when girls start to behave as they are expected to by society – to be caring, to like dolls and to dress like other girls. This is why the 'tomboy' image is quite hard for girls as they are not living up to their gender expectation. On the other hand, boys' self-portrait begins to revolve around 'masculine' behaviour – being interested in football, playing games involving physical activity and so on.

Boys and girls who do not fit the gender stereotype may suffer some confusion about who they are and what their self-concept is.

> **...WORD CHECK**
>
> **role models** – looking at someone else to copy/set an example.
>
> **self-concept** – how we think about ourselves.

CASE STUDY   Amber

Amber is eight years old. She has grown quite tall over the last two years. She likes looking at herself in the mirror. She thinks she looks like her mum. She enjoys going to school as she likes learning new things. She has started to learn Spanish and she is quite good at the subject. She also likes playing with her friends in the playground. She goes with her friends to junior youth club on a Friday evening. They enjoy the activities such as basketball and table tennis. In the summer the group are going away to a camp. Amber is looking forward to this.

1. How will attending junior youth club help Amber's intellectual and social development?

2. Describe Amber's emotional development in this life stage.

3. Explain how Amber's intellectual and physical development is being helped through attending junior club.

4. Why is 'emotional stability' important for a child?

5. Find out about the physical, intellectual and social development of a child who is eight years of age. As a group, discuss the questions you could ask the child's parents to find out about the child's growth and development.

   Produce a short questionnaire that could be used when interviewing the parents about the child's physical, intellectual, emotional and social development. Use the questionnaire to interview the parent(s) about the growth and development of the child. You could (with your teacher's permission) invite the parent to your centre to find out the answers to the questions or you could base the information on yourself.

6. Assemble all the information you have collected about the child and produce a 'Child Study'. Draw some conclusions about the growth and development of the child against the milestones for physical, intellectual, emotional and social characteristics.

▶ ▶ ▶ ▶ ▶ **ASSESSMENT PRACTICE**

Section One

1 ▶ Which is a social characteristic of childhood?

☐ **A** playing ball games   ☐ **B** painting a picture for their father's birthday

☐ **C** doing a jigsaw puzzle by themselves   ☐ **D** meeting other children at school [1]

Section Two

2 ▶ Malik is five years old. Describe **two** physical, **two** intellectual, **two** emotional and **two** social changes that Malik is likely to experience over the next five years. [8]

3 ▶ Explain the meaning of the terms 'growth' and 'development'. Give **one** example of each. [6]

4 ▶ Describe **three** ways in which an effective social relationship with a parent could have a positive influence on Malik's development. [3]

5 ▶ Malik enjoys the following activities. Identify whether each activity is physical, intellectual, emotional or social. [6]

Activity	Physical, intellectual, emotional or social activity?
1. Playing on a swing	
2. Learning to spell correctly	
3. Chatting with friends	
4. Being comforted when falling over	
5. Watching TV	
6. Counting marbles	

6 ▶ Explain how being bullied could affect Malik's development. [5]

7 ▶ Explain how Malik's parents could encourage his emotional development. [6]

WHAT ARE THE KEY FEATURES OF GROWTH AND DEVELOPMENT IN ADOLESCENCE (9–18 YEARS)?

Adolescence begins at the age of 9 and ends around 18 years. It is the life stage in which a person achieves sexual maturity or **maturation**, which is often called **puberty**. In the adolescent life stage intellectual skills are developed, for example, being able to think in an abstract way. The adolescent starts to become independent and develop a sense of their personal identity. They also want to make their own decisions and are often torn between the advice they receive from parents and what they actually want to do. As a result, it is often said that an adolescent is very 'moody'.

◀ Adolescence can be a very difficult time.

Physical growth and development in adolescence

Both boys and girls have a **growth spurt** caused by the production of **hormones** by the pituitary and other glands. Hormones are chemical secretions that pass directly into the blood from the endocrine glands. These hormones affect the thyroid gland at the neck and the pituitary gland located at the base of the brain. The boys' growth spurt is usually greater than the girls', and this is why adult men are usually taller and heavier than women.

The most important physical development in adolescence is puberty, when adolescents become sexually mature. Girls usually start puberty between 11 and 13 years while boys start about two years later.

Changes that take place in adolescence:

Physical development in girls	Physical development in boys
• Develop breasts • Grow pubic and underarm hair • Hips widen • Start to menstruate (have periods) • Growth spurt	• Penis and testes grow larger • Larynx (the voice box) grows and the voice breaks and becomes deeper • Grow pubic, facial, chest and underarm hair • Muscles develop and chest and shoulders broaden • May have wet dreams, which shows they can ejaculate sperm

Human physical development usually follows a **predictable** or normal pattern. Some individuals may find the changes occurring slightly earlier, while others may find they happen slightly later, but this period is usually one of great physical change.

Intellectual development in adolescence

Adolescence is a time when there is a growth spurt in the mind as well as in the body. It is a time when adolescents learn to think in different ways. They can understand more difficult concepts than children. They learn to synthesize information. That is to blend information together from several different sources. They can also use their imagination to solve problems in their heads. This is known as **abstract thinking**. Sometimes this new ability to think for themselves leads to arguments between the adolescent and their parents or others.

Adolescents want to exercise their intellectual ability to make their own decisions. Within a peer group, someone who has developed the ability to think independently can exercise power over other members of the group.

Adolescence is a period of time when examinations are important, which will mean learning new skills and knowledge that, often, have to be applied to real situations. It is a very busy and intense period, which can at times cause stress.

▶ Adolescents and their parents often have terrible quarrels.

Emotional development in adolescence

Group Activity

Work with another person and think about what makes each of you feel secure.

What could improve your feeling of security?

Have a whole-class discussion to note the similarities and differences of what makes individuals feel secure.

The hormone changes that cause puberty also affect adolescents' emotions. They often experience mood swings. An adolescent may be excited one moment and depressed the next. They may be very moody and get angry very easily. It is sometimes difficult for adolescents and their families to cope with these mood swings.

At the same time, adolescents are looking for a sense of personal identity, or to discover 'who' they are. One way of doing this is to react against their parents' ideas and values. These may be ideas about politics, religion, or smoking and drinking. This time can be particularly difficult for adolescents.

Insecurity can be a part of an adolescent's emotional development, so parents and friends need to be very patient and understanding. Adolescence is a time when an individual's personality is developed. This means that characteristics, habits and experiences come together to form that person's personality.

Social development in adolescence

▸ First love.

...WORD CHECK

decrease – get smaller; mean less..

peer group – the group of people who are the same age as ourselves.

cliques – groups.

experimental – to conduct tests/to try out.

During adolescence, relationships between parents and peers change. Peer groups become increasingly important, while parents' views and opinions **decrease** in value to the adolescent.

Adolescents need to grow to be independent from their parents. It becomes very important to the adolescent to fit in with their **peer group**. Peer-group approval becomes very important. It may be important to wear the right kind of clothes, for example, Goths, or listen to the right kind of music to fit in with friends. Peer groups serve a positive function in that they allow adolescents to interact with members of the opposite sex in a non-intimate way. For those who are left out of such **cliques** or who do not have a strong friendship group, the outcome is not bright! In early adolescent years, teenagers tend to form groups and do things together. It is in the safety of the group situation that **experimental** behaviour takes place.

With increasing sexual maturity, adolescents begin to look for a partner of the opposite sex and may start to experiment with sexual relationships.

The need for attachment is very important in adolescence, particularly where new attachments are formed with opposite sex partners. John Bowlby researched the relationship between the infant and the main carer and found that where the attachment was secure there was evidence of a healthy personality and development. Similarly, with adolescents, those who are able to form secure attachments in childhood are usually able to form new close relationships in adolescence with the ability to 'give and take'. They tend to be able to negotiate more easily.

Those who were insecurely attached in infancy tend, during adolescence, to be dependent, clingy and jealous. Or they may put up invisible barriers to stop people from getting to know them well. These adolescents are more likely to have a strained relationship with their parents and are likely to attach themselves to a delinquent peer group.

Self-concept

During adolescence an individual's self-concept becomes very important. Teenagers are at the stage where they become very conscious of their appearance. How a boy or girl sees themselves begins to be defined as how they think the opposite sex see them. Girls in particular become aware of their physical characteristics and this can cause problems with self-confidence and self-belief. With so many female role models in the media presenting the 'perfect image' of being female, teenage girls can easily begin to think that they are unattractive and want to change the way they look. This can lead to physical issues such as wanting to lose weight or change the shape of their body.

Particular difficulties with self-concept can often arise when teenagers are physically attracted to individuals of their own sex. This can be very difficult for a young person to deal with as they are often made to feel 'different' or 'guilty'.

> **...WORD CHECK**
>
> attachment – forming a close relationship with someone.
>
> delinquent – someone who does not obey the rules or laws.

CASE STUDY Nehal

Nehal is 17 years old and has a small group of friends who are mainly from his own culture. When he is with his friends Nehal likes to listen to their ideas but he is very quick thinking himself. He also likes to have a joke.

Nehal is not getting on very well with his parents. He goes out a lot and does not get home until one o'clock in the morning. His group does go clubbing but Nehal and his friends of the same culture do not drink alcohol. The group often try to bully people while they are coming home and chase them around side streets.

Nehal's parents are not pleased that he is out most evenings and doesn't get home until late. They have heard rumours of what happens on the way home, made worse when Nehal comes home with bruises on his face. He tells his parents that he fell on a rough piece of pavement, but family friends who live on the route that Nehal takes have seen what happens and tell Nehal's parents about it. Nehal's parents want him to do well at college and to go to university to become a surgeon.

1. Why do you think Nehal likes being in a group?
2. How could Nehal's parents help to improve their relationship with him?
3. Describe the physical, intellectual, emotional and social development of an adolescent.
4. Why do you think Nehal and his friends 'bully' other people while on their way home?
5. What could the possible result of such behaviour be?
6. How do feelings of insecurity affect the emotional development of adolescents?

▶ ▶ ▶ ▶ ▶ **ASSESSMENT PRACTICE**

Section One

1 ▶ Which is an emotional characteristic of an adolescent? [1]

☐ **A** growing taller

☐ **B** preparing for examinations

☐ **C** having mood swings

☐ **D** joining a weightlifting club [1]

Section Two

Joanne is 14 years old. She is doing well at school and enjoys playing netball and rugby. She is beginning to want more independence from her parents but they are worried about her possibly mixing with the wrong friends.

2 ▶ Describe **four** characteristics of Joanne's intellectual development. [4]

3 ▶ Describe **three** social changes that Joanne is likely to experience. [3]

4 ▶ Describe **five** physical changes that Joanne will go through. [5]

5 ▶ Describe the changes that may take place in the relationship between Joanne and her parents. Explain why the changes are happening. [5]

6 ▶ Explain why Joanne wants to be part of a group of friends. [5]

7 ▶ Explain what is meant by the phrase, 'adolescence is the time when an individual's personality comes together'. [10]

WHAT ARE THE KEY FEATURES OF GROWTH AND DEVELOPMENT IN EARLY AND MIDDLE ADULTHOOD (19–45 AND 46–65 YEARS)?

Early and middle adulthood are the periods where an individual achieves physical **maturity**. Compulsory education is finished and the young adult either tries to find work or go on to higher education. Settling into a career becomes a very important aspect in the life of an adult and during this period, **promotion** will be sought. Additionally, most people find a partner, leave home and start their own families.

Physical growth and development in early and middle adulthood

✓ **...WORD CHECK**

maturity – to reach the age where wisdom is probably evident/older adult stage/grown up.

promotion – to take on extra responsibility at work.

sedentary – a sitting down job/not active.

There is little physical growth during adulthood. Adults tend to gain weight as they age, but this is probably due more to a **sedentary** lifestyle than the ageing process, although the current emphasis and encouragement to 'keep fit and healthy' has led to more adults taking up walking, cycling and other sports in order to reduce weight gain. Physical development is completed early in adulthood and decline starts quite early, although at first it is too gradual to notice.

An important physical development for women towards the end of this life stage is the menopause. Usually between the ages of 45 and 55, women's periods stop, and they are no longer able to have children. This is caused by hormonal changes in the body. Sometimes a woman may feel a sense of loss when the menopause occurs, while others will be glad that they no longer have to worry about becoming pregnant and so have a sense of freedom.

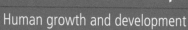
Intellectual development in early and middle adulthood

Intellectual development continues throughout adulthood. Getting a job involves learning new skills. If a person wants to progress in a career, these skills have to be developed and extended. Most people will have more than one job throughout their lives. This is because old jobs go and new ones are created, which frequently means that adults are required to retrain in order to learn new skills. Lifelong learning enables people to learn new skills and keep old ones up to date.

Even outside of work, adulthood is a period of intellectual development. You need a lot of skills to leave home and live independently:

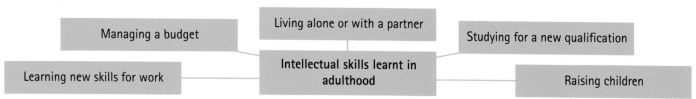

As adults age, they react more slowly and find it more difficult to remember information under pressure. However, to balance this, they have learnt from experience and are, often, better at problem solving and making decisions. This more than compensates for any sluggishness in intellectual ability over the life stage.

Emotional development in early and middle adulthood

The statement 'behaving in a mature manner' usually means that individuals are controlling the way they respond to the emotions they are feeling, such as being angry or being very fond of another individual.

When an individual leaves home, they have to be independent and self-reliant in order to cope. They have to not only be able to consider how they feel themselves but also how other people might react to specific situations. Living with a long-term partner takes a high level of emotional maturity if the relationship is not to break down when problems arise. People have to understand their own emotions and those of their partner. They also have to be able to control the way they respond to their emotions. If they cannot, the result is often the breakdown of the relationship and, in extreme cases violence, if one partner cannot control emotions such as jealousy and anger.

For younger adults, aged between 19–45, the arrival of children means accepting new responsibilities. Babies are very demanding, and can cause a lot of stress to the people who care for them. Adults have to be emotionally mature to cope. Emotional maturity involves:

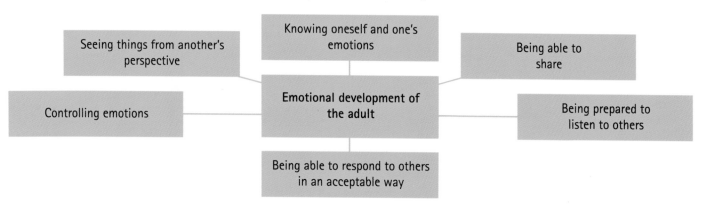

CASE STUDY — Joanne

Joanne enjoys spending time with her friends Pauline and Sophia and their families. Their children are around the same age and attend similar clubs, so the three of them have a lot in common. They meet at weekends in one another's homes for either barbecues or supper, and often go camping together for half term or the summer holidays. Their husbands also appear to get on well and have quite a lot to talk about, except that George, Joanne's husband, never joins in the conversations very much; he just listens.

One evening, after spending a lovely afternoon together, George seems very quiet when he reaches home. Joanne, having put the children to bed, asks him if anything is wrong.

George stands up and walks up and down the living room talking about how he is 'fed up with having to listen to how good Paul is at this and how Adrian's children are so good at that'. He becomes very angry and tells Joanne it is 'all her fault, as she is the one that arranges the family get togethers'. He then slams the door and walks out.

1 What are the emotional issues raised in this case study?

2 How is Joanne likely to feel about this emotional problem?

3 Explain possible solutions to the problem.

4 Explain the likely effects of this emotional upset on the other families.

Social development in early and middle adulthood

▲ Adults learn to accept responsibility.

When young adults leave home, they have to develop new and different types of relationships. They may have a partner or get married and this means making decisions, accepting responsibility and sharing. Relationships with parents change as the young adult starts to relate to them more as equals. Parents realize that their offspring are now taking responsibility for themselves, and maybe others as well, and may speak and treat them with more respect.

Starting work involves developing working relationships with people. These are a different type of relationship. The same choice is not available with working relationships as with other social relationships, as it is compulsory for individuals to work with those with whom they are employed. Sometimes the relationships are distinguished between by calling them **formal** (working relationship) and **informal** (family and friendship) relationships. Working relationships can be formal as some people have authority over others, for example, if they are the employer or the supervisor.

3 How does socializing at work contribute towards an individual's social development?

4 How are working relationships different from social relationships?

Settling down with a long-term partner brings about many changes to people's social lives. Even if people are just living together, this often involves building new relationships with their partner's family. Also people often find that the way they socialize changes when they settle down with a regular partner, and that they tend to mix more with other couples.

5 How might the arrival of their first child change the relationship between two people who are partners?

As adults near later adulthood, they may find that their parents are declining physically, and may begin to depend on them more. This could bring increased responsibility as the older adult may require physical help, such as shopping, or may have dementia, which may mean that they forget things easily and are not safe to live on their own.

...WORD CHECK

formal – a relationship that has rules that must be followed/a framework.

informal – not professional.

Self-concept

Many people develop a clear sense of their self-concept during this stage. An individual might be happily married with a family and have a fulfilling job. Such a person will feel good about themselves and have a positive approach to life. However, factors such as gender and appearance may still play a part in this self-portrait. The search for the perfect body may grow ever more as age begins to damage the way an individual thinks they look. The increasing use of cosmetic surgery by both men and women suggests that they are searching to restore the look they had in the past or create a new look for the future. Whatever the reason, it indicates they are not happy with their self-concept.

▶ ▶ ▶ ▶ **ASSESSMENT PRACTICE**

Nikita and Jack are both in their late twenties and have been living together for four years. Nikita has discovered that she is pregnant and she is worried about telling Jack as they were not planning to have children until much later.

Section One

1 Which of the following is a social development of early adulthood?
- [ ] **A** settling down with a partner
- [ ] **B** learning new skills
- [ ] **C** having mood swings
- [ ] **D** having a growth spurt [1]

Section Two

2 Explain how the pregnancy may affect Nikita and Jack's relationship. [5]

3 How could a child influence Nikita and Jack's physical, intellectual, emotional and social development? [10]

WHAT ARE THE KEY FEATURES OF GROWTH AND DEVELOPMENT IN LATER ADULTHOOD (65+ YEARS)?

Retirement from work is a major feature of this life stage. An adult in later adulthood has to get used to the idea that they are no longer a wage earner and, usually, that they are not responsible for others. This new role can cause some people to feel distressed if they have not prepared themselves for retirement. They may feel useless if they are no longer making decisions for others and have to rely on others for financial and physical support themselves.

Physical growth and development in later adulthood

Individuals in later adulthood often experience a reduction in height as their posture becomes less upright and their spine becomes compressed. A person can lose up to 3 inches in height! The physical decline that started in early adulthood becomes more obvious, especially after the age of 75 years.

Some examples of milestones of the physical aspects of development in later adulthood

Sight worsens as the eyes' lenses stiffen and are less able to focus on close objects, so reading is more difficult.

Hearing declines with the gradual deterioration of the mechanism of the ear.

Mobility may be affected as joints stiffen and become worn or inflamed. Balance is often poorer and falls are more likely.

Those in later adulthood are more vulnerable to cold, making older people susceptible to hypothermia.

Sense of taste and smell are poorer. Teeth may decay and cause problems with eating, which contributes to a lack of confidence.

Bones are more fragile as thinning makes them lighter and more brittle, particularly in women.

Body organs continue to become less efficient, including the heart, lungs, kidneys and liver.

Skin wrinkles because of a loss of elasticity in the tissues.

Hair thins and goes grey, and men often experience hair loss, which could progress to baldness.

▲ Exercise can help to maintain health and well-being if done on a regular basis.

Many of these problems can be overcome or managed so that the older adult can enjoy a better quality of life. Keeping fit can help to maintain our health and well-being, and may help to prevent or delay some aspects of physical decline. Activities such as swimming, walking and jogging can all help to maintain our health and mobility, if undertaken regularly.

Glasses and hearing aids can compensate for deteriorating sight and hearing. New technology means that those in later adulthood have a range of products from which to choose. If joints become damaged, particularly hips and knees, they can now be replaced. Such operations are now common and are not the major events they used to be, but older adults are asked to wait as long as possible before having treatment as the new knee or hip joint will wear out.

Intellectual development in later adulthood

Because of the gradual deterioration of the nervous system, older people have difficulty in remembering things quickly, particularly when they are under pressure. Their reaction times are also slower. However, they may have more experience than a younger person, and could make better decisions as a result.

Older people can become confused and may be unable to manage their own affairs. Confusion is not a normal part of ageing. Confusion is different from dementia, as with dementia actual brain cells cease to function. These cannot be restored. Confusion is temporary and usually passes when the person is less flustered. The occurrence of confusion and dementia is more frequent and this is becoming one of the major health issues of the twenty-first century.

CASE STUDY | **Edith**

Edith is living in Portesham View residential home. She is 75 years old and has the early signs of Alzheimer's disease. Edith wanders around the residential home at night and during the day, going into other people's bedrooms and taking bright objects. These are often found in her own room. She also wanders into the small kitchen and takes snacks that have only been partially prepared and puts them on the table for lunch.

One of the care workers who works part time shouts at Edith when she finds she has been up to her 'old tricks' again and threatens her by saying, 'I will tie you to a chair if you do this again. You are a stupid old woman.' When this happens Edith goes to the locked front door and tries to get out.

1. Carry out research to find out how Alzheimer's disease affects older adults.

2. How could Edith be helped to ensure that she has some meaningful social interaction?

3. How could people in later adulthood be affected intellectually by the ageing process, other than having Alzheimer's disease?

4. What actions should the care assistant take to empower Edith?

Social and emotional development in later adulthood

Poor physical and mental health can also have a harmful effect on social aspects of development.

Mobility problems, whether the result of muscular-skeletal problems or circulatory dysfunction, can result in increased isolation as a service user may be unable to go out for everyday activities, for example, shopping or social events. The impact is likely to be that the service user may not have the opportunity to talk to other people or share views, opinions and ideas. This could mean that they rarely see others and become very inward looking. Their emotional health may deteriorate as a result and they may become withdrawn and lonely. Additionally, because they are not meeting other people, they will not be using their skills of communication and may talk to themselves or become isolated.

Self-concept

Such behaviour could lead to the service user not valuing themselves and having poor self-esteem. Loss of self-esteem could mean that the service user starts to think that nothing is important. Intellectual stimulation is not available, socially they are not meeting others and, consequently, they become demotivated. Some older service users could just sit in a chair watching television all day, but even then they may not be actually registering what the programmes are about.

This type of behaviour is to be avoided. Michael Argyle (1994), a psychologist, puts forward, as part of his theory, that an individual's self-concept and development of personal identity is formed by looking at the reaction of others towards themselves and that people judge themselves according to this. Argyle also indicates that people commonly regard their social role as part of who they are. Older people, if they are withdrawn and socially isolated, will therefore not have any social role with which to compare themselves and, consequently, will feel that they have nothing to contribute.

Cummings and Henry (1961), who are also theorists, defined the state of older people cutting themselves off from society as 'disengagement'. They considered that this was 'an inevitable process in which many relationships between a person and other members of society are severed and those remaining are altered in quality'. This involves the reduction of life activities and ego in old age.

A person who is prone to isolation because of mobility problems is likely, therefore, to be encouraged to visit day-care centres, luncheon clubs and to join in other recreational activities that are beneficial for older people, to avoid them spending too much time looking inward or backwards to events that have happened in previous life stages. The aim is to provide a purposeful role and interest, and to help them become socially integrated.

Some of the illnesses and conditions that can be experienced by people in later adulthood, which influence social and emotional development, are:

Illnesses	Effect on the individual
Stroke	Paralysis, lack of mobility, loss of speech, loss of vision
Incontinence	Lack of bladder and bowel control
Diabetes	Erratic behaviour if it is not controlled
Dementia/Alzheimer's disease	Inability to remember in the short term

▶ Talking to others can stimulate the mind as well as being a social occasion.

After retiring, some people in later adulthood miss the regular contacts with workmates but others enjoy having more time to devote to hobbies and interests. How people are affected may depend on their income. Many older people with pensions from jobs are well off. Others who do not have an occupational pension may find it hard to make ends meet. Many people who can afford it use their retirement to travel around the world or start new activities during later adulthood.

As people get older, they suffer more **bereavements** of friends, close relatives and perhaps their partner. This means they also have to adapt to a smaller social circle.

⊘ ...WORD CHECK

disengagement – to withdraw.

bereavements – sudden deaths.

CASE STUDY — Mr Simkins and his family

Mr Simkins is 70 years old and lives with his wife in their own home. He has a good pension from his job and considers himself quite well off. Their two children are married and live nearby. They have five grandchildren, who they see regularly.

Mr Simkins drives but he is thinking of giving up his car. He took up painting when he retired and he enjoys doing this now, but he has given up hill walking.

He is a member of a number of local organizations. He sometimes says he doesn't know how he found time to go to work.

1. Explain why painting is a better hobby for Mr Simkins than hill walking.
2. Why do you think Mr Simkins is considering giving up his car?
3. Describe the social development for the Simkins in the life stage they are in.
4. How does an individual's relationship with their child change during the older adult life stage?

ASSESSMENT PRACTICE

Section One

1. Which are two positive factors that could contribute to the development of a person in later adulthood?

    1. joining a luncheon club
    2. friends dying
    3. missing work colleagues
    4. learning a new language

    ☐ A 1 and 2
    ☐ B 2 and 3
    ☐ C 3 and 4
    ☐ D 1 and 4 [1]

Section Two

Gwen is 75 years old. She has just suffered a slight stroke, which has caused some paralysis and speech difficulties. Her husband, Joe, is concerned and worried about what the future holds for them both.

2. Describe **two** physical developments and **two** intellectual developments that will affect Gwen. [4]
3. How will Gwen's stroke affect her socially? [4]
4. What impact will Gwen's stroke have upon her husband, Joe? [4]
5. In what ways could Gwen and Joe try to cope with their changed situation? [6]

Factors affecting human growth and development

▶ Getting started

You will gain an understanding of:

a physical factors such as genetic inheritance, illness, disease, diet, exercise, alcohol and smoking

b social, cultural and emotional factors such as family, friends, educational experiences, employment/unemployment, community involvement, religion, gender, ethnicity, sexual orientation, culture and relationship formation including marriage and divorce

c economic factors such as income, wealth, employment status, occupation, social class, poverty and material possessions

d physical environment factors such as pollution, noise, housing conditions and rural/urban lifestyles

e psychological factors such as stress, relationships within the family, friends and partners

f how these factors are related to the formation of, and possible change in, an individual's self-concept

g how genetic and environmental factors can affect an individual's pattern of growth and development.

FACTORS AFFECTING HUMAN GROWTH AND DEVELOPMENT

> **...WORD CHECK**
> detrimental – negative.

Human development can be influenced by a number of factors that may have a positive or **detrimental** influence. It is these factors that help to shape our personality.

Group Activity

Work with another person and think about factors that have influenced your own development, for example, family. Try to make a list of five different factors between you that have influenced your development.
Discuss how these have affected your development.

Now make a list using these headings: physical, social and emotional, economic, environmental.
Place the factors you have in your original list under these headings. Try to have at least one factor under each.
Discuss as a whole group the factors that have influenced all individuals in the group, placing them under the headings given.

PHYSICAL FACTORS THAT CAN AFFECT GROWTH AND DEVELOPMENT

Physical factors affecting growth and development include genetic inheritance, illness, disease, diet, the amount and type of exercise we undertake and smoking and alcohol consumption.

How can genetic inheritance affect growth and development?

◀ Our genes make us who we are.

Genetic inheritance is having a mixture of genes from our parents, which acts as a plan of what we will be like when we grow. Genes are bits of information inside every cell in your body. They are the instructions that the body uses to build itself. The human body is very complicated and it needs a lot of instructions to build itself properly. Genes help decide things like your size, build, facial features and hair and skin colour. They also decide whether you are male or female.

We get half of our genes from our mother, and half from our father, but they mix differently each time a child is conceived. That is why children often look like their parents, and brothers and sisters often look similar, but never exactly the same. The only exception to this is identical twins. This is where a single fertilized egg splits and produces two embryos, which grow into two babies with identical genes.

 6 How do our genes influence development?

The rate at which we grow or mature is genetically determined. Maturation is the rate of physical growth and starts at conception. All normal foetuses develop at approximately the same rate (the norm), and after birth we all learn to crawl, walk and run within approximately the same time scales. All people pass through the same stages of maturation in the same order. However, we don't all mature at exactly the same rate. For example, some children stand at six months, but others not until ten months. Children are not all the same, and this is because each person's combination of genes is different.

 7 Why are all children not the same?

Some genes cause illnesses that affect the way that people develop. These illnesses are called **hereditary** or genetic disorders. They can cause physical and learning disabilities, and sometimes result in the early death of people who have them.

...WORD CHECK

genetic – passed from parents or grandparents down through the generations.

genes – part of a chromosome that controls a particular characteristic, for example eye colour.

features – an aspect or characteristic.

hereditary – passed down from parents or grandparents.

 Group Activity

Work with another person to find out about two different support groups that would help an individual who has a genetic disorder.

Produce a handout to provide information about each support group.

Share the information with others in the group.

How can our experience of illness and disease affect growth and development?

Group Activity

Carry out research to find out what is meant by the nature versus nurture debate.

...WORD CHECK

immunity – resistance to a disease.

prejudices – being biased; making up one's mind about someone or something before really knowing what they are like.

All illnesses have physical effects on the people who have them. Sometimes we can have diarrhoea, we may vomit, have spots or ache all over. These symptoms are going to affect our development, but for only a short time. On other occasions an illness will take us longer to recover. An example would be glandular fever. Experience of illness and disease is sometimes linked with our diet. For example, we may get food poisoning or we may not have had enough iron in our diet and as a consequence we could feel tired and lethargic. In our life time, however, we are bound to have some experience of illness and disease.

Because infants grow so quickly, most illnesses affect their physical development for a short while. Examples of these types of illness are chickenpox and mumps. The infant usually makes up for any loss in growth and development when they recover. Some common childhood illnesses can have long-term effects. Some illnesses have serious developmental effects, sometimes leading to death.

Babies are to some extent protected from infection in the first few months of their lives. This is because they have immunity in the form of antibodies. These have been passed to them from their mother while they were in the uterus before birth. Their immunity to illness can be further boosted through breastfeeding, as antibodies are passed on during this process. After a short while the baby will start to produce their own antibodies in response to infections.

Physical illness and disease can affect our emotional, intellectual and social development. For example, if a child misses a lot of school, they miss learning opportunities as well as the opportunity to mix and socialize with other children.

Serious illness in adulthood may mean that an individual cannot work, so they lose social contacts. This may also have emotional effects, and people may experience depression and lowered self-esteem if they are unable to work.

Some illnesses, such as AIDS, will have social effects because of people's prejudices. AIDS sufferers may be avoided by people who have unrealistic ideas about how the illness is passed on.

CASE STUDY   Sid

Sid is 53 years old. He is single as his partner left him because she could not put up with his heavy drinking habit. Sid worked, but his diet was very poor as he had lots of chips, beef burgers and takeaways. He seldom had any fruit and vegetables. He always had plenty to drink, however. He never cleaned his teeth.

Over several months Sid developed severe toothache. His gums started to bleed badly and lumps developed at the sides of his mouth. Eventually he visited the dentist as he could stand the pain no longer.

The dentist immediately sent Sid to the hospital for x-rays. When the results came through it was decided that Sid would have to have immediate surgery to take all of his teeth out and to remove the parts of the gums that were diseased.

Sid was ill for a long while and could only eat food that was liquidized.

Sid's severe condition was the result of:

- not eating a healthy diet
- drinking a lot of alcohol
- not cleaning the teeth properly
- not visiting the dentist regularly.

Sometimes illness and conditions are the result of our own neglect!

8 Which aspects of Sid's lifestyle caused his health problems?

9 How could this situation have been avoided? Who could have helped him in his younger years?

In later adulthood many people have **degenerative** illnesses such as arthritis or rheumatism. These have the physical effect of making it difficult for them to care for themselves. Other illnesses, such as Alzheimer's disease, have intellectual effects such as confusion and memory loss. Having to rely on others for everyday care tasks may have emotional effects. People who are unable to care for themselves may become depressed. This is likely to happen if their carers are not careful to offer them choices. If illness makes people less mobile, they may find it difficult to leave their homes. This will have social effects and they may become isolated.

> **⊘ ...WORD CHECK**
> degenerative – where a body organ or system slowly begins to break down.

It should be remembered that:

- happy and contented people are less likely to be ill
- a balanced diet can contribute to good health
- having sufficient physical activity can contribute to the absence of illness and disease.

How can diet affect growth and development?

Diet is an important influence on growth and development. Food is needed for two reasons:

1 so that the body can grow and repair itself when it is damaged
2 to provide energy, which is needed to do the work of building and repair, to maintain temperature and to enable us to carry out physical activities.

Pictures of people who have not enough food or water to help them stay alive have probably been seen by all of us on TV and other forms of the media. We see pictures of children who are caught up with war or famine. Their bodies are misshapen through lack of food or not having a balanced diet. Many children in other countries die because they are suffering from malnutrition.

Our physical needs change as we go through different life stages. What we need for a balanced diet depends upon:

- our age
- our size
- our sex
- the amount of exercise we do
- factors such as pregnancy and breastfeeding.

If we do not have a balanced diet, this can have serious effects on our growth and development. To remain healthy, we need to make sure that our diet contains the correct nutrients. These are:

- proteins
- fats
- carbohydrates
- vitamins
- minerals
- water
- fibre.

Look at Unit 3 to find out in detail what each item in the list does in the body and why each is essential to promote good health.

What is a healthy balanced diet?

A healthy diet contains all of the nutrients needed by the body. Nutritionists and the government have worked out a rough guide to show what a healthy diet should include. One of their recommendations is that we should eat five portions a day of fruit and vegetables.

Remember, it is diets, not foods, that are unhealthy and it's the food you eat over months and years which is a factor that will contribute to development. Make changes for life, and don't be influenced by 'fad' diets. When deciding to make some changes to your diet, think carefully about what changes you will be able to follow. It may make more sense to make small changes over time, rather than major changes to your entire diet, if this means the changes are more likely to be permanent.

◄ Five of these foods should be eaten each day.

CASE STUDY   Ellie, Rupert and family

Ellie is 6 years old, Rupert is 13 years old and their mother and father are both in their late thirties. They have all been putting on a lot of weight and Ellie's mum has decided that they must change their lifestyle and food choices. They have been used to eating quite a lot of fried fatty foods, cake, bread and junk food.

1   Carry out research to find out what each member of the family's food intake should be.

2   Plan **one** day's menus for both Ellie and Rupert, showing how they are nutritionally well balanced.

3   Plan **one** day's menu for Ellie's father, who works on a building site. Show why it is well balanced.

4   Produce **ten** questions for a quiz about healthy foods, what they do and where they can be found.
Work out the answers to the questions on separate paper.
Take part in the quiz with the rest of the group.

How can the foods we eat influence our development?

8 ▶ What is a balanced diet?

- If we do not get enough nutrients, it will affect our body's ability to grow and repair itself. We will be less resistant to infections, and it will take us longer to recover from injury and illness.
- If we take in more energy than we use, we gain weight. If we take in less energy than we use, we lose weight. Being very overweight (obese) or very underweight is bad for our health and also affects our appearance.
- If we take in too much energy in the form of fats, it can increase our risk of heart disease.
- If we take in too much energy in the form of sugar, it can increase our risk of tooth decay.

You have all probably heard the saying 'we are what we eat'. If we eat a well-balanced diet, keeping to regular patterns of eating, we are more likely to be healthy. If we eat excessively or have an unbalanced diet, we are more likely to develop conditions and illnesses that will affect our development.

It is unlikely that one diet-related factor would cause a major health problem. It is when poor diet is combined with other factors, such as lack of exercise, stress or poor living conditions, that ill-health is likely to result.

Group Activity

What do they need to eat?
- **a** Miranda is one year old. Plan a diet for **one** day for Miranda.
- **b** Gaye is pregnant. Plan a diet for her for one day.
- **c** Murray is an older adult. How will his diet vary from that of an adolescent?

How can exercise affect growth and development?

Taking part in physical activity regularly throughout our lives is very important. The type of exercise that is right for us will depend on the stage of our physical development. Different types of exercise will suit people in different life stages.

	Mobility is improved	
Bones are strengthened		Less likely to become overweight
	The benefits of physical activity	
Improves the immune system	Improves breathing and circulation	Strengthens muscles including the heart
Relieves depression		Reduces stress
	Improves self-esteem	

Exercise should be taken for 30 minutes, five times each week in order to build up and maintain fitness. Exercise changes the body's composition as it increases the amount of muscle the body has and reduces fat levels. From the moment they are born, babies begin to exercise their muscles. Children will exercise as part of their sports activities and as a major part of growing up. Exercise helps to protect against disease. Regular exercise will improve **endurance** and muscular strength.

...WORD CHECK

endurance – staying power.

Babies exercise quite naturally, even before they can move around. We have all probably seen young babies kicking and stretching in their cots or at bath time. As babies develop they learn to crawl and walk, and to explore their surroundings.

Children should get enough exercise through physical activity such as walking to school, sports, games and play. There are worries that children may not be getting enough physical activity. As a result, more children are becoming unfit and obese. This could be because more parents have cars and drive their children to school instead of letting them walk or cycle.

Also, children may be more interested in activities such as television and computer games and as a result they might be doing fewer physical activities.

Adolescents may also be getting less exercise because more of them are able to drive, and so they walk less. They may also have less-active interests, such as computer games.

Fewer adults work in jobs that require physical effort. Many more people now work in office jobs. Some jobs are physically easier because most of the work is done by machinery. This means that most types of work do not provide the amount of physical activity that is needed to keep healthy. Adults can make sure that they get some physical activity through housework, gardening and walking to the shops. If they do not do a lot of these things, they may have to take care that they get sufficient exercise, perhaps by playing sports, running or going to the gym.

For older people physical activity could be painful because of rheumatism or arthritis. They do still need exercise, for the same reasons as people in any other life stage. They may need specially organized exercise programmes that are within their physical ability.

▸ Physical activities such as gardening help to keep us active and healthy.

How do alcohol and smoking affect growth and development?

Group Activity

In pairs, discuss why too much smoking or drinking might be considered anti-social.

Regularly consuming too many units of alcohol or smoking can seriously affect development.

The effects of alcohol and smoking

Alcohol (short term)	Alcohol (long term)
• vomiting	• cirrhosis of the liver
• headaches	• kidney failure
• lack of concentration	• heart disease

Smoking (short term)	Smoking (long term)
• coughing	• hardening of the arteries
• breathing difficulties	• lung infections
• dizziness	• cancer
• weight gain	• lack of mobility

Too much smoking and drinking can have adverse intellectual effects, as the brain may become slower and not able to function normally. Socially, people who smoke and drink too much may lose support from their families and friends for their habit.

▶ ▶ ▶ ▶ **ASSESSMENT PRACTICE**

Section One

1 To keep healthy, exercise should be taken:

☐ **A** twice each week for 20 minutes
☐ **B** three times each week for 30 minutes
☐ **C** five times each week for 30 minutes
☐ **D** four times each week for 20 minutes [1]

2 To maintain health it is recommended that an individual should eat:

☐ **A** one portion of protein and two portions of carbohydrates
☐ **B** five portions of fruit and vegetables
☐ **C** two portions of fibre and five portions of minerals
☐ **D** one portion of fruit, fibre, protein and carbohydrates [1]

Section Two

Mike is aged 45 and he has a sedentary job working in an office. He lives on his own and he finds cooking boring, so he often eats microwave food and takeaways. He always stops off at his local pub after work for two or three drinks. He drives his car to the office, which is one mile from his house, every day.

3 List **three** physical factors that could influence Mike's development, describing how each could affect his attitudes and behaviour. [6]

4 Describe how illness and disease could affect Mike as he gets older. [5]

5 Identify and explain three changes in Mike's lifestyle that would benefit him. [6]

6 How could participating in regular exercise help to promote Mike's health and well-being? [5]

7 Use theory to help explain how physical factors could affect Mike's development. [8]

SOCIAL, CULTURAL AND EMOTIONAL FACTORS THAT CAN AFFECT GROWTH AND DEVELOPMENT

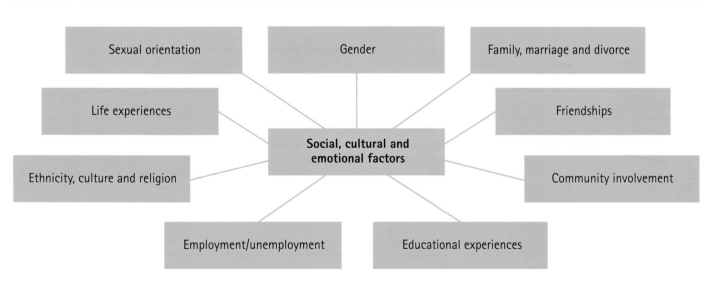

Primary socialization occurs as a result of our home life and the people that we meet first in our lives: our parents, our immediate family, our extended family.

Secondary socialization refers to those things that affect us as we grow and develop, for example, the things we learn from the wider society.

How can family relationships affect growth and development?

⊘ ...WORD CHECK

nuclear – a group of people comprising mother, father and children.

gender roles – how men and women are expected to act in particular situations.

The home is the first place where an individual is socialized. This is known as primary socialization. Socialization is almost like having a series of lessons that prepare a child for its adult role. Whether the family is a nuclear unit, where mother, father, brothers, sisters and extended family exist, or whether it is a single parent family or commune, it is the family who are the main people that contribute to learnt attitudes and beliefs. A child will learn the way of behaving according to the particular culture of the family in which they live. The values and norms of the society in which the child is being brought up become the accepted way for the child. The family is responsible for primary socialization. The family develops the 'conscience' of new members. Once a bond has been formed between a child and its parent or main carer, any threat to that bond will cause the child anxiety. Therefore, rather than losing the close association that it has with its parent or main carer, the child will adopt the norms and values taught by them. This includes the young child's learning and experiences of prejudice, gender roles and the skills of language. For example, if the family has the attitude that some people are inferior to their own family, then the children in the family are likely to follow their example.

Our position in the family can be an influence on our development. If we are the youngest family member, brothers and sisters might protect us from others. Or, on the other hand, we could be blamed for all their wrong doing!

 11 ▶ How does our position in the family affect our development? Why?

The views and opinions that we hear within our own family may also influence our growth and development. Many people tend to adopt these family views and opinions in their own lives. Examples are: our families' views on politics, religion, punishment, law and order and how services should be run. We may hear these views many times within our homes and may agree with them. We could even support the same football team because this is the team that members of our family support. In other words we often follow family tradition.

How can friendships affect growth and development?

Friendships are important to people's growth and development in all life stages. We have close friends. These are people that we share personal things with. Then we have other people who are friends and whom we like doing things with. Our friends give us emotional and social support. They are the people:

Who listen when we have a problem

Who we share our happy times with

With whom we share activities and interests

◄ Friends.

Hopefully we are there when they need us as well!

Sometimes friends can be a bad influence on us. We may do things that we know are wrong because we do not 'want to let our friends down'. We are 'led' by our friends. It could be that our friends want us to stay away from school or encourage us to get drunk. Our friends influence us because we do not want to be 'different' and we want to keep their friendship. Sometimes it is very hard to say 'no'!

Whether our friends influence us for good or bad, it has to be remembered that anything that results from the actions that we take could influence our growth and development. For example, if a friend persuaded us to vandalize people's houses on a regular basis, and if were caught, one possible effect on our development would be that we could be sent to a young offenders' prison or receive an ASBO, depending on our age and the severity of the crime. The effect on our development would be that we would lose our freedom, be taken away from our family who support us and that we could lose our job and our other friends.

 12 How can friends have a negative effect on our development?

Most of our friends will have a positive effect on our development. Some of the features of a positive friendship are:

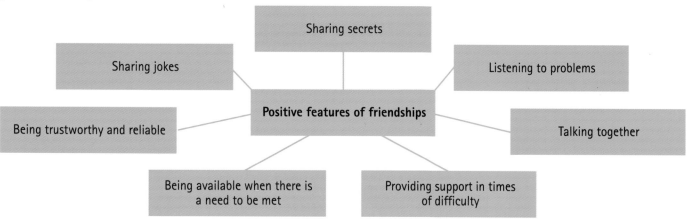

Sharing secrets

Sharing jokes

Listening to problems

Positive features of friendships

Being trustworthy and reliable

Talking together

Being available when there is a need to be met

Providing support in times of difficulty

CASE STUDY   ## Wes and Christiano

Wes is 15. He had been going out with Katy for three months. He was very happy and looked forward to their dates. Katy texted Wes during the lunch hour at school. On reading the text Wes discovered Katy had dumped him.

Wes was very upset. Christiano, Wes' friend, had noticed the text and guessed from Wes' expression what had happened. He went over to Wes and asked him if he would go with him down to the local shop.

Christiano asked Wes what the trouble was. Wes told him what had happened. They talked. Christiano suggested that they meet that evening to talk some more. He also offered to talk to Katy to find out what the problem was.

1. What role did Christiano play as Wes' friend?

2. Which of the features identified in the diagram above are linked to Wes and Christiano's friendship?

3. Do you have a friend like Christiano? How important is he or she to you?

This is an example of a positive effect of friendship on development. Christiano saw that his friend was upset. He provided support and a chance for Wes to talk about his problems. He didn't want his friend to be alone that evening so he offered practical support by asking to meet him. He also tried to give support by talking to Wes' ex-girlfriend.

The effect was probably that Wes felt that someone cared about his situation. He trusted his friend and was willing to share his secrets with his friend.

How can educational experiences affect development?

Within the education system, children and young people have the opportunity to learn new skills, gather information and pass a number of national examinations. Such examinations are important as they allow the individual to access employment, which in turn can lead to a consistent income. While in the education system children and young people learn about history, the world around them, and different cultures and attitudes. It is through becoming aware of such topics and the people met while being educated that secondary socialization takes place. Attitudes and opinions can change quite drastically as a result.

The educational experience

Parent and toddler groups

Playgroups/nursery schools

Infant schools

Secondary schools

Further education

Higher education

Life-long learning courses

Educational achievement can, however, be influenced by particular factors, some of which are genetic, others of which are environmental. Intelligence is partly an inherited factor passed down from parents, while environmental factors are linked to where you live. Both genetic and environmental factors can affect educational success. One of the current debates is 'what causes underachievement' in education. Research has shown that gender, race and social class can affect educational success.

Secondary socialization is also affected by teachers and peers. If you were to observe the same students with two different teachers, it is possible that behavioural changes would be apparent in each class. Some teachers allow the students to talk within class and to have more freedom. Others do not permit talking and demand 100 per cent concentration. Through this tolerant/non-tolerant approach, children are being socialized, although in different ways.

> **...WORD CHECK**
>
> **environmental** – to do with the surroundings.
>
> **self-concept** – the image we have of ourselves.
>
> **subconsciously** – without thinking about it.
>
> **stereotyping** – to consider people from a particular group to be the same.

How can employment/unemployment affect development?

Having a job is important as it provides an income, security and helps an individual to feel fulfilled. It can have physical, intellectual, emotional and social benefits. Learning new tasks also provides intellectual stimulation. What someone does for a living can affect their emotional development as it is an important part of their **self-concept**, that is the picture they have of themselves. They will **subconsciously** compare themselves with other role models.

How can community involvement affect growth and development?

Many people become involved in projects within their own local community. Such involvement can benefit both the individual and the community. For example a person interested in reducing crime could become a member of the Crime Prevention Panel, while an individual with artistic flare could participate in organizing community plays or local arts displays. Those who do join such activities can use their organizing skills, their problem-solving skills, can work as a member of a team as well as meeting and sharing with people who have the same interests.

How can gender affect growth and development?

Gender is not the same as sex. An individual's sex depends on their genes. Gender is about the way society expects people of each sex to behave. In other words, gender affects an individual's life opportunities because some jobs, sports or activities will be seen as being appropriate for males, and others for females.

It is difficult for people to be different if everybody around expects them to behave in certain ways according to their gender. For example, a boy may be provided with different toys from a girl. They may be given a train, while a girl is given a doll. The child will have no choice about some of the toys they are given. Since part of their intellectual and social development happens through play, their development will be affected as they may start to think that dolls are for girls to play with and trains are for boys. This is known as 'stereotyping'.

Gender socialization is also associated with culture. This influences the roles that we are to take for the future. It is thought that gender roles are learnt depending on what is taught as being acceptable to the male and female. However, in today's Western society this has changed

▸ Stereotyping.

Group Activity

Work with another person and think about when you went to playgroup, nursery school or a childminder. Were you given specific toys to play with that were considered to be more suitable because of your gender?

Did you ever want to do something that was considered more suitable for the opposite gender? What was it? Were you allowed to do it? How did you feel when you were originally prevented from doing it?

enormously and if you were to walk into a nursery class or a playgroup, it would be possible to see males playing with dolls and girls playing with building equipment. The roles between males and females are no longer clearly defined and are often merged.

13 ▸ Why is it important to encourage boys and girls to play with toys that interest them when at nursery school?

How can ethnicity and religion affect growth and development?

Ethnicity and religion are aspects of someone's culture. Ethnicity refers to the group to which people feel they belong. If a number of people of the same ethnic group live in a country where the culture is different, they are called an 'ethnic minority' group.

...WORD CHECK

ethnicity – to be related to culture or race.

culture – the way of life of a whole society or particular groups within that society; it would include the norms and values of that group – the way they live.

▸ Religious belief is an important part of some people's identity.

Religion is often, but not always, part of ethnicity. It is a system of beliefs about the spiritual aspects of life. The main religion in the UK is Christianity, although only a minority of people go to church. Other major religions practised by ethnic minorities in this country are Islam, Sikhism, Hinduism, Buddhism and Judaism.

When people are members of ethnic or religious minority groups, their growth and development is often influenced by **discrimination**. This means being treated unfairly because of your race or religion, or some other characteristic. Discrimination is considering a race or culture, or type of person, to be of less value than one's own. To deliberately act against a group of people or to favour one group above another is also discrimination.

Society is made up of different types of people, each having their own traditions, beliefs and cultures. Some people consider their own race or culture to be **superior** or better than others. They have a narrow view and think the beliefs and values they hold are the only correct ones to have. They are not prepared to be open to the values and beliefs of people from other cultures.

There are two main forms of discrimination. These are:

- **indirect** discrimination, for example, only printing information in one language, which could exclude a number of people from accessing it
- **direct** discrimination, for example, talking to someone disrespectfully.

Indirect discrimination is less obvious and more subtle. Sometimes it is unintentional, arising because a person has not given a situation sufficient thought.

Direct discrimination is where individuals are treated differently in an open manner. Obvious unfair treatment shows prejudice and is intentional.

14 ▶ How are indirect and direct discrimination likely to be shown in a residential home or nursery class?

Whether discrimination is direct or indirect it can lead to depression, low self-esteem and can completely destroy a person's belief in themselves.

> ⊘ **...WORD CHECK**
>
> **discrimination** – to show bias or intolerance.
>
> **superior** – to consider oneself to be above others.
>
> **indirect** – not directly responsible; not obvious.
>
> **direct** – open and deliberate.

CASE STUDY   Cass

Cass is a Muslim who lives in England. He is 18 and is the eldest child in a family of five. He has stayed on at college to get his qualifications so that he can become a primary school teacher. His family are very supportive and have encouraged Cass as much as possible.

Cass has a small group of friends at the college with whom he gets on well. He does not go out with them at the weekend, however, because of his family and religious commitments. He would very much like to go with them sometimes but thinks that some of the friends they meet might not accept him because of his culture.

Cass is very pleased when he passes his examinations and is accepted for teacher training. He starts to worry, however, about having to move away from home.

1 What are the social and emotional factors that are affecting Cass' growth and development?

2 In what ways are Cass' friends not being sensitive to his cultural and religious needs?

3 Explain how Cass could help his friends to understand his cultural and religious needs.

4 How are Cass' educational experiences going to affect his growth and development?

5 Explain how ethnicity and religion could influence an individual's development.

How can sexual orientation affect growth and development?

▲ Same-sex partners can now be legally joined in a 'civil partnership'.

From adolescence onwards, people experience sexual feelings towards others. During adolescence, many people experience sexual feelings towards others of the same sex. This is a common stage of their development. Most people go on to develop sexual feelings for people of the opposite sex. A significant minority continue to be sexually attracted to people of their own sex. Whether you are attracted to individuals of the same or the opposite sex determines your sexual orientation. It is an important part of self-concept.

Males who are attracted to other males and females who are attracted to other females are homosexual. Male homosexuals usually prefer to be called 'gay', and female homosexuals usually prefer to be called 'lesbian'. People who are attracted to the opposite sex are called 'heterosexual'.

Gay and lesbian people are usually in a minority in the community. The effect of sexual orientation on self-concept is similar in many ways to that of a minority culture. If you are a member of the dominant group, in this case heterosexuals, it is quite easy to see your sexuality as a valuable part of your self-concept. This is more difficult if you are in the minority.

✅...**WORD CHECK**
prejudiced – to be biased against someone without knowing them.

Same-sex partners can marry or form a legal agreement and often remain together for life. As society becomes less **prejudiced** and discriminatory towards gay or lesbian people, it is becoming easier for them to be open about their sexuality and accept it as a positive part of their self-concept.

CASE STUDY   Sandy and Max

Sandy and Max, same-sex partners, have been living together in a stable relationship for 25 years. They are now both in their seventies and are finding it difficult to cope. They have decided to move into a residential home. They have requested that they have a double bedroom, just like any married couple.

Some of the care workers and a few of the residents at the home are not happy about the arrangement.

1 What could be influencing the attitude of the care workers and service users who have objections to Sandy and Max having a double bedroom?

2 How is this type of discrimination likely to affect Sandy and Max?

How can culture affect growth and development?

Culture is shared beliefs, customs and values

Culture includes:

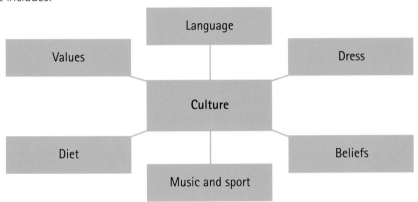

Culture binds societies together. It gives people a shared identity and a sense of belonging. This is why it is important for someone's self-concept.

Understanding culture is quite simple when there is only one culture in a society. Things are more complicated in a **multicultural** society. People from minority cultures may not feel that their differences are respected. They may feel that they are **stereotyped**, and that people are not treating them as individuals. These attitudes can have a negative effect on someone's self-concept. People from minority cultures can suffer discrimination in this country, even though there are laws such as the Race Relations Act to protect them.

> **15** How does our culture affect our self-concept?

A person's self-concept can also be affected if health and social services are not provided in a way that is appropriate to them. They may not get information about services in their preferred language. Their dietary needs may not be met, or their ideas about personal care may be ignored. They may feel that the people providing the services did not think that they are important or valuable and this may contribute to low self-esteem.

> **...WORD CHECK**
>
> **multicultural** – made up of many different people from a wide range of races.
>
> **stereotyped** – to consider people from a particular group to be the same.

CASE STUDY   Kaz

Kaz lives in a residential home. He is not able to eat the food provided because of his faith. Kaz needs a place set aside for him to pray several times each day and where he can follow the needs of his faith, but no one has responded to his request for this.

Kaz has become angry because of the discrimination. He has started shouting at other residents and at some of the care staff. He also cries a lot.

1. Explain how the residential home could meet the cultural needs of Kaz.
2. How is Kaz's self-concept likely to be affected by the discrimination?
3. Explain how this discrimination could affect Kaz's relationship with the other residents.
4. Explain the effect on Kaz's self-concept if the care workers met his cultural needs.

How can marriage and divorce affect growth and development?

▶ Celebrating their marriage.

Group Activity

Work with another person in the group to think about why quite a number of couples prefer to remain as 'partners' rather than getting married.

Make a list of the advantages and disadvantages.
Take part in a whole-class discussion on this topic using some of the items included in the lists you have made.

...WORD CHECK

mutual – two people providing support for one another.

partner – people who choose to live or work together; to do things together.

Marriage and divorce are two experiences that will affect growth and development. Quite a large number of people will marry. When this event happens, a person becomes legally joined to the person they are marrying. They become responsible for one another and any children that they have together.

A successful marriage promotes the development of both individuals because they offer each other **mutual** support. Some relationships are abusive, with one **partner** trying to control the other, or using violence against them. These relationships can be very damaging to an individual's development.

Not all marriages are successful. If a marriage fails, because it is a formal contract, there has to be another formal process for bringing it to an end. This is called divorce. Divorce may have positive effects on an individual's development if they are freed from a relationship that was making them unhappy. It may also have negative effects. Some people may find it very difficult to adjust to being single again. They may feel lonely and isolated. They may also feel that they have 'failed' in the relationship and this could lead to them having low self-esteem. They may feel that they are not able to trust another person again and this could prevent them from forming new relationships.

Currently more people are living together as 'partners' instead of getting married. Some individuals prefer having a **partner** than being legally joined. Often they are as happy as a married couple. Some partners are same-sex partners while others are different-sex partners.

ECONOMIC FACTORS THAT CAN AFFECT GROWTH AND DEVELOPMENT

Economic influences can have a major effect on development. When we talk about economic factors, we mean 'those linked to money'. Our health and well-being is affected by the amount of money we have. Economic factors are:

Income, which is usually from wages, private pensions, or state benefits such as child benefit, jobseekers' allowance, sickness and disability benefits, and the state retirement pension

Savings, which people have because they had more money than they needed to meet all their commitments and were able to put some of it away

The essential bills people have to pay, such as rent for their housing, community charge, gas, electricity and water bills, and transport costs

Debts, caused by borrowing money, to buy a house (a mortgage) or an expensive piece of household equipment. Sometimes people have debts because they have had problems and not paid essential bills in the past

Material possessions are all the things that people need to live comfortably

How can wealth affect growth and development?

Wealth is very important for human growth and development. The more money someone has, the more choices they have, and the better they are able to meet their physical, intellectual, emotional and social needs.

People with a high income can afford good quality clothing, and will not have to worry about fuel bills. This means that they can meet their own physical needs and the needs of the people dependent on them.

> ✅ **...WORD CHECK**
>
> **wealth** – assets such as a house or owning shares in a company.
>
> **vulnerable** – to be at risk of harm.

How can poverty affect growth and development?

A person who has a low income may have to be careful about the amount of gas and electricity that they use. They may not be able to keep their home as warm as they would like it. This may be particularly important for families with young children, and for older people who are more **vulnerable** to the cold.

Some people may not use their income wisely. They may put things like alcohol, cigarettes or drugs before paying their bills. This could mean that, eventually, because they owe so much money, they lose their home and their family.

People with lower incomes do not usually have the choice of private health care; they have to wait their turn on the waiting list as they cannot afford to pay for private treatment.

Savings are important because they help people meet their needs. If people have some money in a bank or building society, then they are prepared when something happens. If a child needs an expensive new pair of shoes, or a vacuum cleaner breaks and has to be replaced, this is much easier to do if someone has some savings. If they do not, and don't have enough income to pay for the things, they either have to go without or borrow to get them.

CASE STUDY — Roger

Roger is 14. He lives with his family on an estate in rented council accommodation. Most of the families on the estate have low incomes.

Roger has three sisters all between the ages of 5 and 11. His father works in a car factory but recently his hours have been reduced as cars are not selling very well. His mother works in a bingo hall during the afternoons, which is also part time.

Roger's parents are very short of money. They have to pay the rent and they are in debt. They have to pay off some of what they owe for a car they once had. This leaves very little left for bills, such as gas and electricity, or food.

Roger has asked if he can have an MP3 player for his birthday but his family cannot afford to get him this.

1. Give **two** economic factors that are affecting Roger's growth and development.
2. Identify **three** essential items of expenditure for Roger's family.
3. How are economic factors going to affect Roger's growth and development?
4. Roger's classmates can afford good clothes and equipment for school while Roger does not have all the things he needs. How do you think this may affect Roger's growth and development?
5. Explain how poor housing and low income could affect Roger's development.
6. Explain how not being able to have an MP3 player could affect Roger's intellectual, emotional and social development.

Debts are an important factor because they have to be paid, and the more debt someone has, the less of their income is available to spend on things they need now. Many people are drawn into debt through advertisements that encourage individuals and families to put all their outstanding debt on one account. In the long run, the amount paid back could be far more!

A parent on a low income might not be able to afford school trips or books and equipment that a parent on a high income could afford. People with higher incomes can also afford to help their children through higher education, but children from lower income families may have to go into debt to pay for their child's higher education. Parents' income affects a child's educational opportunities, and success in education improves a person's chance of getting a good job.

> ✓ ...WORD CHECK
>
> economic – linked to finances.

How can employment status, occupation and social class affect growth and development?

The class we are in will influence, in some ways, the opportunities that we have. Our social class is often based on **economic** factors and the job we do. For example, a GP could be considered to be in a higher social class than a lorry driver. The economic status of a person enables them to have opportunities that others may not get.

In Britain the system is known as the 'class system', the differences between the classes being in terms of educational success, the type of work that is being undertaken and the money earned. A person's occupation is therefore used to assess the importance of people. These differences are recorded in scales. For example, the Registrar-General's Scale:

Class	Definition	Example
A or 1	Higher Professional & Higher Managerial	lawyer, accountant, doctor, minister, bank manager
B or 2	Lower Professional & Lower Managerial	nurse, teacher, farmer, school teacher, MP, police officer
C or 3	Skilled Manual and remainder of Non-manual Workers	plumber, shop assistant, typist, mechanic
D or 4	Semi-skilled Worker	lorry driver, assembly line worker, postman, bus conductor, agricultural worker
E or 5	Unskilled Worker	window cleaner, labourer, messenger, road sweeper, cleaner

C is often sub-divided into two, known as **C1** and **C2**.
Classes **1, 2 and 3**, are middle classes, **4** and **5** are working class.

▲ The Registrar-General's scale.

This scale is often considered to be 'top heavy', with more middle class type occupations than working class jobs. On the other hand, the 'Hall Jones Scale' has seven categories rather than five and is therefore thought of as being fairer by many people.

Class	Definition
1	Professional and high administrative
2	Managerial and executive
3	Inspectional, supervisory and other non-manual, higher grade
4	Inspectional, supervisory and other non-manual, lower grade
5	Skilled manual and routine grades of non-manual
6	Semi-skilled manual
7	Unskilled manual

▲ The Hall Jones Scale.

16 In what way is the Hall Jones scale different from the Registrar-General's Scale?

CASE STUDY   Mandy and Greg

Mandy is training to be a lawyer like her father. Both her mother and father are encouraging her to go to university and study for a degree in law.

Greg's father and mother have their own business and hope that Greg will join the firm when he has finished his A2 qualifications in Business.

1   How are the families affecting the development of Mandy and Greg?

2   Explain how social class can influence development.

3   Compare the Registrar-General's class scale with the Hall Jones Scale. What are the similarities and differences?

4   Why do you think some working-class families would encourage their children to go on to higher education?

How can material possessions affect growth and development?

Material possessions are also important for meeting physical needs. Life is much more pleasant for adolescents and young adults with MP3 players, high definition TVs and the latest in console games. People who have been able to buy these things may have spent a great deal of money on them over a period of time and would have much pleasure in showing them to their friends. People on low incomes may have been unable to do this.

Economic factors affect the way that people can meet their physical needs, but they also affect their intellectual, emotional and social needs. This is because being able to afford things can make individuals happy. Not being able to buy the things they need can make people unhappy and resentful. Individuals could also become socially isolated if they can't afford to socialize with their friends.

▶ ▶ ▶ ▶ **ASSESSMENT PRACTICE**

Section One

1 ▶ Primary socialization is

☐ **A** what we learn from our family ☐ **B** reading a book

☐ **C** collecting information from websites ☐ **D** what we learn from school [1]

Section Two

Robert is the youngest of three children. His father, Ian, is a bank manager and his mother is a teacher. The family live in a small village that is five miles from the town where his parents work. The family live in a detached four-bedroomed house that has a large garden.

Robert has just started at the local primary school. He has frequent epileptic fits. Some of the children in his class are calling him names and refusing to sit next to him.

2 ▶ Explain how a caring home life can affect Robert's socialization. [5]

3 ▶ Identify **two** secondary socialization factors that could influence Robert's development. Explain how each are likely to influence him. [5]

4 ▶ Identify **one** form of discrimination experienced by Robert. Give two examples to illustrate how this occurs. [3]

5 ▶ Identify **two** likely effects of discrimination on Robert. Explain how each is likely to affect him. [6]

6 ▶ Explain the difference between 'direct' and 'indirect discrimination. Give **two** examples to illustrate how each could occur. [5]

7 ▶ Explain what is meant by the term 'self-esteem'. Explain **two** ways in which Robert's self-esteem is likely to be affected positively and **two** ways in which it is likely to be affected negatively. [5]

8 ▶ How could Robert's father help him to understand why others were discriminating against him? [5]

PHYSICAL ENVIRONMENT FACTORS THAT CAN AFFECT GROWTH AND DEVELOPMENT

Environmental factors include the conditions people live in, such as:

Housing

Pollution

Rural/urban lifestyles

How can pollution affect development?

Pollution means the release of harmful things into the environment. By the environment, we mean the earth, air and water. Clean water is essential for healthy living. This particularly applies to drinking water, which is a need for all individuals. The main source of freshwater pollution is

218938/361 FIS

from the discharge of untreated waste and dumping of industrial **effluent**. Water-borne infectious diseases include hepatitis, cholera, dysentery and typhoid. Exposure to polluted water can cause diarrhoea, skin irritation and typhoid.

...WORD CHECK
effluent – pollutant; sewage waste.

Air pollution can cause conditions such as asthma, irritation to the eyes, bronchitis and pneumonia, and other respiratory problems are likely to be activated when the air is polluted. This is because the pollutants in the air cause a reaction in the lungs, making smaller airways constrict. As a result, breathing becomes more difficult. The effect on the individual can be:

- poor health
- low self-esteem
- social isolation
- depression.

There are three sorts of pollution that people are most concerned about. These are:

 Chemicals

 Radiation

Noise

How can housing conditions and rural/urban lifestyles affect growth and development?

Housing and the location where people live can strongly influence the development of individuals, particularly that of children. For example, if a person lives in a rural area, this could determine the number of health, social care and early years services they are able to access, and the recreational

▼ Different types of housing.

activities they can join in could be limited. Visiting friends and extended family members may be more difficult and they may have to travel to receive their education. However, living in a rural area could provide easier access to natural environments, which can enhance learning and development, and provide the opportunity for walking or community activities.

Children and people living in an **urban** area could experience social **deprivation** as they could be exposed to higher crime rates or vandalism and may be fearful of going out. Access to services may be easier when living in a town or city and there may be more activities in which to participate.

Housing in inner cities and towns may take the form of flats with which there are no gardens, whereas in rural areas, houses are more likely to be detached, semi-detached or terraced, with their own gardens. There is likely to be less traffic in a rural area and, consequently, pollution is likely to be less of a problem.

The effects of these environments on development are likely to be:

Effects of living in a rural area	Effects of living in an urban area
Good health promoted because of natural open areas	Illness treated quickly because services are easier to access
May be reserved as social activities may be restricted	Could be more comfortable in social situations and with people
May be physically fitter as open countryside enables walking, cycling and so on	Could be less fit as there are fewer open spaces or these may be more difficult to reach
May be more economically aware as money is needed to reach urban areas for shopping, leisure activities and so on	May be able to spend more money on wants as travelling costs do not have to be taken into account

Good quality housing will usually have a positive effect on people and poor quality housing is more likely to have a negative effect. For instance, a high-rise flat may suit a single person, a couple/partners without children or adults who do not want a garden. It would not be suitable for a single parent or two people with young children or for older people who could find access difficult.

 17 What is meant by inadequate housing?

An infant or child being brought up in cold, damp conditions may suffer physical effects as if the home is damp and difficult to heat, the infant or child will be more likely to have respiratory illnesses, which might affect their development as they will not be fit and healthy.

There may also be intellectual effects on an infant or child, particularly if the home is cramped, and it is not easy to get outside as there will not be a stimulating environment to explore. The parents of children who live in such conditions will probably be under stress because of the conditions they live in, and this may affect the way they provide care for the infant or child.

Older people often have less resistance to infection and have more difficulty maintaining their body temperature if their homes are not adequately heated. A bungalow is also considered to be more suitable for some, as mobility problems may make it more difficult to access upstairs levels.

 ...WORD CHECK

urban – town area; heavily populated.

deprivation – lacking the basic essentials such as food and shelter.

 Group Activity

You have been given the opportunity to decide where you will live, for example, a rural or urban area. Which would you choose? Give advantages and disadvantages. What are the likely effects on development?

CASE STUDY — Elaine and family

Elaine is a lone parent with three children, Olivia, aged one, Rebecca, aged four, and Benjamin, aged six. They live in an upstairs flat in an old house with no access to the garden. The flat has been badly converted, has poor heating and the windows don't fit properly. The cooker is not working, as only one ring heats, and the oven tends to burn food if put on the recommended temperature and so the family often eat takeaway food.

The house is on a busy road, and the nearest play area is some distance away. Elaine has put up with these conditions for a long time because she has no alternative solution and has become frustrated, angry and depressed. The children are boisterous and she is always yelling and shouting at them. Sometimes she hits them. Benjamin has missed a lot of school through illness. When he goes, his teacher often complains that he is unable to concentrate.

1. Think about Elaine. How is her physical, intellectual, emotional and social development being affected by her environment?

2. What would the advantages and disadvantages be to Elaine and the family if they lived in a rural area?

3. How might Benjamin's development be affected if he is being physically punished?

4. How is Olivia's development likely to be affected by the living conditions?

5. Suggest ways in which Elaine could have support to help the family in their present living conditions.

HOW CAN PSYCHOLOGICAL FACTORS AFFECT GROWTH AND DEVELOPMENT?

When factors have a positive effect on us, we feel happy and pleased. When the effects are negative, this may lower our self-esteem.

Effects on our development could be positive:

happy	confident	fulfilled	valued
high self-esteem		high self-worth	positive
pleased	elated	responsible	

Effects on development could be negative:

worthless	worried	low self-esteem	unhappy
undervalued	depressed	disheartened	gloomy
having no authority or influence	insignificant	sad	dejected

It should be remembered that psychological factors can cause an individual to:

- have high or low self-esteem
- have poor mental and physical health or good physical and mental health
- have excellent employment prospects or a poor chance of gaining employment
- achieve well in education if they are feeling content and happy or not succeed if they are worried or anxious, or have poor mental and physical health.

Group Activity

Work with another person in the group to find out the meaning of the words in both the positive and negative boxes.

Write a sentence for each to show that you have understood the effect on development. One example has been done for you:

Faith had low self-esteem when she was not given the promotion at work and was very sad as she felt she was useless.

How can stress affect growth and development?

All life events provide the opportunity for personal growth. They can also cause stress, which can have emotional effects such as anxiety and depression. If this happens, it is a sign that changes are necessary in our lifestyle so that we can live comfortably with the new circumstances. The changes we have to make are one reason that life events promote personal development because we can learn from the experiences and this contributes to our personal development.

The table below shows how stressful different life events can be. Each life event is given a score. The higher the score, the more likely it is that someone will become ill because of the stress. If someone goes through more than one life event at the same time, the scores are added together.

This table is adapted from the Holmes–Rahe Social Adjustment Scale.

Holmes–Rahe Social Adjustment Scale

Life event	Score
Death of partner	100
Divorce	73
Separation from partner	65
Death of close relative	63
Serious injury or illness	53
Marriage	50
Losing job	47
Reconciliation with partner	45
Retirement	45
Pregnancy	40
Birth in family	39
Death of close friend	37
Taking out a mortgage	31
Child leaving home	29
Partner beginning or stopping work	26
Beginning or ending education	26
Moving house	20
Changing schools	20

From the list it can be noted that there are quite a lot of 'life events' that can affect an individual's life.

How can factors inter-relate (work together) to affect an individual's development?

It is not often that any one single factor will affect development for a long period of time. It is only when several factors join together that an individual may be more permanently affected by them.

Which types of factors could inter-relate?

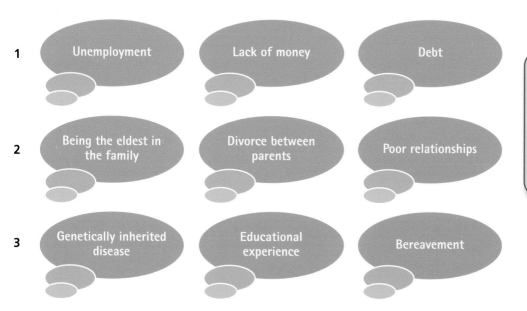

1
- Unemployment
- Lack of money
- Debt

2
- Being the eldest in the family
- Divorce between parents
- Poor relationships

3
- Genetically inherited disease
- Educational experience
- Bereavement

Group Activity

Using the three factor links on the left, write three case studies (for three different individuals) to show how the factors in each are linked and how they could effect the development of each individual.

Let us consider the first combination of three factors: unemployment, lack of money and debt.

CASE STUDY — Angus

Angus works in an estate agent's and has done so since he left school ten years ago. He is now the deputy manager and enjoys going out with his many friends. Suddenly houses are not selling very well and he is eventually made redundant. He has a large mortgage on the house, a loan on his car and money that he owes the bank for a holiday.

At first he manages to keep up all his payments as he was given some redundancy money. He tries hard to find another job but is without any luck. He gradually uses up all his money and is very anxious about what is going to happen next as his credit cards are spent up to the limit. His friends have stopped asking him out as they realize he has no money.

1. Explain how Angus is affected by the links between unemployment, lack of money and debt.

2. In what other ways is Angus' personal development going to be affected by the changes taking place?

Unemployment was the first factor that affected Angus. He had been used to a steady income each month and was not at all worried about money, so he spent what he had, was very happy and had lots of friends whom he often went out with. When he was made redundant he felt quite confident that he would get another job but, as time passed, he found he could not get one. He used his redundancy money to pay his mortgage and loans and for everyday living such as food, heating and clothes. Gradually the money ran out and Angus used his credit cards until he was up to his credit limit.

From being a happy and independent individual who did not have to think before spending, and having high self-esteem because he was in a good job, he found himself, within a short period of time, worried about what he was going to eat, how to pay the mortgage and loans, and the outstanding amount on the credit cards. He was unable to afford to go out with his friends and become isolated. His self-esteem is now low, he doesn't feel valued and he is extremely worried. One event led or inter-related with another to get Angus into this position to which it is very difficult to find a solution.

▶ ▶ ▶ ▶ **ASSESSMENT PRACTICE**

Section One

1 ▶ Which **two** are cultural factors that can affect development?

1 being religious
2 attending a university
3 going to nursery school
4 wearing 'chav' clothes

☐ **A** 1 and 2
☐ **B** 2 and 3
☐ **C** 3 and 4
☐ **D** 1 and 4 [2]

Section Two

2 ▶ Paula and Suzie are identical twins. Their parents read them stories and played with them quite a lot and taught them to play musical instruments. They both went to playgroup and enjoyed meeting other children.

When she was six years old, Suzie had an accident and missed two months of school. This put her very much behind her sister and she found it hard to make progress.

Their father spent a lot of time with both girls, teaching them to use the computer. Paula and Suzie are18 years old and now have jobs working with computers. They both still like to read, and enjoy activities such as badminton, swimming and dancing. They go out quite a lot with their friends.

a Explain **four** factors, other than genetics, that have influenced the development of the twins. [8]

b Explain how the emotional development of the twins has been affected. [3]

3 ▶ Amir is 18 years old and is a Muslim who lives in England. He is studying at a sixth form college to get qualifications that will help him train as a doctor. His family are very supportive.

Amir has a small group of friends at college. He does not go out with them at the weekends because of his religious commitments. His friends often try to persuade him to go out with them but he is reluctant to do so in case he is not accepted by others.

a Explain **three** ways that educational experiences could affect his development. [6]

b Other factors that have influenced Amir's development are:
  • being the eldest in a family with four other children
  • his father being made unemployed
  • living in an urban area with lots of pollution.

Explain how these factors could inter-relate (work together) to affect his development. [8]

4 Explain **three** ways that ethnicity and religion could affect development. [6]

5 List **three** different types of abuse that could take place, explaining how each could affect development. [12]

HOW THESE FACTORS ARE RELATED TO THE FORMATION OF, AND POSSIBLE CHANGE IN, AN INDIVIDUAL'S SELF-CONCEPT

Self-concept is our sense of who we are and the way we see ourselves. It is the picture we have of ourselves. This picture is made up of three parts:

1

Self-image – based on a description of who we are. This includes knowledge from our social roles, for example, mother, father, aunt; the personality traits we have, for example, whether we are clever, have a sense of humour; and how we see our body, for example, brunette, tall, fat.

2

Self-esteem – an evaluation of how we see ourselves, which includes how much we like ourselves.

3

Ideal self – the sort of person we would like to be. The person we admire.

ACTIVITY   Who am I?

Self-image	–	Write a description of yourself.
Self-esteem	–	Evaluate how much you like yourself.
		What do you like?
		What don't you like?
Ideal self	–	How would you like to be?

Think about what you have written and keep it to develop further in this section.

In this activity you may have considered your physical appearance, your intellectual strengths, your personality, thoughts, hopes or fears. Everything that you considered has been evaluated through how you have been reflected back to yourself through other people's actions. Cooley (1902) called this 'the looking glass self'. This means that if people tell you that you are attractive or clever or good at netball enough times, you believe them and take on that role. This is particularly so if you are given this information by 'significant others', who are people like parents, teachers, best friends, whose opinions you trust and value. This does, of course, work with negative aspects of your self-concept as well, hence the labelling of the 'naughty' girl, the 'uncooperative' boy or even the person who is 'useless at maths'!

Self-concept develops as a person grows. Babies do not distinguish themselves from their mother or primary carer. They do not have any understanding of where their mother ends and they begin. An infant will put their fingers into their mother's mouth or bite their mother's finger, having no concern for how their mother will feel. Infants need to develop intellectually before they can understand that they are an individual and that there are other people in the world. It is not until around 18 months old that they begin to realize that they exist as a separate entity to anyone else. They need to develop emotionally before they can understand that other people

▶ Babies cannot know where they stop and where their mother begins.

...WORD CHECK

high regard – to think very well of.

fluid – flexible; having no boundaries.

have feelings of their own. Until they understand this, they can't understand that other individuals have opinions about them. This is why young children cannot play cooperatively with others, and why the infant having a tantrum in the street is not embarrassed to lie on the floor kicking and screaming.

For a very young baby, their main carer is their world. They are helpless and depend on their carer to meet all their needs. Whether they are treated kindly, neglectfully or harshly affects how they think about the world and how it values them.

Our self-concept is important because it affects all our relationships and interactions with others. It is only having a good opinion about ourselves, holding ourselves in **high regard**, that will enable us to value ourselves and to enjoy good relationships with others. If we have a poor self-concept, it is likely to impact on our behaviour, for example, we could become withdrawn from others, may not achieve in examinations or become a bully towards others. Having a high self-concept is, therefore, a very important feature of development.

Unless a person values themselves and has a sense that other people value them, they are not likely to function very well. A person who does not place any value on themselves will not like or 'love' themselves. Most people are often in a muddle about whether they like themselves or not. People are often unclear about how they see themselves or how others view them, particularly in adolescence.

18 ▶ Why do you value yourself or why do you not value yourself? How has this affected your behaviour?

Self-concept is also **fluid**, meaning that it can change as we grow older, meet new situations and people, and take on new roles. As individuals we are part of a cultural group and we will not want to be too far away from the values held by that group. To do so would produce an uncomfortable feeling, a feeling that you do not belong, that you do not fit in.

We all need to have a realistic view of ourselves. We need to feel comfortable with people with whom we work or enjoy leisure time. When this happens, we feel secure enough to allow other people's perspectives of us to have an influence on the way we see ourselves.

How other people react towards us is very significant in how we view ourselves. As young children, it is our parents to whom we look and admire, and this is a very important aspect of our development. Later, as we meet others, for example, teachers and peers, they too become significant and influence our own self-concept as we emulate the characteristics we observe in them that we like. The effect of parenting on self-esteem lasts with us throughout life.

It is from our parents and primary carers that we learn basic social rules and values.

What are the values that children learn?

The difference between right and wrong

To respect others

A sense of 'fairness'

When a child does something well, they are usually praised. When they do something that is unacceptable, they may get a good telling off. In this way the child will add to the picture they are developing of themselves.

Children do not just do the things they are taught to do or the things they see happening around them. They will think about what is happening and decide what their own values are to be. This is called 'internalizing' or examining themselves from the experiences they are having.

 19 How does a child add to the picture they have of themselves?

A child's self-concept is also affected by what society expects from them. We take it for granted that being a child involves certain things. For instance going to school and being protected from certain things, for example, using alcohol and tobacco, and having sex.

An adolescent sense of self is very strong. An adolescent wants more independence. They want to make their own decisions. They may not feel very secure in making these decisions but they have an internal picture of themselves and they try to project this picture so that others can see who they are.

> **...WORD CHECK**
> internalizing – to absorb into the self-conscious; to understand and then to be able to discuss the subject with understanding.

◀ Individual identity is important.

Adolescents often identify themselves by their membership of particular groups. These groups have often identified themselves by hairstyle, clothing, tattoos, body piercings and the type of music they like. This has been a way of expressing their self-concept. It is a way of demonstrating rebellion and rejection of adult values, and independence, showing that they are no longer children.

A good self-awareness will help adolescents develop a secure sense of self. They will need this to be able to:

- make difficult decisions
- form social and sexual relationships
- develop confidence in work roles or in a chosen college course.

20 What else will influence the development of self-concept?

How we learn to value ourselves in childhood and during adolescence can affect us as adults. Adults are recognized by society as being fully independent. Unlike children, they are fully responsible for all their actions. We are surrounded by images of young, attractive people in advertisements, newspapers and other forms of the media. This will greatly influence our internal image of how we think we should be.

In later adulthood it is important that we still keep a clear sense of our self-concept. The image that we have of ourselves will be influenced by the life events we have experienced. Such events that influence self-concept could be getting married, starting a family or experiencing divorce. Some of these life events will reinforce the positive image we may have of ourselves. Others may have a negative effect on our development. A few people may have experience of accidents that change their lives from being 'able bodied' to 'disabled'. This can be very challenging for the person and it can be very hard to keep a positive self-image in these circumstances.

21 Why may it be hard to keep a positive self-image if disabled as a result of an accident?

CASE STUDY   Sedu

Sedu is 37 and is a college lecturer. He has a wife and three children who are 7, 5 and 3. Sedu's wife works part time as a teacher. The family are always very busy taking the children to and from school, and to their various clubs and activities during the evenings or at the weekend. They are happy.

Sedu always cycles to college to make sure he gets enough exercise. On the way home one day he is knocked off his bicycle by a car. He is taken to hospital with spinal injuries. He has a three-hour operation to remove pieces of bone from his spinal cord.

Three months after the accident, Sedu is told that he will never be able to work again. He can shuffle around the downstairs rooms at home but he cannot walk properly. He cannot get upstairs and he is in pain most of the time. He cannot work at his computer for longer than ten minutes because of the pain. The worst thing is that he is unable to help his wife with the daily chores and he cannot play with the children. Sedu becomes very depressed about his state of health.

1. How has Sedu's intellectual development been affected by the accident?

2. How do you think Sedu's self-concept has been affected as a result of the accident?

3. How do you think the accident will affect Sedu's wife's self-concept?

4. Explain how the self-concept of Sedu's children could be affected as a result of the accident.

5. Assess the possible effects Sedu's accident could have on his self-concept in the future.

Some people could experience discrimination in the workplace. They may find that employers prefer younger staff whom they may see as more flexible and adaptable. People over 50 may feel that they are not as valued as younger people. A person with a strong self-concept will probably be able to find other areas of their lives where they are valued, such as being a member of a club or the leader of a committee. However, they could be affected in some way by discrimination. For example, they may feel:

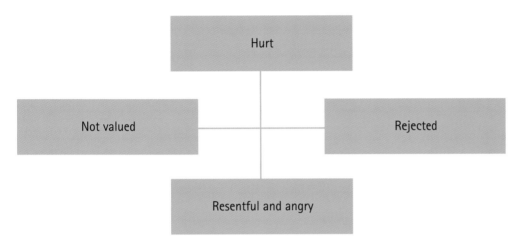

When our self-concept has been lowered, the effect may be that we withdraw from social activities because we are afraid we may get hurt again. We may not want to trust people again. We may find that we communicate less with people. In some circumstances people become so angry that they physically hurt the person with whom they live.

Such actions are going to contribute to developing a negative self-concept. We may need help to see ourselves in a different way and to cope with the situation we find ourselves in.

In later adulthood some people may feel that they are not valued, particularly as they have lost their work role. The effect may cause them to become withdrawn and depressed. They may feel that others think they have nothing to contribute.

CASE STUDY   Malcolm

Malcolm is 63. He has worked as a salesman in a furniture store for 30 years. Malcolm loves his work. He lives on his own, so he enjoys meeting customers and chatting to his colleagues. Sometimes he goes out with his work colleagues for a drink and a game of darts. This is his main social life.

He is called in to see the manager when he arrives at work one day. The manager tells Malcolm that the firm would like him to take early retirement. This is because they are going to introduce a number of changes and feel that he would benefit financially if he were to leave at the end of the month. The manager makes it clear that he expects Malcolm to accept the package being offered.

1. How will Malcolm's social development be affected by taking early retirement?
2. How do you think Malcolm's self-concept may be affected by taking early retirement?
3. List **three** negative social aspects of retirement. Describe how each could affect Malcolm's self-concept.

How is self-concept affected by emotional development?

Emotional development is very important to the individual's self-concept because it determines how the individual thinks about themselves and what they believe others think about them.

If early experiences are positive, then the individual will feel good about themselves and will expect other people to value them.

Sometimes early experiences are not good. A child may be neglected or abused by carers. This child may have low self-esteem and feel worthless or not valued. They may not expect other people to like them. Their emotional development has been harmed.

The way parents discipline infants, children and young people will also affect their emotional development and self-concept.

CASE STUDY — Praise and punishment

Carer A tries not to punish a young child unless it is absolutely necessary. When their child is doing something dangerous or naughty, they distract them by offering them something interesting to do. When the child does something good, they are praised and rewarded. The child is often praised.

Another child is shouted at and sometimes hit when they do something that Carer B thinks is wrong. They are often criticized and told they are naughty, or a nuisance. They are never praised for things they do. They are often put to bed hungry as a punishment.

Discuss: Which is the best option? Why?

For each case study, state how each individual's self-concept is likely to be affected.

Group Activity

Work with another person to find a solution.

A four-year-old child has hit his friend with a toy and made him cry.

Explain **two** different positive ways of disciplining the child, giving reasons for the actions suggested.

Someone who has had a positive experience in their emotional development will have a strong self-concept. If someone is confident that they are valuable, then they will believe in themselves and won't depend on the approval of others. They will have more confidence in everything they do, whether it is sitting an examination, asking someone out or applying for a job. They will be able to accept that sometimes things go wrong, and it is not necessarily their fault. When they are criticized, they will be able to accept it if it is justified, and learn from it. They will be optimistic about life. They will be able to present themselves confidently and have a realistic view of their abilities.

Someone with poor emotional development will have a negative self-concept. They will feel anxious about taking risks. This may make them shy and self-conscious. They may find it difficult to make friends because they are not sure what they have to offer. They may find it difficult to get a partner because they are reluctant to take the risk of asking someone out. They may feel guilty and responsible when things go wrong, even when it was not their fault.

They will be afraid of confrontation with others because they will not be confident in their own opinions. They may put themselves down. They may not be able to react positively to criticism and will either resent it or see it as a personal attack. They will not have a very good opinion about life and undervalue their abilities.

CASE STUDY   Chantelle

Chantelle is aged 5 and lives with her mother and older brothers Ethan, aged 10, and Mark, aged 13. Chantelle cried a great deal during the first few months of her life and constantly disrupted family life. As a result, her father left home and her mother blamed her for this.

As a toddler, Chantelle spent a lot of time playing on her own, as her mother was too depressed to play with her. As a result she is a quiet, withdrawn child who does not speak very much to others in the reception class.

Chantelle's mother compares her with her brothers, whom she praises a lot. She often tells Chantelle that she is a nuisance and that having to look after her prevents her from having any life of her own.

Chantelle's father takes both boys to football matches at the weekend but she is not invited to go with them. Chantelle's brothers often tease her and say it's her fault their father left and that he doesn't want to know her.

When at school Chantelle does not make any effort to make friends and spends a lot of time just daydreaming.

1. Explain the factors that have influenced Chantelle's development of self-concept.

2. How do you think Chantelle identifies herself? What has influenced this?

3. How do you think Chantelle compares herself to others? What has influenced this?

▸ ▸ ▸ ▸ ASSESSMENT PRACTICE

Section One

1. The effect of discrimination against an individual could cause:

    ☐   **A**   an individual to feel respected
    ☐   **B**   an individual to feel valued
    ☐   **C**   an individual to feel worthless
    ☐   **D**   an individual to feel confident   [1]

Section Two

2. Patricia had a car accident while she was on the way to work one morning. She was badly hurt and needed to have an arm amputated.

    a   Explain **three** effects Patricia's physical disabilities may have on her self-concept. [6]

    Patricia's husband, Andy, is a teacher.

    b   Explain **three** ways that Patricia's accident could affect Andy's self-concept. [6]

3. Sasha likes buying clothes and making sure that she looks good when she is out with her friends. She is a member of several recreational clubs and joins in a number of different activities.

    Explain how having nice clothes can influence self-concept. [5]

Continued on next page ▸

◀ *Continued from previous page*

4 ▶ Sakina, 71 years of age, has recently moved to this country from India. She is now in a residential home because she is not very mobile and cannot look after herself. Sakina is a Muslim and likes to practice her faith and follow her cultural beliefs. She is the only Muslim in the residential home and the care workers do not make any different provision for her. In fact, they talk about her to the other residents as though Sakina is not in the room and leave her out of their activities. She cannot always eat the food that is provided.

Explain **three** ways in which Sakina's self-concept is likely to be affected by the discrimination she is experiencing. [6]

5 ▶ Brenda cannot look after herself any longer. The local authority have arranged for her to visit the day-care centre twice each week and for a care assistant to call three times a week. The care assistant is to help with a little tidying and hand ironing and to do the shopping.

Explain **three** ways that Brenda's self-concept could be affected by visiting the day-care centre and being visited by a care assistant. [6]

6 | Use theory to help explain how self-concept develops from childhood to older adult life stage. [20]

HOW GENETIC AND ENVIRONMENTAL FACTORS CAN AFFECT GROWTH AND DEVELOPMENT

All of the factors that have been discussed in this section can affect the way that people grow and develop. These factors are often categorized into two groups: genetic and environmental. As we have discussed, an individual's development could be affected by a genetic factor, such as an inherited illness, or an environmental factor, such as the family relationships they experienced when they were a child. The consideration of which has more influence on an individual's development is called the 'nature versus nurture' debate. Nature refers to the genetic influences on our development and nurture refers to all the other environmental influences on an individual, such as family, education and where they live.

Most people suggest that an individual's development is significantly influenced by both their genetic make-up and the influences around them. As illustrated throughout this section, it is how an individual's unique combination of nature and nurture affects their development that determines their health, well-being and life opportunities.

CASE STUDY   Sheila

Sheila is an identical twin. She is very close to her sister, Mary. They both have fair hair and blue eyes. When they were children, they had the usual childhood illnesses but Sheila also developed a mild form of meningitis and was away from school for several weeks.

At school they both did quite well in their examinations but Sheila found the language classes quite difficult. When she was ill she missed quite a few lessons and found it hard to catch up.

Both Sheila and Mary like playing the piano and enjoy jogging. When they were younger they used to go running with their father at the weekends. He was a member of the running club. Their father also taught them how to use a computer when they were six years old.

Sheila now has a job as a computer programmer. Mary also works with computers but in an office at the other end of the town. They meet for lunch twice a week and bring a friend with them. They usually have a snack such as a jacket potato and salad.

On Thursdays they play badminton in a group of four and on Saturdays they go swimming. They are members of the swimming club.

1   Sheila's growth and development has been influenced by several factors. List **six** factors that have influenced her development and give an example of each.

2   Explain how Sheila's family could have influenced her development.

3   Using the case study for Sheila discuss the nature versus nurture argument. Give examples to illustrate the points you are making.

4   Think of your own development **or** find out about the development of a friend. Describe **four** factors that have influenced either your or their personal development. Give examples for each.

Effects of relationships on personal growth and development

▶ Getting started

You will gain an understanding of:

a the different types of relationships:
   i   family relationships, such as marriage, divorce, parenthood, sibling relationships and blended families
   ii friendships
   iii intimate, personal and sexual relationships
   iv working relationships

b the importance of the effects these relationships have across the six life stages, on an individual's growth and development

DIFFERENT TYPES OF RELATIONSHIPS

Family relationships

Most people will, at some time in their lives, live with or in a family. The family is a group of people of various ages who are usually related by birth, marriage or adoption. Members of a family usually feel that they have a special relationship with one another. This is often known as 'family ties'. The family plays an important part in the development of individuals. How we feel about our family and how we get on with the members of our family will influence the way we think and relate to people throughout our lives.

 What do you think contributes to members of a family feeling they have something in common?

There are different types of family. For example:

Lone parent families

This is where one parent, either the mother or the father, has decided to bring up a child on their own. This could be because the parents have decided to separate or divorce, or it could be because of the death of one parent. Sometimes it is because the mother has decided that she wants to stay single and bring the child up herself without any support from the child's father.

Nuclear families

These live as a self-contained family unit in a single household. They consist of parents and their children. When the children in the family are young, the whole family live together, sharing and supporting one another. When children grow up they may move away from home and set up their own home.

Blended families

These often happen when there has been a divorce or the death of one parent, followed by re-marriage. The child or children will be the natural child of one person in the marriage or partnership. An example of a blended or step family is:

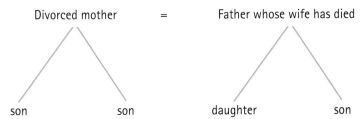

Divorced mother = Father whose wife has died

son   son   daughter   son

The increase in marriage breakdowns means that families are separating at an earlier age.

Re-marriages are taking place when people are younger. As a result it is likely that the new partners may have children of their own as well as children to care for from previous marriages.

Children from different families in a blended family situation can find it hard to get on with one another in the early days of the new arrangement. This situation is sometimes resolved after the family settle down and become used to each other's ways.

An extended family

This is a large family group that includes parents, sisters, brothers, grandparents, uncles and aunts. The members of the family all live together in the same building or very close to each other. Such a large group can give support to each other by helping to bring up the children. They can give advice when there is a problem and will help by contributing to the daily living expenses for the group. Extended families are not so common in Western Europe as the pattern of family life has changed in recent years, but they are common in other parts of the world.

▶ Blended families occur when people re-marry and children from previous marriages all live together.

'Looked after' families

Residential homes provide family life for children who cannot live with their natural parents. The care or key workers who look after the children try to make sure that the pattern of the children's life is as similar as possible to children who live in single households. In a residential children's home there may be six or seven children living with main carers.

23 What relations could exist in a residential children's home?

24 Why do you think there are fewer extended families in Western Europe now than there were in previous years?

Each member of the family will have a number of different relationships. For example:

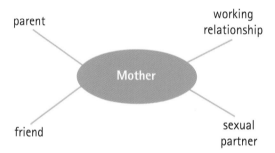

- As parents the mother and father will provide for and support the family. They will provide safe and secure surroundings for their children to grow up in.

- As sexual partners the mother and father will develop intimate and loving relationships with one another.

- The father and/or the mother may go out to work and may be an employee or an employer and will have a working relationship with others.

- As well as providing for the family, the mother and father will also have friends of their own age with whom they can talk and share activities.

25 Why do you think a number of people will want to wait until they have a stable home before having a family?

The main features of a positive family relationship are:

love	protection	care
responsibility	sharing	mutual support

Negative family relationships can develop for a variety of reasons. For example, partners may fall out of love or lack of money can put a strain on family relationships.

When relationships break down, whether it is between adult and adult, children and children or children and adults, the people involved often get hurt.

CASE STUDY — The Clay family

Jon Clay works hard as an environmental health officer. He brings home a reasonable wage each month. The family are able to afford a car and they are buying their semi-detached house. Pauline works part time as a teacher, so the money she earns helps to pay for some basic necessities, for outings for the children and holidays.

The family have bought an outdoor slide, a swing and trampoline for the children to play on. They have made sure that each play item is put up properly and is securely fixed to the ground.

After the family have had their evening meal they always spend time playing with the children. The children tell their parents what they have done during the day and Jon and Pauline tell the children something about the things they have been doing. Before they go to bed the children have a story read to them and each parent gives them a big hug.

1. From the case study select an example to show how Jon and Pauline showed the following features in their relationship with their children:
   - protection
   - love
   - friendship
   - providing
   - sharing.

2. Describe how Jon and Pauline are showing mutual support in their relationship.

3. Explain how a loving, caring relationship is likely to affect the development of the two children.

4. Write a short case study of your own based on a family who have a teenage son. You should make sure that you have included examples of how the family:
   - provide support
   - give protection
   - share.

   Exchange case studies with another person in the group.

What are siblings?

'Siblings' is another way of saying 'brothers and sisters'. They are other children who are in the same family. Most people who have brothers and/or sisters are very protective towards them. They may quarrel from time to time but they would not want any harm to come to them.

When a new baby is born into the family, an older sibling, who has previously been either the youngest child or the only child, can become very jealous. Jealousy can be shown in many ways, such as snatching a toy away from the new arrival, behaving badly, having a temper tantrum and demanding attention. It is in these situations that parents need to remember to give love and support to the child who is jealous.

◀ 'Why are they bringing him here?'

Relationships experienced by infants

Infants (0–2 years) and children have relationships with others. When they are first born, the infant will start to develop very close relationships with their mother and then their father. This is known as 'bonding'. As the child grows and develops, they will form relationships with a much wider group of people.

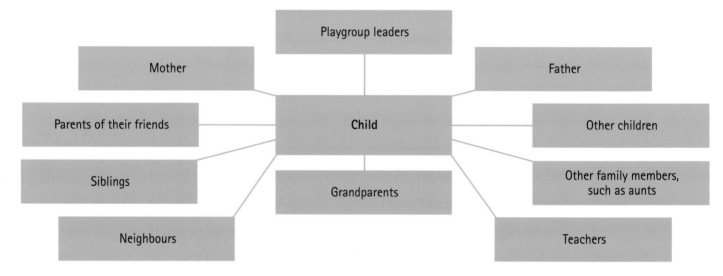

By the time the child reaches the age of eight years the relationships it has with others will have widened quite a lot. For example:

CASE STUDY   Brittany

Brittany is eight years of age. She plays with her four-year-old brother while her mother gets their breakfast. She can dress herself ready to go to school. On some mornings she quarrels with her mother because she wants to take dolls and toys to school with her. She wants to take far too many.

Brittany's mother walks with her to school each day. As soon as they reach the school gate she runs off to meet her friends. She enjoys school and likes the work she has to do. Her teacher is pleased with what she does. Brittany cooperates well with her teacher and tries hard to follow her instructions.

After school Brittany, her mum and brother call at the local shop. Brittany has her own pocket money to spend and likes to choose her own sweets. Sometimes she shares them with her brother.

1   Describe the positive relationships Brittany has with the individuals in her life.

2   Which other individuals not referred to might also influence Brittany's development?

Let us consider some of Brittany's relationships. She has a relationships between:

- her mother and herself
- her sibling and herself
- herself and the friends at her school
- herself and the teacher
- herself and the shop assistant.

Some of the benefits of these relationships are:

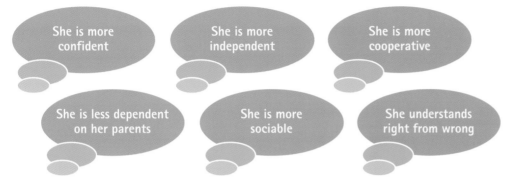

She is more confident

She is more independent

She is more cooperative

She is less dependent on her parents

She is more sociable

She understands right from wrong

ACTIVITY   Relationships

1. Carry out research to find out the meaning of the following features of a relationship:
   - independence
   - confidence
   - being more sociable
   - being less dependent.
2. Explain how a mother still provides protection for an eight-year-old child.
3. Describe the relationship between an individual and a teacher.
4. Describe **two** features of a relationship between an eight year old and their grandparents.
5. Describe **three** ways that a child's relationship with their friends could affect development.
6. How is going to school likely to affect an individual's development?

Friendships

Friendships support our need to have companionship and self-esteem. There can be different types of friendships such as:

- a close friend – someone you will trust and share secrets with. You are likely to share the same interests and do things together
- other friends – these are people who you might meet quite often and whom you like. But you will probably not share things with them that are confidential or secret.

When do friendships start?

Can you remember who was your first 'best friend' and at what age you made this friendship? Close friendships can help fill a 'gap' in our lives. If a person is an only child then they may need someone to share with and do things with. Lots of people have one or two 'best friends' with whom they share their happy times and the times when they are sad or hurt.

▸ Friendships can start quite early.

Friendships are often formed when one person is attracted to another person and likes the way they do things. Their **personality**, for example their sense of humour, the fact that they are dependable or the way they are prepared to work with others on school work or hobbies, could be the attracting feature.

In friendships people communicate with one another. Communication skills enable individuals to express their feelings and emotions to each other and to share information. Some people define friendship as 'groupings of people who come together voluntarily'. Features of friendships are:

Sharing

Giving reassurance

Giving mutual support

Making us feel valued

Being honest

Loyalty

Providing stimulation

Trusting one another

Group Activity

Work with another person in the group and try to work out the features of a close friendship.

Now work out the features of an associate relationship.

Share your findings with another pair in the group.

 ...WORD CHECK

personality – a person's character.

peers – people who are the same age.

In adolescence, both boys and girls are influenced quite strongly by their **peers**. This is known as 'peer pressure'. For example, some boys, in particular, will not answer a question in class if they think that this action would make them look too enthusiastic to their peers.

26 Why do you think boys like to be in larger groups of friends and girls prefer to be with small groups of friends?

Adolescents often have disagreements with their parents and appear to 'break' friends with the family. This is usually because they want to be more independent and make their own decisions.

During adulthood, friendships are more lasting. For example, we could become friends with our immediate neighbours. This might just be by speaking when we see each other. Sometimes neighbours can develop close friendships and may go on holiday together. People with whom we work can also become friends. We may enjoy going out with a group of people from work to a concert, for a shopping trip or to a football match.

When people retire from work they often miss the company and the friendships of their work colleagues. They may decide to have a pet to keep them company. By having a dog, for example, older adults may make new friends, as they are likely to take the dog out for walks. While walking the dog they may stop to speak to people. They may take their dog to training classes and make new friends through such activities.

27 How are adolescent friendships different from those formed by adults?

◀ Close bonds can be formed between grandparents and grandchildren.

Individuals in later adulthood often form friendships with their grandchildren. They may help to look after them while the parents are at work or may baby-sit in the evening, if they live close enough. Some grandparents have their children to stay for a holiday, and firm friendships are formed that last throughout life.

Older adults may, as time passes, lose some of their friends through illness or death. This could make them feel lonely and isolated. As they themselves get older, they may not be able to travel as much as they used to do to meet their friends. They may also have to cope with the death of a lifelong partner who was a very close friend.

28 What do you think the effect would be to lose a life-long partner who has been a friend?

> ✓ **...WORD CHECK**
> **intimate relationships** – very close sexual relationships.

CASE STUDY · Changes in relationships

Barnaby used to live with his two brothers but each has died and now he is on his own. When the brothers were alive, Barnaby did the cooking and kept the house tidy. The brothers could not help because they were ill. Barnaby used to read the newspaper to them. In the evening they would play chess or dominoes.

Barnaby now has mobility problems and cannot walk very far. He used to visit his friend, Zac, every day. Zac lives two streets away. Zac cannot visit Barnaby as he has Parkinson's disease and cannot get out. When they were able to meet, they used to spend a long time chatting and would enjoy a game of cards and a pint together.

A home care assistant visits Barnaby twice each week to help keep the house tidy. A social worker has arranged for a volunteer to visit Barnaby to chat to him on three evenings each week.

1. Think about the relationship changes that Barnaby has had in this life stage. Give **three** examples of the changes that have occurred. For each, explain the effect you think they would have on Barnaby.

2. Barnaby used to enjoy meeting his friend Zac. Describe **three** features of their relationship.

3. A volunteer friend is visiting Zac each week. Describe **three** features that could develop in this relationship.

4. Explain the effect on Barnaby's relationships of not being able to go out so often.

5. What other actions could be taken by the social worker to improve Barnaby's relationships? How could they help?

Intimate, personal and sexual relationships

There are many different kinds of love. We use the word 'love' quite often. For example, a person might say 'I love my dog' or 'I love going on holiday' or 'I love my dad'. The love felt for a boyfriend or girlfriend is a different type of love from the love expressed for family and friends. This is because it has a sexual attraction to it.

Intimate relationships involve being very close to someone. Sexual feelings start to develop during the early teens. This means that teenagers fall in and out of love quite often. These early 'first relationships' often do not last because adolescents have not matured sufficiently to be sensitive to the needs of others. Falling in and out of love, however, can be a very painful experience!

Sexual love often begins with physical attraction. Two people may find, as they get to know one another better, that they have the same interests. The relationship may deepen and sexual love develops out of a close friendship. Sexual activity is one of the most powerful expressions of intimacy that two people can share.

▲ Very much in love.

Forming sexual relationships

Touch plays an important role in sexual activity. Warm and friendly touches that show care and concern for one another are different from the very physical kissing and cuddling that happen in sexual relationships. Touch is the main language of sexual relationships when 'falling in love'. Having sexual intercourse is the expression of emotional and physical attraction.

Our parents are often role models on whom we base our own relationships.

Adults learn to be sensitive to the needs of others. As a result they are less likely to be thinking about themselves but instead consider the best interests of the other person. Both people in the relationship are considering the needs of the other person first. As a result the relationship is more likely to last.

 29 Why is it necessary to be sensitive to the needs of a partner?

As two people live together they become more aware of the needs of their partner. Interest in sexual activity does not necessarily decease with age. Many people who have lived in a partnership or marriage for a long time say that sexual activity is the result of emotional closeness and not a physical desire. The essential ingredient for a good sexual relationship is 'emotional sensitivity'.

Working relationships

Individuals spend quite a lot of their adult, waking life working. The relationships that are formed with people while working are an important part of our lives. Working relationships are different from other relationships such as friendships because they have a specific purpose. In a working relationship often one person is in a position of power over another.

Working relationships can include, for example:

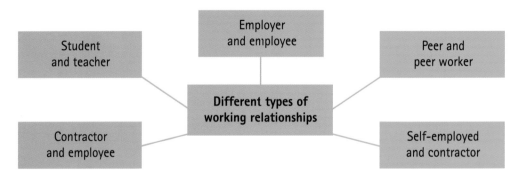

As early as five years of age, or even before if a child attends playgroup or nursery, children learn to work with others. These could be other adults or other children. Learning to work with others means learning to cooperate. The playgroup leader or teacher will ask a child to do something. The child does what has been asked and a working relationship has been formed.

Another feature of a working relationship is trust. This is particularly true when working relationships are made with children, as the child is dependent on the teacher and trusts them not to harm them in any way.

Adolescents studying for their examinations are also working with teachers and tutors. A feature of this type of relationship is a partnership. The student and the teacher will work closely together exchanging knowledge and ideas. While there is power in the relationship as the teacher or tutor is 'in charge', there is also a sharing of information.

Peers, who are people who are usually around the same age as ourselves, can influence us in good ways or in bad ways. This is known as having a positive or negative influence. Working relationships with teachers and lecturers can be greatly influenced by the attitudes of our peers.

 30 Why do you think peers influence our behaviour?

31 Are employer and employee relationships different from other types of relationship?

Good working relationships help to keep employees and employers happy and this contributes to good health. Good communication is a feature of successful working relationships. Friendships can develop between people who are working on the same tasks or who have the same job status.

▲ Following the employer's instruction is important.

It is more unusual for people who work at different levels or who have a different status within an organization to make deep friendships. This is because there is often an 'invisible barrier' between staff levels. For example, a manager or supervisor who is friendly with a care assistant could not easily reprimand the care assistant if this became necessary. It is not often that a person in charge of a department shares a problem they may have with a junior member of staff. This is because they may feel that the junior will think they are not able to cope. Not many people are able to 'choose' the people they work with.

A good atmosphere in the workplace depends on mutual tolerance and valuing the contribution that others are making. An employee who shows respect for another employee is likely to be respected in return. An employee who shows respect for the employer is likely to receive back that respect.

Some employees may feel that an employer may have power over them. They may desperately need the work because they have a large mortgage or bills to pay. They may feel that they have to do whatever their employer asks because if they don't they will not keep their job. If they don't keep their job then they will not be able to pay the bills. This type of attitude does not help to make good working relationships.

Good working relationships depend on:

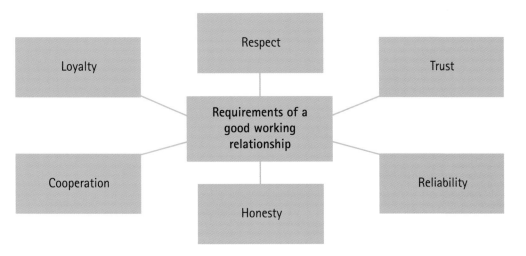

If these are present the effects are likely to be:

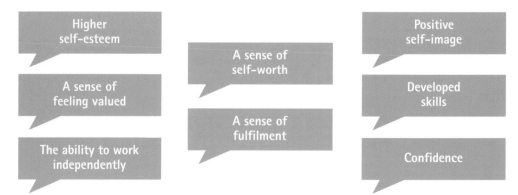

Higher self-esteem

A sense of self-worth

Positive self-image

A sense of feeling valued

Developed skills

A sense of fulfilment

The ability to work independently

Confidence

CASE STUDY   Samera

Samera has worked at the hospital for 20 years. She used to like work, but now she finds it quite hard as so much is expected of her. She never seems to have enough staff and equipment and materials are never enough. She has made lots of requests for more equipment and materials and even more staff, but her line manager has not been able to provide them.

When she first started at the hospital Samera really enjoyed the work. She also liked the people she worked with, as they were able to talk about things together. Sometimes they went out as a group in the evenings or at weekends. They always has a good time and seemed to laugh a lot. At work they would help one another, particularly if one person needed help to manage their work load. They all helped one another.

Now she is a sister in charge of a ward, Samera feels that she cannot be quite so friendly with the other nurses. She expects them to do a good job and will not allow standards on her ward to be lowered. There are one or two staff that she would, if she could choose, prefer not to work with. Samera knows, however, that in her professional role she needs to treat her staff equally.

Samera has to work as she is divorced and has a mortgage to pay. Her children are at university and they always need more books or help to pay for their accommodation.

1. From the case study show how Samera demonstrates the following features in her relationships:
   - mutual support
   - sharing
   - dependency
   - loyalty
   - respect.

2. Explain how Samera showed that she valued those with whom she worked.

3. What effect could financial pressures have on Samera's relationships at work and with her family?

4. If Samera gave up work, how could her relationships with her children change? How do you think this would affect Samera?

THE IMPORTANCE OF THE EFFECTS THESE RELATIONSHIPS HAVE ACROSS THE LIFE STAGES

It is likely that in each day of our lives we will experience both positive and negative relationships and these will affect us in some way. Positive relationships will help us to have a good self-image. A negative relationship is likely to lower our self-esteem and make us have doubts and a lack of confidence.

A positive relationship can mean:

- having someone to share an interest with
- knowing that you are loved and liked
- having someone for whom you can provide support in times of stress
- having someone to support you when you need help.

Positive relationships are essential if we are to have high self-esteem. We need to feel good about ourselves. This happens when we feel we are valued. For example, we feel valued when we have done a job well and someone tells us so. We will also feel good in ourselves because we know we have achieved the task that has been set and this will give us a good feeling of self-worth.

Good relationships contribute to our own sense of identity and help us to know about the direction in which we are going. Positive relationships often lead to other activities. People who relate well may have a good social life doing things together. They will enjoy being together and sharing one another's company. There are always times when we will want to be on our own. But if we have positive relationships with others, there will be a good balance in our lives of being with other people and choosing when to have time to ourselves. We are likely to be able to:

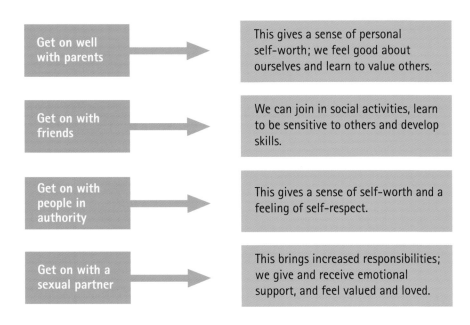

Get on well with parents	→	This gives a sense of personal self-worth; we feel good about ourselves and learn to value others.
Get on with friends	→	We can join in social activities, learn to be sensitive to others and develop skills.
Get on with people in authority	→	This gives a sense of self-worth and a feeling of self-respect.
Get on with a sexual partner	→	This brings increased responsibilities; we give and receive emotional support, and feel valued and loved.

Negative or poor relationships are likely, after a period of time, to contribute to poor health. Negative relationships mean not being able to get on with other people. An individual may find it difficult to get on with their family, friends or people in authority. When a person does not get on with others they are likely to become socially isolated and will not want to join in activities or meet with others. Their sense of identity and self-esteem may be affected negatively. An individual may find that they have a feeling of worthlessness and may fail in the tasks that they are given to do. This could lead to poor examination results or loss of a job. This in turn could lead to not being able to pay the bills or eat properly. None of these events are going to help anyone to be successful in their lives.

Negative effects could include:

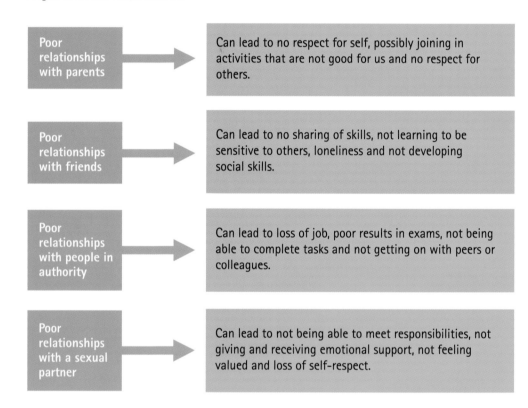

Poor relationships with parents	Can lead to no respect for self, possibly joining in activities that are not good for us and no respect for others.
Poor relationships with friends	Can lead to no sharing of skills, not learning to be sensitive to others, loneliness and not developing social skills.
Poor relationships with people in authority	Can lead to loss of job, poor results in exams, not being able to complete tasks and not getting on with peers or colleagues.
Poor relationships with a sexual partner	Can lead to not being able to meet responsibilities, not giving and receiving emotional support, not feeling valued and loss of self-respect.

ASSESSMENT PRACTICE

Section One

1 Which one of the following is an example of a nuclear family?

- **A** a mother looking after her two children
- **B** grandparents, parents and children all living together
- **C** a mother and father living with their children
- **D** two women living together with their children [1]

Section Two

2 John, aged 17, and Sarah, aged 16, are going out with each other and have started having a sexual relationship. Explain why this type of relationship is important to both John and Sarah at this stage in their lives. [6]

3 Jasmine has just started work at her local hairdressers. She has been friends for some time with Jo, who owns the salon. Explain how Jasmine's relationship with Jo will be different at work compared to when they meet socially. [6]

4 Frank, aged six, has noticed that recently his parents have been arguing over money and his father's drinking habits. This seems to happen every night and at weekends. Explain how this situation might affect Frank's social and emotional development. [8]

5 Discuss why relationships are important for individuals in all the life stages. [10]

The effect of life events on personal development

▸ **Getting started**

You will:

a   study how expected and unexpected life events impact on human growth and development, including:
   i   relationship changes such as marriage, living with a partner, birth of a children, death of a partner, relative or friend
   ii   physical changes such as puberty, menopause and the possible effects of accidents and injury
   iii   changes in life circumstances such as starting school, starting further education, relocation (national and international), entering the employment market, promotion, retirement, redundancy and unemployment
b   develop knowledge and understanding about how these life events affect personal development and lead to new learning
c   need to develop knowledge and understanding about how to manage change and of the support networks which can be accessed and used to support people through change. These include:
   i   partners, family and friends
   ii   professional carers and statutory services
   iii   community, voluntary and faith-based services.

⊘ ...WORD CHECK

expected – something you know is going to happen.

unexpected – sudden.

LIFE EVENTS AND HOW THEY AFFECT PERSONAL DEVELOPMENT

 Group Activity

Think about a life event that has occurred in your life or the life of your family. Was it expected or unexpected?

How did you or the family feel at the time? Were you able to get any support?

Life events can affect an individual's personal development and at such times support will be needed.

Some life events are **expected**. This means that we can be almost certain that they will happen to us. For example, everybody starts school around the age of five. Everybody goes through physical changes such as puberty. The death rate is 100 per cent and is expected!

Other life events are **unexpected**. This means they take us by surprise, and we have no way of knowing when or if they might happen. An example of this is a serious road accident. A number of people will be killed or seriously injured on the roads each year, but we have no way of telling who it will happen to, or when.

32 ▸ What is the difference between expected and unexpected experience of life events?

Relationship changes

Many of the most stressful life events are to do with relationship changes. These are the events that are often most difficult to **adapt** to. Relationship changes include getting married, moving in with a partner, the birth of children and the death of a partner, relative or friend. Look back in this unit to remind yourself about these relationship events.

The death of a partner, relative or close friend is very upsetting and can have a negative effect on development:

P.I.E.S.	Negative effects on development
Physical	May lose their appetite, be unable to sleep and lose the will to look after themselves properly.
Intellectual	May lose interest in things around them. They may not be able to concentrate on a task.
Emotional	The person could feel a sense of grief, loss, depression, and possibly shock if the death was unexpected. They may feel isolated and alone. They may not feel valued.
Social	The person could have lost companionship and support of their partner. They have also lost their role as someone's partner. They must adapt to a new way of life as a single person.

Group Activity

Work with another person to find out about the 'stages of grief'.

Make a handout to tell others about the stages of grief.

...WORD CHECK

adapt – be flexible; adjust to.

CASE STUDY   Hanan

Hanan and her partner, Mike, have three children. All are healthy and appear to be happy. Erin, the youngest child, appears to have a cold, but soon she develops a fever. Purple spots appear and Erin can't bear any light near her eyes. Her parents become quite worried and call the GP.

The GP immediately arranges for Erin to be admitted to hospital. She is given a great deal of medical help, but unfortunately Erin dies. The doctors tell her parents that the cause of death is meningitis.

1. What is the term used to describe this sudden death?
2. How are the parents likely to express their grief?
3. How is the loss of a child likely to affect the development of the parents?

ACTIVITY — Life events

1. List **three** relationship changes that could occur as life events.

2. For each relationship change given in question 1, describe how the change could affect the development of an individual.

3. Explain how divorce could have both a positive and negative effect on personal development.

4. Anita is four years old and runs out into the road. She is killed by a passing car. Is Anita's death an expected or unexpected life event? Give an explanation for your answer.

5. Explain the difference between 'marriage' and having a 'partner'. Explain how marriage or having a partner could affect development.

6. Melissa has to move into a residential home because she can no longer look after herself. How is moving into a residential home likely to affect Melissa's development?

7. Explain how the birth of a sibling could affect the development of an only child.

Physical changes

Puberty

Puberty is a time of physical and emotional changes. It is the stage between childhood and adulthood, the attainment of sexual maturity. Both boys and girls experience puberty. There are changes in body size and shape. The reproductive organs develop. Boys usually experience a sudden voice change and both sexes start to grow more hair on the body. Weight problems sometimes occur during this period. These could be due to natural changes or they could be the result of over or under eating in response to emotional problems. Some teenagers develop skin problems

▲ Puberty is a time of changes.

such as acne or eczema as a result of rapid changes in hormone levels. Concern about appearance can lead to a lowering of self-confidence in teenagers.

These changes will not occur in all adolescents at exactly the same time. Some will experience the changes very early in their teenage years. For others changes will occur more gradually.

Changes during puberty are considered to be main life events as they can affect the development of individuals, having positive and negative effects.

33 ▶ Why does puberty not occur at exactly the same time in all adolescents?

CASE STUDY   Jackie

Jackie is 13. She thinks there may be something wrong with her. All her friends have developed very shapely bodies and are dating boyfriends. No one of the opposite sex seems to be at all interested in Jackie. She feels left out of conversations because everyone else is talking about their boyfriends and where they are going clubbing at the weekend.

Jackie cannot understand why her body has not developed like her friends. She wonders if dieting would help, but she didn't think she was overweight. She becomes very depressed and stops trying to join in any of the group conversations.

1. Explain what is meant by the term 'puberty'.

2. What advice would you give Jackie about her physical development?

3. How is Jackie's emotional and social development likely to be affected by the delayed onset of puberty?

4. Describe **four** physical developments in males during puberty.

The menopause

The menopause is the end of a woman's reproductive life. She may have to come to terms with the fact that she can no longer have children. The menopause can be a main life event for some women. It will affect their development differently. Some will be pleased that they no longer have to worry about having children, others may feel a sense of loss.

 Why might a woman feel a sense of loss when the menopause occurs?

Accident or injury

Becoming physically disabled through accident, injury or illness is a major life event. It is not usually expected. A person who becomes disabled will have to adapt their lifestyle, depending on the degree of disability. They may lose some of their independence, and they may have to rely on others for daily living tasks that they were once able to do for themselves. An extreme example is someone who becomes completely paralysed and requires help with all their bodily functions. Perhaps the biggest problem that many people have to face in adapting to disability is the prejudice of others. People with disabilities often complain that they are treated like children. They say that people often speak to their carers rather than to them. This makes the person who is not able bodied feel inferior and as though they do not count. It is almost as though they are not present in the conversation.

Becoming disabled may involve losing a job, and having to retrain. It may involve a loss of income, or moving to more appropriate accommodation. It may also require changes in hobbies or interests.

Changes in life circumstances

All changes in life circumstances have some common features. The most important is that they involve changes in existing relationships, and a need to develop new ones. Moving house, changing schools and changing or losing a job all involve leaving some relationships behind – neighbours, friends, teachers, bosses and colleagues. To adapt successfully to the change, the individual must make new relationships, sometimes in a new role.

▲ Starting school might be frightening.

Starting school

Starting school may be the first time that a child has been away from their main carer for a whole day. It means that the child has to become more independent of their parents, and make relationships with other children. This could be quite a frightening experience for the child if careful preparations are not made. Parents who have previously been close at hand will no longer be available. Relationships with new adults and new children will be formed. Rules will have to be followed. All these changes can have a negative effect on the child's development.

A child may become very 'clingy' to the parent and make a fuss when it is time to leave. They may become withdrawn and sit in a corner away from the other children, refusing to join in the activities. The child may behave like this because they do not understand what is happening. They may think they have been abandoned or that they are being punished. This may lead to the child having nightmares or bedwetting. They may become aggressive towards their parents. It could lead to the child disliking school and underachieving in their work.

If preparation is done with the child before having to start school, the child is more likely to have a positive experience. The parent could talk to the child about school, read them stories about school or take them to meet someone from school. Most schools invite children to attend for a morning or two before the child has to do an all day session. This can help the child to prepare for longer all day school hours.

 3 ▶ Why is it important to prepare a child for starting school?

Starting further education

Starting college or university is a very exciting time. It can also be daunting even if the person has been looking forward to it for some time. The result of having to leave home to go to college could be isolation and a sense of grief and loss, or it could bring feelings of joy and satisfaction as well as mental stimulation due to the new challenges being presented.

CASE STUDY   Lindsey

Lindsey has been successful in her examinations. She is moving away from home to go to university to study midwifery. She has lived with her family in a rural area all her life. None of her friends are going to the same university and she is sure she will miss them.

At university Lindsey will be sharing a house with three other girls whom she has not met before. She is very nervous and anxious about the move, but it is something that she wants to do.

1 Describe the difficulties Lindsey might have to cope with when she moves to university.

2 List **four** ways in which Lindsey could help to prepare herself for the move.

3 Explain how Lindsey's development is likely to be affected by moving away from home.

4 If Lindsey has an accident that affected her ability to walk, how is her development likely to be affected?

5 How is Lindsey's leaving home to go to university likely to affect her parents' development?

Relocation

When someone moves house or moves away to start a new job or college, they leave behind familiar friends, neighbours and neighbourhoods. Leaving friends and neighbours matters because you lose the physical, emotional and social support they offer. Life is much easier with these networks to help. Parents, for instance, have to know who they can trust to baby-sit for them. Good neighbours can help in all sorts of ways, for instance by watching the house when you are away on holiday, or helping you when you are ill. When you move house you have to build new relationships to replace this.

A person will know a lot about where they live if they have been there for a period of time. They know where shops and services are, what buses to catch and their location. When moving to a new area, everything is new and has to be learnt again. New friends, new teachers or employers will be introduced and the individuals will need to learn how to get on with new neighbours.

Starting work

Starting work involves intellectual development because a person will have to learn what the job involves so that the job can be done properly. They will have to learn new skills and knowledge. Emotional developments will also take place when starting work. This is particularly true if working in the health, social care or early years sectors. For example, as a carer when working with someone who is rude and bad tempered, or very slow, it will be necessary to deal with your own anger or impatience in a mature way. At work an individual will meet new colleagues and have the opportunity to make more friends. Social development will therefore also be affected.

As working means earning money, an individual will become financially independent. This means they may no longer be totally dependent on parents for money. Managing finances is an important aspect of intellectual development. Physically work may be more challenging.

Starting work is usually considered an 'expected' life event, as most people at some time during their life will have the opportunity to do this. If the work done is something a person likes doing, they will be mentally stimulated and happy and will have a sense of fulfilment. Work can give a positive direction to our lives. If a person earns a promotion because of the good work that they have done, this success can have a positive effect on confidence and self-esteem.

During an adult's life they are likely to spend many hours at work. If they do not like the work they do, they could become depressed and physically ill. Many people today suffer from stress as a result of work. This could be because they are asked to do too much or they may find the work too difficult or because the work does not suit their characteristics. Whatever the reason, the negative effects can make a person feel that they are a failure.

 36 ▶ Why is it important to like the work we do?

 Group Activity

Work with another person to make a list of **three** negative results of retirement.

Describe the likely effects of these negative aspects on individuals.

Share your results with others.

Retirement

Retirement is when a person stops working. Some people are entitled to an occupational pension, while everyone is entitled to a state pension. When an individual retires, they could lose the physical, intellectual, emotional and social stimulation provided by work. Some people are very sad when their working lives come to an end. Others are very happy. Whether retirement is a positive or negative development depends upon how people deal with it. People who are happy to retire are those who find other ways of getting the stimulation that they used to get from work. This might involve:

Participating in voluntary work

Helping to care for grandchildren

Returning to education to learn something new

Positive elements of retirement

Travelling to new places

Gardening

Taking up new hobbies

Redundancy and unemployment

Unlike retirement, redundancy and unemployment are often unexpected life events. Unemployment means not having a job. Redundancy means losing your job because the job has disappeared, perhaps because a company has closed down.

Like retirement, unemployment and redundancy mean losing physical, intellectual, emotional and social stimulation provided by work. Redundancy is different from retirement because it often happens unexpectedly and without warning. It can affect development because people worry about how they are going to manage financially. Too much worry can make us ill both physically and mentally through stress.

Some people who are made redundant, particularly older workers, find it very difficult to get another job before they reach retirement age. This may make them feel under valued and lack confidence in themselves.

37 What is the difference between retirement and redundancy?

Many people who are unemployed will feel bored because they do not have enough to do to fill their time. They may get depressed if working is very important to their sense of identity. They may find it difficult in their relationship with their partner. This may be especially true for men who are used to providing for their family. They may find it very difficult to be dependent on their partner or on benefits.

38 How can unemployment affect development?

Life events do not come along one at a time. One life event may be related to several others. For instance, someone who is in a relationship and has children is offered a promotion at work that involves moving house. They will have to learn new skills and their partner may have a job of their own that they have to give up. The children will have to change schools, and everyone in the family will leave friends behind when they move.

HOW EXPECTED AND UNEXPECTED LIFE EVENTS CAN LEAD TO NEW LEARNING

This is discussed in more depth in Unit 4. However, it is possible to see some positive benefits from what, at first, appears to be a devastating change in life. For example:

Redundancy – Learning new skills for re-employment.
Divorce – Finding a new partner to spend one's life with.
Having to change school – Meeting new friends and teachers.
Retirement – Taking on new interests and hobbies.
Suffering a serious injury – Taking on new challenges, for example, competing in the Paralympics.

It is always pleasing to see how some individuals overcome the most serious life event changes and become even happier and more successful. It is all about adopting a positive approach to life rather than just sitting back and thinking that there is nothing one can do. Look at the examples of individuals who have turned adversity into achievement (see Unit 4, pages 240–241).

◀ Being born blind, David Blunkett's life could have been very limited. However, he used this disability to lead to new learning opportunities. He obtained a place at Sheffield University and went on to become a successful Member of Parliament. Eventually he became Home Secretary in Tony Blair's government.

HOW TO MANAGE CHANGE AND THE SUPPORT NETWORKS WHICH CAN BE ACCESSED

Partners, family and friends

In difficult times, partners, family and friends can help by providing physical, emotional and social support to make it possible for us to cope with the effects of life events. They are often called **informal carers**.

By talking about our problems with others, they sometimes appear to be smaller than we thought. Sometimes talking to someone can bring clarity to the situation.

Friends are important because they are people with whom we can share our problems and will listen and understand why we are upset. Social support is also important. For example, after a divorce or bereavement an individual or a family may be lonely and isolated. Friends and neighbours can help by:

▶ Friends and neighbours can help us to cope.

✔ **...WORD CHECK**

informal carers – those who look after individuals but who do not hold the qualifications to do so, for example, parents, spouses, partners, family.

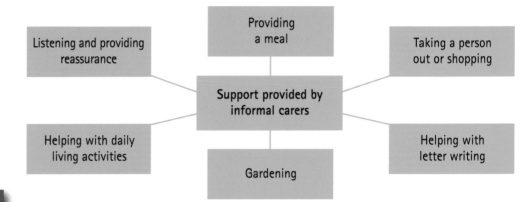

Listening and providing reassurance

Providing a meal

Taking a person out or shopping

Support provided by informal carers

Helping with daily living activities

Gardening

Helping with letter writing

Group Activity

Work with another person to research the differences between informal carers and professional care workers. What different tasks are each likely to do? Compare the two groups.

Share your findings as a whole group.

 39 Who are informal carers?

Informal carers can help a person to face up to the changes in their life. They can do this by setting short- and long-term goals or targets. Informal carers can encourage the individual to spend time in a positive way; for example, helping with charity work or learning a new hobby. They help by giving both practical and emotional support.

 40 How can informal carers help people cope with change?

Professional carers and statutory services

Group Activity

Work with another person to find out information about:

- **three** different health professionals
- **three** different social care professionals
- **three** different early years professionals.

Find out how each would help in the case of a life event. How would each help an individual to cope? Share your research as a whole group.

Professional carers are people who are paid to look after individuals when they need help, for example, GPs and counsellors.

The role of a GP

- make an assessment of need
- talk about their needs
- listen
- provide medication/sleeping tablets
- monitor health
- provide advice
- liaise with other agencies/professionals
- write a report
- provide information about all options available.

The role of a counsellor

- listen to individuals
- draw information from individuals
- clarify points
- help an individual to reflect on what has happened
- write reports
- liaise with other agencies/professionals.

Unit 2 provides more information about the different types of professional care workers but other examples are:

Professional	The help they provide
Home care assistant	Helps with shopping, cleaning and preparing meals
Midwife	Helps with the delivery of babies and gives advice
Social worker	Makes an assessment of a person's needs Liaises with other professionals
Occupational therapist	Assesses the adaptations needed to a person's home

While informal carers will do their best to help and provide support, sometimes professional help will be required. People who are professional care workers are trained to deal with some of the complex situations and life events that individuals and families have to cope with.

Community, voluntary and faith-based services

Some examples of voluntary groups are:

Voluntary group	The help they provide
The Compassionate Friends	Help people who are trying to come to terms with the loss of a child.
Age Concern	Help older people adapt to changes in their circumstances.
Alzheimer's Disease Society and Dementia Care Trust	Provide support for carers of people with Alzheimer's disease and dementia.
ChildLine and Kidscape	Give advice and support to children in trouble or danger. This may be because of violence from their parents or problems at school such as bullying.

Group Activity

Work with another person to find out exactly how **three** voluntary groups help individuals. How does this help the individual to cope?

Find out about **two** other voluntary groups not on the list above.

What do they do? How does it help an individual to cope?

Having a faith or a belief gives emotional and social support. Priests and other church workers such as volunteers can be very important in advising and comforting people during important life events.

 41 ▶ How can having a faith or belief help us to cope with life events?

Without receiving help with life event changes some people may not be able to cope, because the life event will have had a major effect on their personal development. The result may be that they have very low self-esteem, may become depressed or even suicidal. They may need medication to help them manage their depression or their inability to sleep. Without help the situation could get worse. We all need to remember that we may need help when life events overtake us. We should not be afraid of asking for that help.

CASE STUDY   Christopher

Christopher had a wife and a daughter aged five. He worked on a building site for 15 years. Christopher earned good money. The family lived in a semi-detached house but Christopher was still paying the mortgage and the family were reasonably well off.

One morning Christopher was told that he was being made redundant as there was a credit crunch and orders for new houses were not coming in.

Christopher tried to get another job, but so many other people wanted jobs. He applied for 65 jobs but didn't get any of them. He became depressed. The money he had been given for redundancy started to run out and arguments broke out between Christopher and his wife. They became so bad that Christopher just walked out and only came back when he knew the family were in bed. Then he started going into the pub when he received his dole money and drank so much that there was no money left for food.

His wife decided that she could not put up with things any longer, so she left Christopher and went back to her mother and took their little girl with her.

Christopher continued to drink. He didn't pay the mortgage on the house or the bills. Eventually the house was re-possessed by the mortgage company. Christopher was homeless. He had lost everything!

1. Explain what is meant by 'being made redundant'.

2. How do you think that being made redundant affected Christopher's emotional and social development?

3. When Christopher was made redundant which voluntary service could he have visited to get support? How would this service have provided help?

4. How could family and friends have helped when he was made redundant?

5. Explain the effect that the redundancy might have had on Christopher's wife.

6. How can faith-based organizations help people like Christopher cope with life changes?

7. Christopher had a child of five. How would the child's personal development be affected by the changes in the family circumstances?

8. What professional support could have helped Christopher cope with the changes in his life? Explain how each would help.

▶ ▶ ▶ ▶ **ASSESSMENT PRACTICE**

Section One

1 Which **one** of the following is an unexpected life event?

- ☐ **A** Going to school
- ☐ **B** Getting married
- ☐ **C** Being made redundant
- ☐ **D** Retiring from work. [1]

2 Which **two** of the following are professional care workers?

- ☐ **A** GP
- ☐ **B** Neighbour
- ☐ **C** Social worker
- ☐ **D** Family friend. [1]

3 Which **one** of the following is a voluntary group?

- ☐ **A** Help the Aged
- ☐ **B** Social services
- ☐ **C** The National Health Service
- ☐ **D** A local comprehensive school. [1]

Section Two

4 Richard and Christine's child, aged four, dies from a road traffic accident. They are provided with support to try and help them cope with the death of their child. The parents are supported by:

- a counsellor
- a GP
- a health visitor.

Describe how each could provide support for Richard and Christine. Explain how the actions of each professional care worker could help the family to cope. [10]

5 While out shopping Mandy is hit by a car. She remains in hospital for several weeks as she is paralysed in her legs. Eventually she is allowed home. She is provided with support by:

- a physiotherapist
- an occupational therapist
- health care assistant.

Describe how each could provide support for Mandy. Explain how their actions could help her to cope. [10]

6 Describe how a hospital social worker and the family could provide support for Mandy, after her serious accident, to assist her through any changes necessary if she returns home. [10]

7 Lenny suddenly has a heart attack after which he finds it difficult to move. Since his heart attack, Lenny has been in hospital, but it is agreed that he will move home. Different formal and informal carers will help his recovery.

Identify **three** different types of informal carers who could provide support for Lenny. Describe how each could provide different types of support. Explain how the support could help him to cope. [10]

8 Sunny had broken ribs and a broken leg as a result of a football injury.

Identify **five** professional health and social care workers who could provide support for Sunny in his own home. Explain the support each would give. Explain how each would help him to cope. [10]

2 Exploring Health, Social Care and Early Years Provision

Contents

About this unit

This unit will be assessed under controlled conditions and internally assessed and externally moderated. You will need to produce **one** report which will be based on an investigation of the needs of **one** service user and how these needs are met by service providers and care practitioners.

Health, social care and early years practitioners need to develop knowledge and understanding of the range of care needs of major service user groups and the services that exist to meet these needs. In your portfolio you must show evidence of:

- the range of care needs of major service user groups
- the types of services which exist to meet service user needs
- how services have developed and how they are organized
- the ways in which people can obtain care services and the barriers which that could prevent service users gaining access to these services
- the main roles and skills of people providing health, social care and early years services
- the principles of care and values which underpin all care work with service users.

You will demonstrate the ability to apply knowledge and understanding to investigate the needs of one service user.

Evidence required for the controlled assessment will be related to service users and settings. This will be drawn from one of the following:

- health
- early years
- care of individuals in later adulthood
- individuals with specific needs.

You will plan and carry out investigations based on an individual in **one** care setting and how service providers and care professionals work together to meet the individual's needs. In addition, you will be expected to analyse and evaluate information, draw conclusions and present reasoned judgements from the research undertaken. The quality of written communication will be assessed in this unit.

The task will be assessed and marked by teachers and moderated by Edexcel.

Tips for preparing a report

To write your report you will need to:

Plan your time and investigation

Produce a bibliography

Analyse information and draw logical conclusions

Produce an evaluation presenting your conclusions

Carry out **primary research**

Choose an individual to investigate

Carry out **secondary research**

Choosing an individual to investigate

One person must be chosen for the focus of the health plan. You could select:

- a friend
- a member of your group
- a member of your immediate family
- a member of your extended family
- a neighbour
- yourself
- a case study.

The table below shows an advantage and a disadvantage for each group.

Group	Advantage	Disadvantage
A friend	You find it easy to talk to them	Your friendship may not last as long as the investigation
A member of the group	You would be with them every day so you could check on pieces of information required	The individual could get fed up with being continually questioned or they may be away for a long period of time
A member of your immediate family	There would probably be others in the family who would know the details if the person had forgotten anything	The family may not want others to know what is personal to them
A member of your extended family, for example, grandparent	They are older and would have the knowledge that you need to collect	They may not want to confide in you
A neighbour	You could contact them quite frequently if you had forgotten something	There may be times when they are not available due to work, holidays or other family commitments
Yourself	All the information is to hand	You may be biased about your own strengths and weaknesses
A case study	You would be able to obtain the information you need from the case study	You may not have sufficient depth of information in the case study to answer the tasks

It will be very important to make the correct choice. You will have to ask yourself some questions before making a final decision, for example:

- Will I be able to access them easily?
- Will they have all the information I need?
- Will they be interested in helping with the topic?
- Do they need to have their health improved?
- Have they got the 'staying power' to see the project through to the end?

Start your plan and bibliography

You will need to start a plan for the investigation of the service user you have chosen. You will need to follow this plan after the teaching has been completed and before starting the controlled assignment. You should include:

- the dates when you propose to investigate and write up the information
- the actions you propose to take
- the reasons for the actions taken.

Draw up the outline plan you intend to use for your investigation. Your plan might look like this:

Date	Actions to be taken	Reason for actions
15 Jan	Research the structure of the health sector	To find out how it is organized at national and local levels

Begin your bibliography – a record of the books, journals and websites that you intend to use. You must include the title, author, publisher and date of publication of each book, and include every website. Your bibliography might look like this:

GCSE Health & Social Care for Edexcel: Double Award Student's Book, Angela Fisher, Stephen Seamons and Mike Ancil, Folens Publishers, 2009.

www.nhs.uk

Primary and secondary research

Researching information from books, magazines, journals and websites is called secondary research.

For your report you will also need to do some primary research, that is obtaining information directly from the individual you are investigating, or from practitioners. You might get this information from:

- an interview
- a questionnaire.

Primary research will produce both quantitative and qualitative data. Quantitative data is expressed in numbers and can be analysed using statistical methods. An example of a question that produces quantitative data is, 'How many times do you exercise each week?' Quantitative data can be displayed using graphs, charts and tables.

Qualitative data concerns feelings, attitudes and opinions and is expressed in words, not numbers. An example of a question that produces qualitative data is, 'How does doing regular exercise make you feel?'

Both qualitative and quantitative data can produce useful and meaningful results.

Interviews and questionnaires both have their advantages and disadvantages. For example, a face-to-face interview might produce good qualitative data. On the other hand, it may be difficult to find a convenient time for both interviewer and interviewee, and if you are asking very personal questions, the interviewee may feel too embarrassed to give a totally honest answer. A questionnaire might be a less intimidating way of getting information, but the answers you receive might not be as complete or as detailed as you'd like. So you may need to decide which is the best method depending on:

- the amount of time you have
- the amount of time your chosen individual has
- the details needed for the investigation.

⊘ ...WORD CHECK

secondary research – using existing material that has been produced by someone else. This might include government statistics, for example, from a census or a book written by another author.

primary research – an investigation that a researcher has carried out themselves using a questionnaire, an interview or an observation, or a combination of all three methods.

quantitative data – information that is based on numerical (numbers) information.

qualitative data – information that is based on spoken or written responses from people. It may provide a lot of depth and detail.

Interviews

An interview involves asking a person questions in a 'face-to-face' situation. The person being interviewed has probably consented to take part beforehand. The interviewer will have prepared questions for the interview that will give the information that is needed. When planning your interviews you should:

- ask permission to carry out the interview
- arrange a mutually convenient date and time
- prepare questions to make sure you gather the required information – you may need to trial questions beforehand to make sure they give you the kind of answers you require (this is called piloting)
- avoid bias – do not lead the participant in the way you ask the questions
- consider recording the interview so that you can concentrate on asking the questions and listening to the responses
- maintain confidentiality – do not use the full name of the participant
- prepare a transcript of the interview so that results can be analysed.

Questionnaires

A self-completed questionnaire is one where the researcher hands out questionnaire forms to the participants, who then answer the questions by filling in the answers in the spaces provided. The forms are then collected by the researcher when they are completed. The advantages of using a questionnaire is that it is cheap, quick, anonymous and a way to collect information without interviewer bias. Participants can also take their time to answer the questions.

When writing a questionnaire:

- Include a short introduction that explains why the survey is being carried out and covers the issue of confidentiality.
- Begin with easy to answer closed questions and work towards questions that need more thought at the end.

Remember:

- Make sure the questions are easy to understand.
- Do not use questions that allow the respondent to repeat previous answers.
- Do not assume the respondents have any previous knowledge of the topics you are asking about.
- Thank the respondents for completing the questionnaire.

...WORD CHECK

closed questions – questions in surveys that give alternative answers to choose from. They are used to collect factual information or simple yes or no answers to questions.

▶ Introducing this unit

All service users will probably need to make use of a number of services during their lives. These will include:

- health services, for example, a health centre or hospital (private or NHS)
- social care services for older people, for example, a day centre for older people, residential homes
- early years services, for example, a nursery, paediatric service, children's centre.

> Work with another person and write down three services you or your family have used. Produce a table with three columns headed 'Health Care', 'Social Care' and 'Early Years'. Place the services that each of you have used under the correct heading. Why did you use the services?
> Compare your table with that of a different pair within your group.
> Are they similar or different?

In this unit you will find out who uses services, why they are used and the different types of treatment that the services can provide.

Was it easy to use the services you have listed or did you have any difficulty accessing them?

While studying this unit you will explore the different types of barriers that can cause difficulty for some people to use them.

> With another person in the group, discuss how an individual with a health need might feel if they were prevented from using the service they needed because of lack of money or being unable to reach it.
> Discuss your findings as a whole group.

> ✓ ...**WORD CHECK**
> paediatric – looking after children.

Providing care for the local community takes a great deal of planning and those who are involved in this process have to think about national targets and standards as well as the needs of individual clients. Planning has to consider all who live in the local community, not just one section of the population. In this unit you will find out how services need to work together in order to provide for the needs of different client groups.

Once services have been established, those who work in them, the professional practitioners, have to respond to the individual needs of clients. These are not just the client's physical needs, but the intellectual, emotional and social needs of individuals. Practitioners have to set targets, maintain standards and use different approaches in order to meet the individual needs of those who require care. While studying this unit you will find out about the ways in which professional care workers apply the care values in their day-to-day tasks and about their job roles. You will also think about the skills they need to carry out their work.

> How did the professional care workers apply the care values in the services you used? How did this make you feel? It is the quality of service that we receive when we are in need of health and care that will influence how we 'rate' the service. How well did the service meet your needs? Make some notes and then discuss this with the rest of the group.

The range of care needs of major client groups

▶ Getting started

In this section you will gain an understanding of who needs to use care services and why.

a You will need to gain an understanding about the following different groups of service users:
i   infants
ii   children
iii adolescents
iv   individuals in early adulthood
v   individuals in middle adulthood
vi   individuals in later adulthood
vii individuals with specific needs

b the physical, intellectual, emotional and social needs across the different groups by considering:
i   the hierarchy of needs
ii   how a failure to meet these needs can affect the development of the individual

c how health, social care and early years services respond to the needs and demands of the different groups including universal services and targeted services, meeting social policy goals and assessing the needs of the population

d why individuals may need to access health, social care and early years services, to include temporary or permanent needs

DIFFERENT SERVICE USER GROUPS

In this unit you will gain an understanding of the physical, intellectual, emotional and social development of individuals in each life stage and how this affects their needs, investigating which services may be able to help meet those needs.

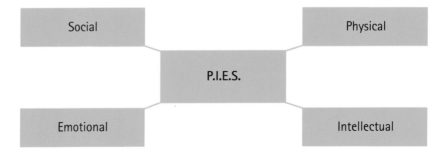

Different groups of service users can include:

Life stage	Age span	An explanation of the life stage
Infants	0–2 years	From birth to two years infants are totally dependent on their parents or main carers. Professional care needs could include vaccinations, inoculations, diagnosis of illness, treatment for specific conditions.
Children	3–8 years	Children start to become a little more independent. Care needs could include diagnosis of illness and treatment, play activities, mental stimulation, fostering, adoption, speech therapy.
Adolescents	9–18 years	Adolescents like to be involved in different types of relationships. Care needs could include counselling, dietary advice, sexual guidance/treatment, behaviour therapy, diagnosis of illness.
Early adulthood	19–45 years	Needs could include diagnosis of illness, vaccinations for holidays abroad, treatment for mental ill-health, services relating to pregnancy and birth, parenting advice.
Middle adulthood	45–65 years	Diagnosis and treatment for health conditions, mental health care, dietary advice, counselling.
Later adulthood	65+ years	Mobility conditions often need diagnosis and treatment, heart conditions or stroke, health monitoring, day care centres, residential or nursing care.
Individuals with specific needs	Any age	Adaptations to the home, aids for daily living, diagnosis and treatment of health conditions, for example, teenagers requiring contraceptives, learning support, employment training, residential care.

Infants

Very young children are often dependent on their parents or someone else, who is called their main carer, who makes sure that they are able to use the services that they need: for example, if they have to go to the GP to have a vaccination against meningitis.

It is important that babies form strong relationships with their parents or main carers. This is called **bonding**. When such relationships are formed, the baby or child will feel happy and secure and this provides the basis of trust, which contributes to their emotional and social well-being. Those who provide services for infants will try to make sure that parents or their main carer are not separated from them when treatment or care is needed. An example, is when an infant has to be admitted to hospital for observation or treatment. The parents are provided with facilities, such as a room with a bed, so that they can stay with their infant in order to help the child feel secure and happy. The parents or carer are also encouraged to participate in the infant's care programme so that they feel valued and part of the care process. For example, they may be asked to feed or to hold the infant while it is being examined.

Infants will also be users of early years services, such as a crèche, a nursery, a childminder and health services. Intellectual stimulation is provided for an infant by talking to them. Emotional support is provided by giving the infant a cuddle and making sure they are safe. An infant's social development is encouraged by playing with them and taking them to mix with others in a crèche or nursery, for example.

...WORD CHECK

bonding – grow(ing) close to someone.

 1 Why is it important to involve the parent or main carer when providing medical care for an infant?

Examples of the needs of infants are:

- fostering and adoption, if home circumstances prove to be difficult on a temporary or long-term basis (social need)
- diagnosis and treatment of illness (physical need)
- health monitoring (physical need)
- vaccinations/inoculations (physical need)
- childcare, for example, nursery, childminder (physical/intellectual/emotional/social needs)
- coping with sibling rivalry (emotional need).

Children

▼ Encouraging young children to learn and play together to meet social and intellectual needs.

The diagram below shows some examples of how the needs of a child can be met. The recognized age for childhood is from 3–8 years of age.

Physical needs can be met by providing food

Intellectual needs can be met by providing mental stimulation, for example stories, games

Emotional needs can be met through providing a safe environment

Social needs can be met by playing with others

CASE STUDY   Nisha

Nisha is six years old. She attends the local primary school where she has lots of friends and where she enjoys doing different activities. She learns how to read, how to form letters and how to write and count. Nisha also enjoys making cakes, painting and building objects.

1. How has attending school helped Nisha's language development?

2. Explain how making items by matching the pieces together and learning to add up are helping with Nisha's development.

Social development will very much depend on the individual child and the family. If they participate in a range of after-school activities, they will meet different people from different backgrounds and this will enable them to learn new skills, to widen their vocabulary and to meet their need for social interactions.

For more information on the physical, intellectual and emotional development of children, see pages 14–16.

Examples of the needs of children are:

- diagnosis of illness
- behaviour counselling
- speech therapy
- dietary advice and treatment
- treatment for accidental injury.

Group Activity

With a partner, discuss which of these needs are physical, intellectual, emotional and social.

Adolescents

The life stage between the ages of 9 and 18 is known as **adolescence**. In this stage of development physical growth is fast. Puberty occurs during this period. During puberty the sex hormones become active and cause physical, emotional and intellectual changes, which in turn will affect the adolescent's social needs. For example, adolescents may fall in and out of love several times during this period.

Adolescents become more independent of their parents and are able to use some services without parental or main carer consent, particularly after they have reached the age of 16. For example, adolescents may decide to go to the family planning clinic for advice on contraception, without needing consent.

Emotionally, adolescents may experience mood swings, for example they may be happy one minute and depressed the next. This is likely to happen more often if a new boyfriend or girlfriend relationship is going well or not so well!

Socially, most adolescents like going out in groups with friends. Clubbing is a new experience for them and a place where they can meet people, talk and have a good time. Unfortunately, on some occasions adolescence can be a time when a young person is introduced to drugs or when they abuse alcohol. This misuse of substances can lead to physical and mental health problems.

...WORD CHECK

adolescence – the period between 9 and 18 years of age.

 2 How does clubbing fulfil an important need?

Examples of the needs of adolescents are:

- counselling services when they feel they have issues that are hindering their progress or relationships
- information and treatment about contraception
- diagnosis of illness
- dietary advice and treatment
- health advice and planning
- drug and alcohol advice.

Individuals in early and middle adulthood

People who are over 18 years of age are considered to be adults. These are people who can make decisions for themselves about the services they wish to use or whether they have the treatments that are offered by health, social care or early years services.

Adults often form partnerships and set up home together. They will provide one another with **mutual support**, which will help to meet their emotional and social needs, as they can express their feelings and share experiences. Adults will often visit health and social care services together when they have a problem. Service providers must, however, respect the wishes of adults if they request that personal information is not to be shared with their partner.

Examples of an adult's needs will include:

- having illness diagnosed
- having vaccinations/immunizations for holiday trips
- seeking health promotion advice
- seeking advice about fertility treatment
- liaising with different agencies when there is a specific problem, for example, depression following an accident.

3 ▶ Give examples of how adults provide mutual support.

Individuals in later adulthood

Individuals in later adulthood often use health and care services more frequently than other service user groups because their needs change and they become more dependent on others.

Older people may need services to help with:

- physical needs, for example, medication, diet, mobility care and support in the home, such as help with preparing meals, cleaning, shopping
- social, intellectual and emotional support to prevent isolation and encourage intellectual stimulation.

Those providing services for older people will make sure that the individual is fully involved in planning their care. They will also try to **empower** the service user by making sure that they are given sufficient information to make informed decisions and choices.

▶ With suitable equipment older adults can often continue to live an independent life.

Individuals in later adulthood may wish to continue living in their own homes in order to be independent. Such service users will require support from health and care providers so they can do this. Other service users will need 24-hour care and support or nursing care and will move into residential or nursing homes.

 4 ▶ Why is 'empowerment' of older service users important?

Individuals with specific needs

Type of condition	Examples of the effect of the condition
Having a congenital condition	Being born with a disability or impairment. That is, they have part of their body that is damaged and is not working properly, for example, a heart defect.
Having a mental disability	This could include a condition that a person was born with or one that has developed through illness.
Having an accident	Someone in a motorcycle accident could lose a leg. Or a person could develop a sensory impairment and become blind. A person could have a swimming accident and become paralysed, unable to move from the waist down.
Having a developmental or degenerative condition	A disease or condition that develops after birth and which may become more severe as they get older. An example would be a person who has Huntington's disease or Retinitus pigmentosa.
Having a learning difficulty	A situation where the brain could have been starved of oxygen, either at birth or through an illness, which affects the brain's ability to function correctly.
Having a specific health need	This could include teenagers who may need advice relating to contraceptives; or individuals who need advice about diets or specific aids to help with daily living.

Group Activity

Find out how conditions such as being paraplegic, quadriplegic and hemiplegic affect individuals.

...WORD CHECK

designed – created; planned.

People who have individual specific needs will require a range of health and care services, for example:

- community care – for example, a special school for children with learning needs
- hospital care – for example, a psychiatric unit in a hospital
- volunteer services – for example, Meals on Wheels
- informal carers – for example, friends and relatives
- private organizations – for example, a private drug rehabilitation centre.

Services will not be appropriate if they do not meet the needs of the individual who uses them; therefore, they must be planned or **designed** so that they do meet these needs.

PHYSICAL, INTELLECTUAL, EMOTIONAL AND SOCIAL NEEDS ACROSS THE DIFFERENT GROUPS

The hierarchy of needs

We all have the same basic needs. Abraham Maslow represented these needs in the form of a pyramid showing which needs must be met first before other needs could be satisfied. Below is a diagram showing Maslow's pyramid of needs.

LEVEL 5
Intellectual needs
personal growth
and fulfilment

LEVEL 4
Emotional needs
love, companionship, respect

LEVEL 3
Social needs
friendship, communication, mixing with others

LEVEL 2
Safety needs
protection from dangers

LEVEL 1
Physical needs
food and water, shelter and warmth

▲ Maslow's pyramid of needs.

Maslow included five levels of need. He placed the levels that he thought were most important at the base of the pyramid, supporting all the rest. Only when the basic needs have been met at level 1 can levels 2, 3, 4 and 5 be met.

5 Give examples of the needs in levels 2, 3, 4 and 5.

6 How are these needs met for you?

7 What basic physical needs do you have in order to keep you alive?
Who tries to provide for these needs?

A GP (doctor) tries to meet the needs of all individuals. Below is a table that shows how some of the needs of different individuals are met by a GP practice:

Service users	How needs are met by a GP and those employed in a GP practice
Infants	Immunizations Vaccinations Monitoring health
Children	Diagnosing illness Prescribing medication
Adults	Health promotion Monitoring health, for example, blood pressure Counselling
Older people	Giving advice about exercise Diabetes clinics Chiropractors Influenza vaccinations
People with disabilities	Liaising with specialists, for example, occupational therapist Providing counselling

How failure to meet these needs can affect the development of the individual

If an individual's needs are not met, they may not develop according to the norms of development. In other words they may not make the progress expected and some individuals may **regress**, which means their development retreats to an earlier stage.

Examples of failure to meet the needs of individuals are:

Example of need not being met	Possible effect on an individual
Physical need not met by lack of feeding correctly, abuse, not providing treatment, physical abuse, neglect	Poor health, failure to develop physically, prone to other illnesses, could become weak/frail or die
Intellectual need not met through not playing with a child, not providing stimulating activities with older adults, keeping someone isolated, shouting at an individual, verbally abusing an individual	Bored, slow in intellectual development, anti-social behaviour, the individual feeling they have nothing to contribute
Emotional need not met by not showing love, not giving praise, not keeping a person company or keeping a person in isolation, continually not making the individual feel valued	Emotional and intellectual regression, bullying, withdrawal, mental ill-health, not feeling confident, feeling worthless
Social need not met by not allowing the individual to mix with others, not talking with others, not allowing individuals to integrate with others, being unable to conform to social norms	Isolation, withdrawal, anti-social behaviour, not confident

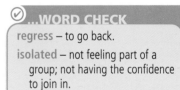

...WORD CHECK

regress – to go back.

isolated – not feeling part of a group; not having the confidence to join in.

HOW HEALTH, SOCIAL CARE AND EARLY YEARS SERVICES RESPOND TO THE DIFFERENT NEEDS AND DEMANDS OF DIFFERENT GROUPS

▲ Providing for physical needs.

All of the services provided could be used by different people in different life stages. The organizations providing care are called **service providers**. Some service providers will meet more than one of our needs, while others may provide for one particular need. You may have visited your GP, or you may have visited the dentist or spent some time in hospital. Perhaps you attended a playgroup?

Universal services are those that are provided by statutory care services, such as GPs, hospitals, clinics and community services. These will be considered in more detail in the next section.

Different services will provide for our needs in a variety of ways. For example, a nurse will provide for physical needs when cleaning a wound and putting on a protective dressing.

The nurse will also satisfy emotional, social and intellectual needs by:

- reassuring the patient and helping to stop them from worrying
- explaining what she is going to do and why and by answering questions
- by being with the patient and talking about things of interest.

A day-care centre for older people will meet physical needs. An example is by providing lunch for them. Their intellectual needs will be met through the different activities such as bingo or community singing. Emotional and social support will be met by making sure older people can talk to friends and to professional care workers about their interests and problems.

Group Activity

Look at the three bullet points to the right. Which is meets social, which meets emotional and which meets intellectual needs?

Compare your answers with someone else in the group.

How a nursery school tries to meet the needs of children

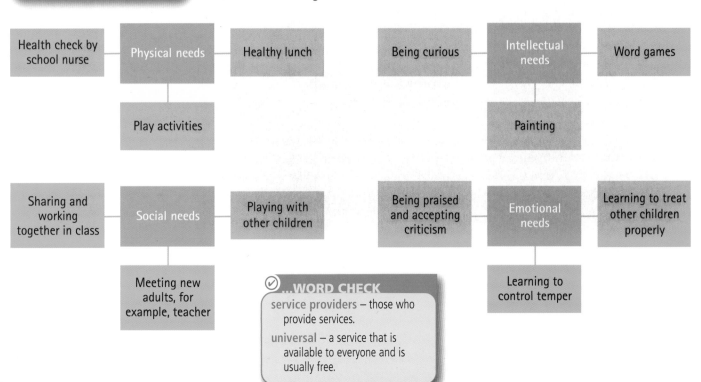

CASE STUDY   **Hebbi and James**

Hebbi is five years old. She lives with her mum, who is divorced, and with her brother James, who is three years old. They have moved away from their family home into a small house many miles away. This means that both Hebbi and James have to start at a new school.

Hebbi is very upset that she is no longer living with her father. She cries a lot, eats hardly anything, has little sleep and does not want to go out and play with others of her own age. She tells her mother that she does not want to start at a new school.

James has made friends with a little boy that lives next door. They play in the garden and enjoy talking with one another. James is looking forward to going to the same nursery school as his new friend, Benjamin.

How will services and friends meet the needs of Hebbi and James?

1. How could a GP practice meet Hebbi's physical needs?

2. How could the reception class meet Hebbi's intellectual needs?

3. How are the emotional needs of James being met?

4. Look at Maslow's pyramid of needs. How could Hebbi's and James' Level 3 needs be met?

Physical needs

Physical needs are most important as without them we would not be able to live. Physical needs include food, drink, warmth and shelter. To be healthy we all need to eat five portions of fruit and vegetables and other foods that contain all the nutrients to help the body to function properly. We need water to drink and clothing to keep us warm. Housing also provides shelter to protect us from the cold, from rain and from too much sun. Safety is a need common to all of us, as we need to be protected from danger.

Intellectual needs

The child in the picture is involved in a stimulating task. She is meeting her intellectual needs and exercising her brain. The brain is used to solve problems that occur in our day-to-day lives, in our work and during leisure and recreational activities. We also use our brains to help us develop new skills and knowledge. We all have our own interests and like different things and so

▸ Stimulating tasks help to exercise the brain and meet our intellectual needs.

as individuals we think in different ways. To make the best use of our abilities we need to use our **intellect** to set ourselves goals and targets. In doing this we will help to develop our **self-esteem**. When we **communicate** with others our intellectual needs are also being met, which helps us to develop and have a good self-image. If we use our brain to help us solve a problem, we will feel a sense of achievement.

8 What do you like doing which might develop your ability to think and learn?

Emotional needs

> **Emotional – how we feel about ourselves and how others make us feel**

How do we feel about ourselves and others? How we feel is linked to our emotions. Sometimes we will feel happy because we have friends who understand us and have the same interests or because we achieved a good grade in an examination. On other occasions we may feel sad because we have had a disagreement with a member of our family or we have to move away from our friends. Being accepted by our family, our friends and by others is very important to us. We all need to be loved and wanted and when this happens our emotional needs are being met. Being treated with **respect** and **dignity** and being given privacy and independence also contributes to meeting our emotional needs.

9 Give examples of emotional needs you have had recently. How is your emotional health likely to affect others who you live with or your friends?

Social needs

How often do you meet with friends to share interests? Sometimes you will just want to talk to one person about the things you have done, rather than being with a group of people. Being able to join in activities and being able to communicate with other people is a way of meeting our social needs. Usually we take part in activities and communicate with people who share the same interest as ourselves. Social needs also include being **valued** as an individual, having friends, feeling a sense of belonging and enjoying being with other people.

...WORD CHECK

intellect – the mind; the brain's activity.

self-esteem – how a person feels about themselves.

communicate – to share information either verbally, in writing, by signal or electronically.

respect – to treat a person with kindness and with value.

dignity – to value a person.

valued – to hold dear; to show respect.

Meeting social needs. ▶

ACTIVITY — Greg

Greg is three years old. He lives with his mum and dad but both have to work each day so Greg attends the local nursery school. Before going to the nursery Greg has breakfast at home. He likes to have a toasted sandwich which is cut up and dipped into marmite. He also has a fruit drink and an apple.

Greg enjoys going to the nursery as he has a special friend that he likes to play with on the large equipment. He enjoys painting and story time as well as making things with play dough.

His mum collects Greg at 5:00pm and they visit the public play area on the way home. After tea Greg has a bath and likes his mum or dad to read him a story before he goes to sleep. They both give him a big hug and a kiss before turning off the light.

1. How are Greg's mum and dad meeting his physical, intellectual, emotional and social needs?

2. How are staff at the nursery school meeting Greg's physical, intellectual and social needs?

3. How could the staff at the nursery school meet Greg's emotional needs?

4. Think about your own physical, intellectual, emotional and social needs. How are these being met by:
   - your family?
   - your leisure activities?

How services are shaped to meet individual needs

The care management process is a system for assessing and organizing the provision of care for an individual. Even when a service user appears to have the same condition as another, their needs will be different because of their circumstances.

When an assessment is requested after consultation with teachers, professionals and family members, a referral could be made to the social services department. Such a referral could come from a GP, from a hospital or from another care professional. A person, for example, a social worker or an occupational therapist, will be allocated to assess the service user's needs.

During the initial assessment a practitioner will:

- talk with and listen to the service user
- talk with and listen to informal carers
- provide information about what is available
- may observe the service user carrying out a variety of tasks
- record information observed or discussed
- discuss with the service users their preferences regarding services that may be needed
- write a report about the outcomes of the assessment.

> **...WORD CHECK**
>
> care management process – making an assessment of need and managing the process.
>
> assess – to make a judgement about how much an individual can or cannot do; to find out about an individual's strengths and weaknesses in relation to the care that is needed.

When undertaking an assessment it will be important to find out what is the least that it is necessary to know, in other words what must be done to enable the individual to cope. This will be done by either a social worker or an occupational therapist, but if a complex assessment is to be carried out, a high level of skills will be needed to determine the breadth and depth of the assessment and this may involve several professional care workers. Assessment is between the person (s) carrying out the assessment and the individual, being a two -way process that involves a great deal of trust. If other professionals are involved in the assessment, consent will need to be obtained from the service user for this to occur.

Care planning is identifying the most appropriate ways of meeting the needs of the service user with the best type of resources available. Responsibility for ensuring that the care plan is **implemented** at the correct pace will be that of the key worker. Implementing means carrying out the plan. While the plan is being implemented, it is important to set out the arrangements for monitoring it. This is essential to make sure that the plan is still on course.

The services supplying care must be carefully monitored to ensure that:

- the expected quality of care is being provided – is the service user getting the most up-to-date treatment?
- the care being provided meets the objectives that were agreed – does the care deal with the illness?
- the care being provided meets the cost agreed – how expensive is the treatment?
- the timing of the service provision is suitable to the service user and the main carer – is the treatment done quickly and in time to stop the illness getting worse?
- any changes from the agreed plan and the reasons for such changes are recorded – during the treatment are there any complications that affect the individual?
- any deficiencies within the plan are checked – does the treatment work?

Monitoring a care plan is important because it ensures that the service user's needs are continuing to be met. A review of a care plan must be made within the first six weeks of the starting date. Evaluation involves:

- looking at the objectives – what is it trying to do?
- considering the nature of the interventions – what action was taken?
- assessing the effectiveness of what has taken place – did the action work?
- considering if there is a need for improvement – how could things be changed for the better?

...WORD CHECK

implemented – put into place; carried out.

It is essential that a balanced view is taken when evaluating. Those involved will need to reflect and to make informed judgements about what has taken place. They will need to analyse and to make judgements about whether aspects of the care plan could have been improved and whether the outcomes actually match with the objectives set.

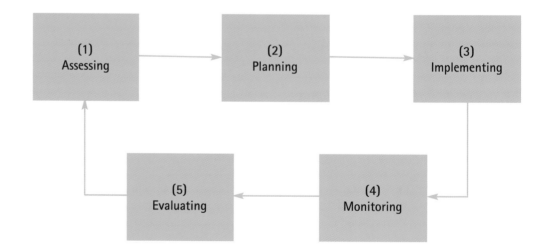

ACTIVITY — Maggi

Maggi is 75 years of age. She is recovering from a broken arm and leg in hospital but is now ready to return to her own home. An assessment of her needs is to be done in her own home before she finally leaves hospital.

1 Identify who is likely to attend Maggi's assessment. Explain the role of each.

2 Explain how the care management process will be applied to Maggi.

3 Explain how Maggi's individual needs will have been identified.

4 Draw up a list of services that could meet Maggi's needs and describe how each could help.

Developing universal services to meet social policy goals

Before making decisions about which services to provide, there is discussion between different members of the government and with other people in the local area, to decide what are to be their **aims** for health, social care and early years services. The group make their decisions and then use these to form a **policy** that will guide them when they make other decisions. Often there is no 'right way' to make sure that people get the best health care, social care or early years services that they need. A policy will provide 'broad ideas' or an **approach** that will be the basis on which other decisions will be made.

10 ▶ Why have a policy?

A government will have a large number of targets or **goals**. Each will be formed to try to deal with a particular problem or **issue** that needs to be solved. They will form a policy about how to deal with the issue. For example, one policy the present government has is to 'reduce child **poverty**'. They have decided that their approach or policy is to try and make sure that fewer children in this country are poor. Having made this decision, the government will then set goals. These are **targets** that they want to meet.

▲ Childcare is such an important matter.

> **...WORD CHECK**
>
> **aims** – the overall target or purpose.
>
> **policy** – guidelines that must be followed; procedures that must be followed.
>
> **approach** – the method used.
>
> **goals** – the outcome to be achieved.
>
> **issue** – problems; difficulties.
>
> **poverty** – to not have sufficient money to meet basic needs; to be very poor.
>
> **targets** – goals; points that must be achieved.

ACTIVITY — Researching child poverty

1 In pairs carry out research about what is considered to be child poverty in Britain. Look up the website for the Child Poverty Action Group.

2 Find out about **two** ways that the government is trying to reduce child poverty in Britain.

3 Explain how the government's policies would affect a child who is in poverty.

One of the government's goals, which will enable them to fulfil their policy to help reduce child poverty, is to make sure that help is given to 'lone parents', who are often poor because they are not able to go out to work. The government is providing help through Children's Tax Credit schemes, after-school clubs and by helping to pay for childcare for low-paid lone parents.

How can the government help?

In 1998 the government introduced the *New Deal For Lone Parents* to help unemployed lone parents get back into work. It is a 'policy goal' to encourage as many lone parents as possible to return to work and so the government is taking actions that will help them to achieve the policy they have made.

 11 How will lone parents benefit from the government's social policy of reducing child poverty?

Every Child Matters identifies that children and young people cannot learn unless they feel safe and that they cannot learn if they have ill-health. Five outcomes are the focus of the policy. These are to make sure that children:

- stay healthy
- stay safe
- enjoy and achieve
- make positive contributions
- achieve economic and social well-being.

This approach makes the commitment that the 'education of the whole child' is the main focus of attention. Education settings will not only be a place for learning but will become the 'gateway' to a number of learning opportunities and activities that offer a range of extended services. Closer working relationships between educational settings, health and social care services and parents will occur earlier and will be effectively supported. The government standard is to 'remove barriers to achievement'.

Within the *'Extended Schools'* programme some areas are specifically targeted, for example, measles vaccinations for children and young people.

...WORD CHECK

lone parents – single people with children.

income – the amount of money coming in.

gateway – a path that leads to another.

extended – more than the basic; extra.

targeted – goals; points that must be achieved.

CASE STUDY — Government policy

Marlene is five years old and is attending Granthall Primary School. Her parents work in a local factory and have to start work at 8:00am. They do not finish work until 5:30 pm.

1 How will Marlene's needs be met by two government targets in the government's policy *'Every Child Matters'*?

2 How could this policy be applied in Marlene's primary school?

3 Find out as much as you can about the government's policy on drug misuse. Show how the policy could help an adolescent.

What other social policies are there?

Other current government social policies are to **reduce** homelessness and drug misuse. To help them do this they have set policy goals – targets they want to meet by a certain time.

Once a policy has been made, consideration is given to the services that will be needed to make the policy successful. For example, if the government has a policy to reduce drug misuse, they will need to make sure that there are sufficient services available to help service users to do this.

They have to think about:

- Who will want to use the services?
- What type of services will be needed?
- Which type of health care workers will be required to run the services?
- Where in the country will the services be most needed?

To find answers to these questions they will **consult** those who are responsible for the provision of services in local areas, for example, **local authorities** and **health authorities**, and other people who may have opinions about the social issue that is being considered. These people will look at the needs of their **population** and then give the government the information they need to make decisions about which services to provide. They will also think about where the services will need to be **located** and whether more people will need to be trained so they can run the services. There will be a lot of **debate** about how the goals will be achieved and who will be involved.

How do pressure groups affect decisions?

Some people may disagree with the ideas that are being put forward and they may try to form **pressure groups** to prevent (or encourage) the government carrying out its goals. The **media** will discuss some of the points made by people and will put their ideas forward.

When everyone has had the chance to make their views and opinions known, the government will make their decisions using all the information gathered. Look at the diagram below to see how the process works:

Goals ⟶ Consultation ⟶ Gathering information ⟶ Returning information ⟶ Policy ⟶ Service provision

...WORD CHECK

reduce – to lower.

consult – to seek the opinion of others.

local authorities – those who are elected/employed to make decisions in the local area.

health authorities – those who make decisions for health care provided in a local area.

population – the people who live in an area.

located – where an individual lives.

debate – to discuss; to talk about.

pressure groups – an individual or a group of people who try to persuade someone that their way is the right or correct approach to use.

media – TV or daily papers, radio.

demographics – the factors that influence the provision of services, for example, disability, unemployment, single parent.

assess – to make a judgement about how much an individual can or cannot do; to find out about an individual's strengths and weaknesses in relation to the care that is needed.

How do local authorities and health authorities assess the care needs of the local population?

Local authorities and health authorities use **demographics** to help them **assess** the needs of the population in their community. Those who are planning health, social care and childcare provision for their local communities must research and find out about the different types of people living in their area, taking their health needs into consideration. For example:

- the number of births that occur in any one year or part of a year and whether there is an increase or decrease in these rates
- the number of single parents
- the number of children below compulsory school age
- the number of children who are of school age
- the number of people living in their area who are registered disabled

- • the migration figures, that is those moving out of their area and those moving into the area
- • the number of people who are unemployed
- • the death rate and ages of those who die.

These are demographic characteristics that will influence the planning of services. For example, if a local population has a high number of children living in its area who are under the age of five years, services such as playgroups, nursery schools and health care for children are likely to be a focus that will need careful planning. On the other hand, if a large number of the population are older adults, that is over the age of 65 years, then residential homes, nursing homes, health care and community care and support will need to be high on the planning agenda.

Very often the demography of a local area will have more than one high priority, particularly if there are, for example, both large numbers of children under the age of five years and large numbers of older adults living in the community.

The people involved in the plan are known as the 'stakeholders'. They are individuals who have the **responsibility** and interest in seeing that the service that they represent has the resources to provide an effective service. Examples of the main planners could include:

Social service purchasers
Representatives who are responsible for buying services

Local authorities
Representatives of local authorities who provide finances for community services

Private fund holders
Insurance companies who pay for care

Patients and public
Includes those who are using the service as well as those who may use it

The stakeholders

Voluntary and community groups
Charities, support groups, forums

GP services
Representatives who purchase services on behalf of local GPs

NHS
Executive members of Primary Care Trusts/groups/organizations who have money for the purchasing of services

Local education departments
Providers of services within Sure Start centres and Full Extended Schools

ACTIVITY   Planning for health or social care

Invite a member of the local planning group to your centre to talk about one health or social care or early years plan that they have developed for the local community. Try to find out:

1. How they assessed the needs of the local population.

2. Who was involved with planning and how the plan was implemented.

OR

3. If you are unable to invite a member of the group to your centre, you may be able to access the information through the internet by accessing your local PCT/PCG/Foundation hospital.

WHY INDIVIDUALS MAY NEED TO ACCESS HEALTH, SOCIAL CARE AND EARLY YEARS SERVICES

Service users may need to access health and social care services for a variety of reasons, which could include:

Physiotherapy, occupational therapy

Diagnosis of illness and conditions, for example, measles, heart disease, arthritis, diabetes

Monitoring health, for example, blood pressure

Adoption for long-term care for children, early years education, health and children's family services, residential or nursing care for older adults

Why people need to access services

Fostering, for example, short-term care for children

Counselling/behaviour therapy

Hospice for those who need 24-hour care

Most individuals have a temporary need that requires them to use one or more of the range of services. For example, an individual recovering from a hip replacement will require the short-term help of a physiotherapist to improve his or her mobility. On the other hand, a young person with Type 1 diabetes will need to use a range of services throughout their life, as they will need a constant supply of insulin and needles in order to stay alive. This will only change if a pancreatic transplant is available, which is a very complex operation.

CASE STUDY   The Mather family

John Mather is 75 and is suffering from dementia and incontinence.
Arthur Mather is 35 years of age and is overweight.
Fiona Mather is 30 and is pregnant.
Boyd, who is 14, is refusing to go to school and refuses to leave his home.
Jessie is 8 years old and has developed a rash.
Grant is 2 years old and has muscular dystrophy.

1. Which service would meet the need of each service user?

2. Explain how each would provide support.

3. Which members of the Mather family have temporary or permanent needs?

ASSESSMENT PRACTICE: PREPARATION

Choose a service user who has used more than one service. The service user can be in any life stage:

- infancy
- adolescence
- early adulthood
- middle adulthood
- later adulthood.

1 Draw up a plan to show:

- timescales, what you need to do, what you are trying to find out.

- the resources to be used, for example, the books, magazines, websites, people you may talk to using questionnaires or interviews.

2 Find out from the service user chosen:

- their needs, to include physical, intellectual, emotional and social needs

- why the service user sought to use the services offered by the service provider

- which specific services were offered by the service providers.

Remember

- Keep aims and objectives for your investigation.

- Make a plan that shows the order in which you will work, giving the dates, actions and the reasons for the actions to be taken.

- Keep a bibliography that shows primary and secondary sources of evidence and any Internet or other material used.

Note: this is only preparation for the controlled assignment that will be issued by the examination board.

How health care, social care and early years services are accessed and the barriers to access

▶ Getting started

You will gain an understanding of:

a   the range of services available to the following service users:
   i   infants
   ii   children
   iii adolescents
   iv   service users in early adulthood
   v   service users in middle adulthood
   vi   service users in later adulthood
   vii service users with specific needs

b   how service provision has developed and how it is organized, including:
   i   types of providers, to include statutory provision (NHS Trusts; integrated children's services; extended services and local authority services), private provision (private companies; self-employed practitioners and outsourcing of indirect care services), voluntary provision (charities, local support groups and non-profit organizations) and informal provision (family, friends and neighbours)
   ii   national and local organization of health, social care and early years services including the relationship between different organizations within the framework
   iii partnership and multi-agency working and how the different service providers work together to meet client group needs and how these services are integrated. Examples which could be considered in detail include Sure Start children's centres, virtual wards, multi-agency disability teams/key workers and local authority extended services provision.

Group Activity

Town Trail: Follow a route organized by your tutor. Note down any health, social care or early years services that are in the area. What services do they provide? Which service users do they provide for? When do they open and close?

When you have completed your walk, mark the services on a map. Make sure you colour code the different sectors to which the services belong.

Alternatively: this activity can be achieved by using telephone directories, guides to health, social care and early years services and local city/town information packs.

THE RANGE OF SERVICES

Which services belong to which sector?

GP practice

Social worker

Chiropodist

Special clinics

Playgroups

Primary Care Trust

BUPA

Dentist

Adoption and fostering

Age Concern

A wide range of services are available to individuals from all life stages in all main sectors. The table below includes a few examples:

Individual service users	Health care services	Social care services	Children and young people's services
Infants, children and young people (including those with specific needs, for example, disabilities)	GP Maternity services Mental health care Speech therapy Dentistry Opticians School medical services Hospital in-patient care Hospital outpatient care, for example, physiotherapy Health promotion Complementary approaches Community services, for example, dietician Hospice	Foster care Adoption Child protection Residential care Child and family support groups Child psychologists Community services Youth workers Health visitors Residential care Counselling Clinics (sexual health, smoking, alcohol and so on)	Childminders Nursery schools Playgroups Family centres Crèches Toy libraries Parent and toddler support groups After-school clubs Holiday clubs Specialist education Training schemes
Adults (including those with specific needs, for example, disabilities)	Hospital in-patient care Hospital outpatient care, for example, radiography GP Mental health care Dentistry Opticians Health promotion Complementary approaches Day care centres Community services, for example, district nurse Chiropody/podiatry Nursing homes Special services, for example, dialysis Rehabilitation Hospice	Residential homes Day care centres Training/resource centres Psychologists Psychiatrists Luncheon club Home care services Community services Counselling Social services, for example, social worker Support groups	
Older adults (including those with specific needs, for example, disabilities)	Hospital in-patient care Hospital outpatient care, for example, radiography/physiotherapy GP Mental health care Dentistry Opticians Health promotion Complementary approaches Day care centres Community services, for example, district nurse Chiropody/podiatry Nursing Homes Special services, for example, dialysis Rehabilitation Hospice Psychologists Psychiatrists	Residential homes Day care centres Training/resource centres Psychologists Psychiatrists Luncheon clubs Meals on wheels (with voluntary sector) Home care services Community services Counselling Social services, for example, social worker Support groups	

MAIN TYPES OF PROVIDERS THAT OFFER CARE

Services that are available to all individuals in England can be from:

- the statutory sector (universal services) – provided through government legislation and usually free at the point of entry but paid from taxes and National Insurance; for example, health and local authority services
- the private sector – paid for by the individual using the service, which provides a source of income to maintain the service, for example, a private hospital or dentist
- early years – those involved with education, health and looking after children
- the voluntary sector – not for profit organizations who on some occasions have paid employees working for them as well as voluntary workers. Some voluntary organizations will work alongside statutory organizations, for example, Meals on Wheels, local support groups
- informal carers, for example, family, friends and neighbours.

Those responsible for statutory services can be:

- primary care trusts
- local authorities.

The structure of health and social care statutory services is currently as shown below:

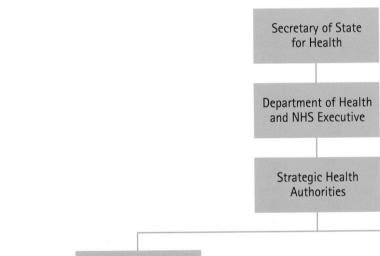

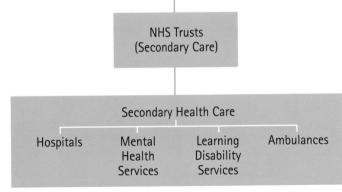

> **Group Activity**
>
> Look for a hospital in your local area and try to find out its status, for example, whether it is a Foundation hospital. With your tutor's permission invite a person from the hospital (training department) to find out about its status and the services it offers. Also find out about the needs of the individuals who use the hospital and how those needs are met.
>
> Make a record of the information given. It could be useful for your portfolio.

The Department of Health is a government department responsible for health and social services. They provide the statutory services we all use, for example, NHS hospitals and dentists. The government decides how much money each year can be given out of taxes to run the National Health Service. As we are all living longer the demand for the services continues to grow and as a result the NHS cannot provide for every need. They have to ration what is available based upon priorities, for example, the government may decide to target an issue such as alcohol addiction, and to put more money into this area.

Increasing numbers of hospitals have become Foundation Trusts. This means the government allocates money to them and the hospital decides which services they will offer.

The Strategic Health Authority looks after the needs of the population in their area. There are 28 such authorities. They use their funding to buy health care for the people who need it in their area. The use this money to:

▾ A Foundation Trust hospital.

Some services are delivered by private and voluntary groups. Examples of such services are:

Voluntary services	Private services
Meals on Wheels	Hospitals
Help the Aged	Shop mobility
Cruse (bereavement counselling)	Complementary approaches

The NHS provides a whole range of services. The chart below shows some of the settings within the NHS and examples of the services they offer.

Health setting	Examples of services provided
Hospital	Maternity, caring for people who are ill, surgery, x-ray, physiotherapy, pharmacy speech therapy, occupational therapy, orthodontal clinic, ophthalmic clinic, outpatient clinic, geriatric care, clinical counselling/psychology chiropody, nutrition clinic
Dentist	Treatment for teeth and gums, oral hygiene, advice
Health centre/ GP surgery	Health diagnosis, physiotherapy, chiropody, health advice, counselling, maternity, family planning, giving prescriptions, monitoring health, vaccinations, immunizations
Pharmacies	Making up prescriptions, advice, health monitoring
Community services (health)	Nursing care, advice about health, psychiatric nursing, medical care, monitoring health
Optician	Eye testing, diagnosis of conditions of the eye, advice, providing glasses and frames

CASE STUDY   Sasha

Sasha has a severe kidney problem and has to take medication every day to keep her condition stable. She collects her prescription once a fortnight. Sasha also has to have regular health checks to make sure that her condition stays stable, and visits the local hospital for this. Sasha also has incontinence problems and is visited at home by a health care assistant.

1   Draw up a table to show all the health services Sasha would use because of her condition. For each show the treatment she would receive.

2   Carry out some research to find out about walk-in centres and hospices. Who are the clients for each?

Local authorities

Local authority social services departments are based in the area in which we live. They are responsible for the needs of people who live in their area. These are those needs that are not 'health' or 'medical'. For example, the local authority has a Families Information Service whose responsibility it is to provide services for people who have care needs on a **temporary** or **permanent** basis.

The structure of the social care services can vary but the diagram below gives a broad outline of the structure and the various departments within it.

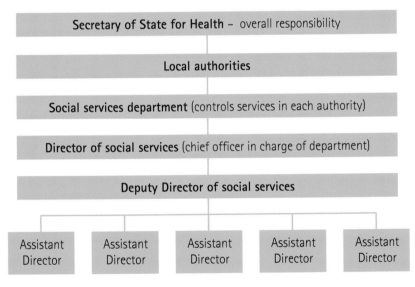

> ✓ ...WORD CHECK
> **temporary** – not long lasting; not permanent.
> **permanent** – for ever; constant.

One of the services provided by the local authority is, for example, fostering services, who provide a short-term home for children and young people. The adoption services arrange for a family to keep a child or young person for life, which is long-term care. Some of the services offered by the local authority for children and young people are:

- child protection, fostering and adoption
- providing for children and young people with disabilities
- children's and young people's homes
- youth justice.

The local authority also keep a register of people who are suitable to work as a childminders and they keep a register of early years groups such as playgroups and nurseries. Local authorities will also purchase places in playgroups and nurseries for children and young people who may be 'at risk' or where the family may need support.

 11 Why is it important for the local authority to keep a register of all the early years providers in their area?

Local authority services for adults

Examples of some of the services made available by the local authority for adults are:

- contributing financially to places for service users within private residential homes and within nursing homes for people who need 24-hour care and support but who may not have enough money to pay for their care

- accommodation and workshop facilities for people with physical and **learning disabilities**

- day centres for service users who may wish to live in their own homes, but who may need to have some social **interaction** with other people.

▲ Learning skills for work and learning to socialize.

The local authority keeps a register of residential and nursing homes in their area and will carry out inspections of these as required by law. Some examples of settings and services made available by the local authority for service users are:

Local authority settings	Examples of services
Day care centre for older people (sometimes these work with the voluntary sector)	Personal support, supervision, advice, chiropody, aids and adaptations, meals
Community care and support	Advice and guidance, counselling, psychiatric support, home care services
Fostering and adoption	Children's and young people's homes (temporary and permanent)
Playgroups/nurseries (sometimes these can work with private and voluntary groups)	Purchasing places in playgroups and nurseries
Family centres	Day care for children and young people Support for adults
Resource training centres for service users with disabilities	Training for work, education, advice and guidance

CASE STUDY — Services

1. Debbie-Ann is in her late fifties. She lives on her own but she is becoming very forgetful. She sometimes leaves the lights on all night and wanders around the road and garden in her nightdress, talking to herself. She is not feeding herself properly and does not often wash herself. She has no one to talk to as her family live abroad and the house next door is empty.

   a) Produce a table to show three services or ways that the local authority could provide support for Debbie-Ann.

   b) Carry out research to identify a voluntary group that could help Debbie-Ann. Describe the support they could give.

2. Andre is four years old. His family are having personal problems and are finding it difficult to care for Andre. Find out and explain the different ways that the local social services department could provide help and support for Andre and his family.

3. What is meant by 'learning difficulties'? Find out about one service for people who have learning difficulties in your area and describe how it provides support.

4. What advice would you give to a parent who has a young child with physical disabilities about how to find out about the early years services available?

How are private services organized?

Private services are not provided by law. They are sometimes called 'non-statutory' services. They are often set up by large companies to make a profit. Some offer medical care and others are involved in giving care and support, for example, counselling.

Examples of private services are:

- private hospitals
- private dentists
- childminders
- playgroups/nurseries
- home care assistants.

People who use private organizations, or use practitioners who accept private patients, have to pay for the services they receive. Some people have insurance policies to help them with the expenses for their treatment. Others will pay for their treatment from their savings.

People often choose to have their medical care carried out by a private organization, for example, a hip replacement operation, because they can choose the time and the place when it can be done. This might be an important consideration if you have a business to run or if childcare is a problem.

Practitioners who treat people privately often work in a private hospital or from their own home. Alternatively, they could have their own premises that have been set up with all the specialist equipment they will need.

 12 How would paying to have private treatment for an operation help someone with childcare problems?

Some service users combine treatment from universal services with that of private care.

> ## ...WORD CHECK
>
> **non-statutory** – not law.
>
> **profit** – to make money on.
>
> **insurance policies** – taking out cover to prevent an emergency, for example, Denplan for dental insurance.

CASE STUDY **Eddi**

Eddi had cancer of the lungs and received treatment in hospital for this. He had a small part of his lung removed and then received chemotherapy. When Eddi came out of hospital, he made an appointment to see a local alternative therapy care worker.

This practitioner gave Eddi some herbal tablets to help relieve his stress. He also recommended that Eddi should have some aromatherapy in his own home. Eddi continued to keep appointments at his local hospital for chemotherapy.

Eddi combined traditional medical treatment with alternative approaches to try to improve his health.

1 How do you think Eddi was helped by the methods he chose?

2 Would you choose alternative approaches for treatment? Give reasons why you would or would not do this.

Examples of other private organizations are playgroups or nursery schools. These are privately organized but are monitored by Ofsted and records are kept by the local authority.

A diagram of how the services are organized is shown below:

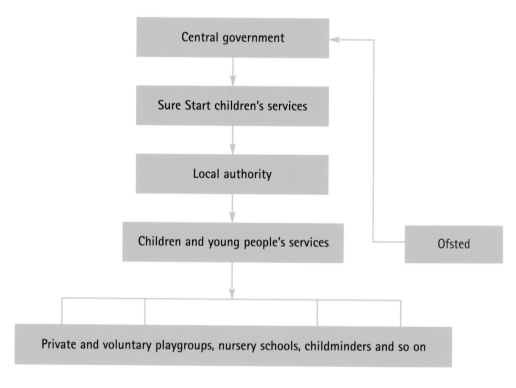

Central government

Sure Start children's services

Local authority

Children and young people's services

Ofsted

Private and voluntary playgroups, nursery schools, childminders and so on

Voluntary organizations

Voluntary organizations are those who provide services or advice about health, social care and early years services because they see there is a 'gap' or a need for these services. Usually services that are made available by the voluntary sector are free of charge, but this is not always the case. Occasionally a small charge is made for the service.

Most of the workers who give the care and advice are 'volunteers', who are not paid for the work they do. Any profit that is made by voluntary organization is used to make the service better or to offer a wider range of services. They are, therefore, often called 'not-for-profit' organizations.

Keep a look out in your local high street for 'charity shops'. You might find Help the Aged, Sue Ryder, Oxfam, Age Concern, British Heart Foundation and others. These shops will be selling clothes, china, books, pictures and other items that they have been given by the people who live in the area. The money that is collected from selling the goods is used so they can organize services for people who have a health or care need.

▶ Which charity shops exist in your local area?

When do voluntary organizations work with other sectors?

Sometimes voluntary organizations will also work together with the statutory service providers. An example is the provision of Meals on Wheels.

In this case, social services make a **contract** with voluntary services so they can supply hot meals for service users in their own homes. This helps when the service users are unable to cook for themselves. Often, when a contract is made between a statutory provider and the voluntary sector, the person who takes charge of the project for the voluntary sector is paid for their skills and expertise. This is a because a large project may require at least one full- or part-time paid employee.

There are times when the private sector and the voluntary or third sector work together to provide services. Below is a table that shows where this could occur:

✓ **...WORD CHECK**

contract – a legally binding agreement.

▶ Meals on Wheels delivery service.

Private and voluntary	Examples of services provided
Day centre for older people	Meals, chiropody, personal support, aids and adaptations, leisure activities, care planning, counselling
Residential homes	24-hour care and support, chiropody, alternative therapies, volunteer friends
Nursing home	Medical care and support 24 hours a day, volunteer friends
Playgroups/nursery schools (private)	Care and education
BUPA hospitals Nuffield hospitals	Surgery, medical nursing, physiotherapy, x-rays, consultations about health conditions, audiology
Help the Aged day centre for older people	Meals, leisure activities, personal help and support, chiropody
Community services	Nursing care in service user's own home, for example, Macmillan nurses
Hospice	Medical care, personal care and support, alternative therapies

How do the universal (statutory), voluntary and private sectors work together?

The *NHS Plan* and the *1999 Health and Social Care Act* made it possible for voluntary partnership to be formed between local health and local social care organizations. In such an arrangement PCTs (Primary Care Trusts) and local authorities both commission and provide services for the people within their local area.

Additionally, statutory, voluntary and private sectors often work together to meet the needs of service users. This approach is being encouraged by the government to help people get the treatment they need more quickly. If a service user has been waiting a long time for an operation or treatment that they need, a Trust Hospital (statutory) will make a contract with the private hospital to carry out a certain number of hip operations or knee operations, for example. This means that the service user will receive their operation and aftercare in the private hospital but they will not pay. The payment will be made by the organization that has made the contract with the private hospital.

Informal carers

Group Activity

Talk to a person who has been an informal carer. Find out what type of jobs they have done. How did this help the individual for whom they were providing support?

Informal support is the care given by those who are not paid to do so. In most cases such people may be unskilled and will also be available at times when professional care workers are not available. Informal care workers are most likely to be individuals who the service user knows and trusts. For example:

- **immediate family members** – husband, wife, sons, daughters. Family members are likely to be involved in the personal care of the service user, for example, washing, changing, cooking and serving meals

- **extended family members** – grandparents, aunts, uncles, nieces. Members of this group could contribute by shopping or sitting with the service user for periods of time or helping to write letters or assisting with the laundry. The way in which they help is likely to be less personal

- **neighbours** – those living near at hand. A neighbour can help by providing a snack, sitting and talking with a service user, making sure that medication is taken if family members are not able to do so or even by shopping for the person who is ill

- **friends** – people who know the service user well and want to help. For example, they may take the service user for a walk or a drive, they may take them to an appointment or just sit and share news about what is happening in the world.

Other groups of people who are classified as informal carers could include:

- **volunteer friends** – untrained, or retired, or people who do not work, who feel they can contribute to the service user's care, for example, by driving them to appointments or collecting books from the library

- **faith groups** – individuals who belong to a faith group who probably know the service user who wish to visit to keep the person company or to pray or to help in any other way that is useful

- **support groups** – these are groups of people who may be experiencing the same problem as the person who is ill or has a particular need, for example, a group of people who have previously had alcohol- or drug-related problems and who meet to talk through how they are feeling and the issues they have faced. By meeting and talking they provide support for one another, which helps them to feel more confident about the future.

Informal carers are invaluable as they can fill the gap left by professional care workers and can deal with all the daily routines which, if not done, could cause the service user to worry.

Partnership and multi-agency working

> **Partnership** is working together to provide an holistic approach to care, and sharing resources, both human and material, to achieve this type of care.

The government wants to ensure that Sure Start Children's Centres are available in every area by 2010. Such centres open from, for example, 8:00am to 6:00pm all the year round and provide **seamless**, **holistic** and **personalized integrated** services for children aged under five years and their families. All Sure Start Children's Centres are part of the government's '*Ten Year Strategy for Childcare*'. This enables all families with children to have access to affordable, flexible, high quality childcare places for their children.

A second target is to put in place '*Full-Service Extended Schools and Extended Schools*'. The former will have key professionals such as health workers, psychologists and youth workers based on education sites, and who will work closely alongside teachers so that children's problems can be addressed without too much disruption. Extended schools, too, will offer a wide range of activities beyond the school day to help meet the needs of children and other individuals who live in the local community. Examples would be after-school clubs, holiday clubs and leisure activities.

The table below shows examples of the objectives for specific targets for '*Every Child Matters*':

Target	Objective
Promote being healthy	Stress management programme for learners and staff Healthier eating options in school canteen Education about leading healthier lifestyles
Staying safe	Peer mentoring programme to reduce bullying Linking with police liaison and crime prevention panels
Enjoy and achieve	Emphasizing the importance of and providing the opportunities for students to achieve a balance between education/work and leisure, for example, running after school clubs and activities.
Making a positive contribution	Setting personalized learning plans Improving access to diagnostic testing Improving the opportunity for assessment Addressing disengagement Befriending scheme
Achieving economic and social well-being	Engagement in mini enterprise projects Developing literacy and team working skills Developing problem solving skills

These examples show how teachers, health and social care professionals, **paraprofessionals** and parents can all work together to improve the quality of life and learning for the child.

Other examples of partnership working and **multi-disciplinary teams** are disability teams with key workers.

A multi-disciplinary approach means that professionals from different sectors, for example, health and social services, work together as a team rather than in isolation. Sometimes the voluntary sector will also be involved, depending on the type of care that is needed.

Group Activity

Find out about disability teams and key workers. Who could be in a disability team? How would they work?

How could a disability team be of benefit to service users?

Who are 'key workers'? What is their role?

...WORD CHECK

seemless – continuous; without any breaks.

holistic – looking at the whole (person).

personalized integrated – for the individual being considered.

paraprofessionals – someone who is trained to provide support for professionals, for example, classroom support assistants.

multi-disciplinary teams – a team from different sectors or areas that work together bringing different skills and thinking to the work they do.

Group Activity

With your tutor's permission, invite a person to the Centre who works with other services/ /sectors to your centre. Find out how this process is managed. What are the benefits? Are there any weaknesses?

Write up the information provided.

...WORD CHECK

diverse – a wide range of different types of people/cultures living in the country.

There are many advantages to both the service user and the care practitioner when care is provided through a multi-disciplinary approach:

- the staff can discuss problems with other colleagues and refer the service user quickly to receive the support they need
- it should avoid tragedies such as the case of 'Baby P' and other child abuse cases where information was not fully shared by all the services working on the case
- regular team meetings can be held to check on the progress of the case
- the service user should know who to turn to for help rather than being confused about which agency to contact
- no individual should 'slip through the net' and fail to get the help they need.

13 ▶ Have you or any of your relatives and friends ever used services that adopt a multi-disciplinary approach?

What does this mean in practice?

The United Kingdom has a **diverse** cultural population. This means that a mixture of people from different ethnicities live together. Within the population there will be people who have different ways of doing things. This will apply to the foods they eat, their beliefs and the way they would like health, social care and early years to be delivered. Services try really hard to meet the needs of all their population by:

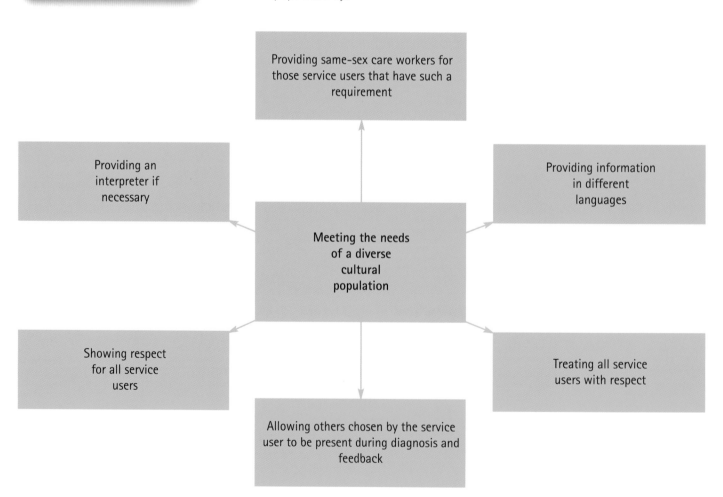

CASE STUDY — Dimitar

Dimitar lives at home with his wife, but he has Alzheimer's disease. He is forgetful and often wanders outside. His wife has to keep the doors locked or he will wander into the road. Dimitar loves to chat with people. He can remember quite a lot from the past but not very much about the present. Sometimes he forgets where the toilet is and just urinates where he is. His wife is finding life very difficult and is quite worn out. His GP arranges for an assessment to be made.

1. Identify which services could help provide care for Dimitar and
   - explain the help they could give
   - explain how this would help Dimitar and his wife to cope.

2. Explain how the services could work together to support Dimitar.

ASSESSMENT PRACTICE: PREPARATION

For the **one** service user chosen in the previous Assessment Practice, produce an information booklet by the service providers to be used as a guide for service users who use these services. The information will include:

1. An explanation of how policies led to the provision of the national and local services.

2. The structure and organization of the services showing how the organization fits into the local and national framework by producing diagrams and explaining them.

3. Show how the service user accesses the range of services offered by and through the local service provider.

4. Any problems the service user might encounter in accessing the provision.

Remember

Continue with the plan that shows the order in which you will work, giving the dates, actions and the reasons for the actions to be taken.

Keep a bibliography that shows primary and secondary sources of evidence and any Internet or other material used.

Note: this is only preparation for the controlled assignment that will be issued by the examination board.

How health, social care and early years services are provided

▶ Getting started

In this unit you will gain an understanding of:

a the ways in which service users access health, social care and early years services, including:
   i self-referral
   ii professional referral
   iii third party referral

b barriers which exist to accessing these services, including:

c physical barriers including stairs, lack of lifts and lack of adaptations

d psychological barriers including social stigma, fear of loss of independence

e financial barriers including services that are means tested, services that are charged for and those which have fees attached

f geographical barriers including distance of services provider from service user residence, poor transport links

g cultural/language barriers including differing cultural beliefs, differing first language

h resource barriers including staff shortages, postcode lottery, lack of local funding, great local demand.

✓ ...WORD CHECK

referral – the method by which a patient is put in contact with a medical specialist.

direct – straight to the person/openly; to be responsible for a person's care.

ACCESSING HEALTH, SOCIAL CARE AND EARLY YEARS SERVICES

Think about the number of times that you have used different services that provide health and social care or childcare. You may have used a dentist, a GP, a hospital, nursery school or social services. How did you access the service?

Self-referral

Self-referral is the name given when a person has gone straight to their GP and not approached through another professional care worker. When wanting to see a GP most of us will gain access by taking ourselves directly to the surgery.

When feeling unwell and when a prescription may be needed to help fight an illness such as 'flu', an individual will probably go directly to their GP or telephone the GP to make an appointment. This is a direct approach.

Professional referral?

The GP, however, may on some occasions want us to make an appointment with a person who specializes in specific types of conditions or illnesses or a person who deals with injuries. He will then either telephone or write to the specialist, who is usually known as a 'consultant', to make an appointment on our behalf.

This method of making an arrangement to see someone else is called a 'professional referral'. Perhaps you have had such an appointment made for you if you have hurt your arm or leg and the GP thinks an x-ray is necessary? Or maybe you have had an illness that the GP needs a second opinion about and has made an arrangement for you to see the specialist at the local hospital?

> **...WORD CHECK**
>
> **consultant** – a person who provides advice, for example, medical advice.

Third-party referral

The third way in which service users can be referred to health, social care or early years services is called 'third-party referral'. This is when another person who is not a professional care worker refers, or draws attention to, an individual. The person who makes the referral could be a relative, another professional, a neighbour, an employer or a friend.

In all educational and care settings for children and young people there has to be a 'named person' who will take responsibility for reporting suspected cases of child abuse. This is a legal requirement and the instructions given within the legislation state that a 'named person' must be in place and should have undertaken the required training. Any suspicions by staff must be reported to the named person, who after considering the facts will probably contact a social worker who would investigate the concerns further.

◄ GP telephoning consultant in a hospital.

Group Activity

Work with another person to decide which method was used by the following three people to access the services:
Person A: GP asked them to see a specialist heart consultant.
Person B: A teacher asked a social worker to visit a student.
Person C: Gemma visited the dentist.
Compare your answers with another group.
Write a short definition of the three different ways of accessing the services.

Group Activity

Try to visit a nursery and a residential home or day care centre to find out the different methods of referral that have been used. You may wish to do this during work experience. Alternatively, your tutor may arrange for two professional care workers to visit your centre to talk about the different methods they have experienced.

After the visit discuss:

Which methods had been used to refer people?

What are the differences between the methods?

Working with another person, write **three** different scenarios as examples of how individuals have been referred.

Exchange your scenarios with a different pair and work out the methods of referral.

CASE STUDY   Fion

Fion, who is four years old, attends playgroup three times each week. The nursery nurse at the playgroup becomes very worried as Fion has bruises on her legs and on her tummy. She notices these when she takes Fion to the toilet. The nursery nurse reports the bruising to the 'named person' at the playgroup.

Two weeks later Fion is found to have more bruises and she seems to be very sad and cries a lot. The named person at the playgroup telephones social services to report her concerns.

1. Why did the nursery nurse report to the 'named person'?

2. Why do settings that provide care and education for children have a 'named person'?

3. Produce your own short case study to include a different third-party referral.

4. Exchange your scenario with another group and check whether it is a third-party referral.

Other examples of third party referral could include:

- a teacher telephoning a social worker because they have concerns about a child
- a neighbour telephoning a social worker or GP because they have concerns about a child that lives next door
- a neighbour telephoning social services because an older person is wandering about in the garden at night or leaving the gas on
- an employer telephoning a GP about a young employee who seems to be very depressed and who he feels may harm himself
- a person telephoning the emergency services for an ambulance to take an injured person to hospital.

15 ▶ Why is it important that people know how to access health, social care and early years services?

ACTIVITY — The Bishop family

Russell and Heather Bishop have three children: Malcolm, who is 13, Naomi, who is 9, and Daniel, who is 4. Heather's mum, Greta, also lives with the family and she is 72 years old.

1 Daniel has a cold, a very bad cough and also a high temperature. His mother takes him to the GP as she is slightly worried about him.

   a Identify the type of referral this is and explain why.
   b What needs does Daniel have?
   c How can these needs be met?

2 Greta is seen by a social worker as she does not see many people of her own age. The social worker refers Greta to a social worker at the local day-care centre to try and encourage Greta to attend twice each week.

   a Identify the type of referral this is and explain why.
   b What needs does Greta have?
   c How can these needs be met?

3 Russell is walking home from work one day when he finds a lady lying injured on the pavement.

   a Identify the type of referral this would be and explain why.
   b What needs does the lady have?
   c How can these needs be met?

WHAT MIGHT PREVENT PEOPLE FROM USING THE HEALTH, SOCIAL CARE AND EARLY YEARS SERVICES THAT THEY NEED?

Sometimes people do not use the health, social care and early years services that they need. This could be for a variety of reasons but is usually because **barriers** prevent them from doing so. Legislation has meant that barriers are not as common as they used to be, since through a number of laws organizations have removed the obstacles to access. Possible barriers are covered in the following sections.

> **✓ ...WORD CHECK**
>
> **barriers** – an obstacle that may prevent something from happening.
>
> **physical barrier** – preventing someone from obtaining access, for example, a lift or operator buttons not in place in Braille for a person who cannot see.

Physical barriers

Imagine you are in your seventies and you suffer from rheumatism, so that you have to walk using a walking stick. You want to go to the dentist but the only way to get to the surgery is by going down some very steep steps.

You would know that you could not make it down those steps, so you would probably not go to the dentist in the first place! You might go without the treatment because of the **physical barrier** presented by the steps.

Quite a lot of people are prevented from using health, social care and early years services because they are unable to enter or leave a building. Or they may not be able to use the toilet because, for example, it is upstairs or the door is not wide enough for a wheelchair to enter.

Some people could be prevented from using a lift because they cannot access the control buttons or if they are blind they may be unable to read the instructions because they have not been given in Braille.

▲ 'How am I going to get to see the dentist?'

Psychological barriers

These affect the way we think. Some people are afraid of going to the dentist; they have a 'fear' of dentists. This is an example of a psychological barrier. Some older people will not agree to going into a residential home because they think they will become **dependent** on others or that people will not have any respect for them because they cannot cope. They think there is a 'stigma' attached to them and will not accept the care offered even though they may know it is best for them.

Individuals who have mental health conditions are sometimes afraid to access the service they need. In their minds they could be afraid of meeting other people or they may think that the professional care worker will immediately make them go to a clinic for treatment. While such fears are unfounded, they still loom large in the mind of the individual.

Financial barriers

▲ 'Can I afford these tablets?'

How often have you been prevented from doing something because it cost too much? Most of us have, at some time or another. But, when people are unable to use a health, social care or early years service because of a lack of money, their health may suffer as a result. If someone lives some distance from health services, for example, the cost of travelling may be too much. If it is a private service, such as a playgroup, a family with several children may not be able to afford to send them all to the playgroup. Cost can stop some people from getting their prescription, if they have to pay for them, and so they do not get the medication they may need.

Some services are **means tested**; this means that an individual will have to declare their income and have this **scrutinized** to make sure that they cannot afford to pay for the service they need. Many service users find this process very demoralizing and feel that they are being 'looked down on' by the people who administer the process. An example of a service that is means tested is that of a home care assistant who would visit a service user in the service user's own home to help with shopping, cleaning and preparation of snacks.

Geographical barriers

Some people live in rural areas and may find that getting to the services they need is difficult because they do not have a car, and buses may run at times that are not suitable. Older people may have difficulty getting on and off public transport and they may not be able to walk the distance to the service they require. They may put off going to see their GP because of this and as a result their condition could get worse. Some individuals and families may not be able to afford a car, particularly with fuel prices being so expensive, so they could be prevented from accessing the service they need because of the geographical location and the cost.

Cultural and language barriers

◀ 'I can't make sense of this!'

In order to find out about services it is most likely that you will need to read signs, leaflets or posters. If these are written in English and this is not the language that you usually use, it may be difficult to understand the information that is given fully and so you may not know what services are available. Also, if a leaflet is provided by the GP or specialist to explain the treatment that is being proposed, the person may not be able to read or understand what is being said in the leaflet. So cultural or language barriers can cause individuals to become worried or frightened.

Resource barriers

The table below gives a summary of the possible barriers that can prevent people from getting the care they need.

Barrier	Examples
Physical barriers	• The service is not available when they are not working • Stairs • Lack of adapted toilets • Lift operating system being out of reach • Lack of ramps • Lack of lifts
Psychological barriers	• Fear of losing independence • Stigma associated with using some services • Not wanting to be looked after by others • Mental health problems
Financial barriers	• Charges/fees • Lack of money for transport • Lack of money to provide the service
Geographical barriers	• Living in a rural area where facilities are limited • Living in a rural area where transport is not available when the services are open • A long bus/train journey may not be practical
Cultural and language barriers	• Using English may deter some people from using services • Not having professionals who are of the same sex, for example, women doctors/consultants for women • Written information not provided in the person's own language • Not knowing what is available • Some treatments being considered unacceptable to certain cultures
Resource barriers	• Lack of staff • Lack of information about services • Lack of money to fund services • A large demand for a particular service

Sometimes we are not able to get the services we want because there is a shortage of staff or money to pay for the service. The lack of such resources can prevent people from gaining access to services when they really need them.

Also, if there is a large demand for a particular service, then people may have to wait, as there may only be sufficient money to provide for some and not all who require the service.

Health care professionals often have to make very difficult decisions about who gets treatment and who does not. They may have one child who needs treatment that will cost a great deal of money. The same amount of money would perhaps cover 50 people who need hip replacement operations. They may not have the money for both -- who should they treat?

CASE STUDY — Coping with barriers

Remus has only been living in this country for a few months. He and his partner, Katrina, are trying to learn English but they are finding it very hard. Remus is unemployed and is finding it difficult to get work, but his partner has a part-time job in a local hotel. Remus and Katrina have two children, Kerry, who is four, and Brendon, who is two years old. It is difficult for the family to get transport into town, where the health, social care and early years services are. A bus leaves twice each day but the costs are high. Katrina and Remus would like Kerry to go to playgroup, but there isn't one in the village. Brendon has to go to the hospital once a week as he has cystic fibrosis and needs treatment to clear his lungs. He is waiting to have an operation to help clear his airways but the hospital has a long waiting list and staff shortages.

1. Katrina and Remus have a lot of barriers to cope with. Use the table on the previous page, which shows the different types of barriers that people face, to help you with this task. Draw up a table of your own, copying the main types of barriers shown on the left-hand side. Complete the examples by using the case study and describe how each barrier will affect the family.

2. Think about all the different types of barriers that can exist when clients want to use health, social care and early years services. Conduct a survey to find out how easy it is for clients to access **three** different services. Record the types of client that use the services, explain their needs and give information about the barriers that may prevent them from using the service. Clearly record your findings and draw some conclusions. You can use graphs, pie charts or other methods to help you do this.

3. How would an individual feel if they are not able to use a service they need?

How can barriers to accessing services be overcome?

Getting past the 'barriers' and accessing health, social care and early years services is important for service users. Service providers, too, want to make sure that they reach all those who need their services.

When new services are developed, those responsible put a great deal of thought into how they can be made accessible to all. For example, if someone lives in a rural area and needs to get to the hospital, but the buses are not timetabled so that this can happen, or if the person who needs to go to the hospital is in a wheelchair and cannot get on a bus, how can this be overcome? In this situation the voluntary care sector will probably be able to help. They would organize a volunteer with transport to collect the person and take them to the hospital.

Lena's first language is not English and she cannot read the leaflet about health services.

Overcome by: having leaflets printed in other languages so that they are accessible to all.

Martin is in a wheelchair. He cannot use the lift because the control panel is too high.

Overcome by: moving the control panel so that it can be reached at wheelchair height.

Amy is blind and cannot use the lift at the hospital as she cannot use the control panel.

Overcome by: putting in a control panel that also uses Braille.

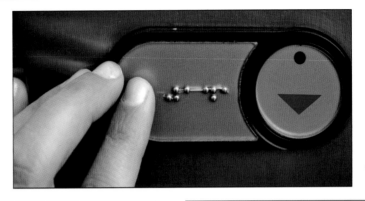

◄ 'Now I have access!'

Kelly has three children and lives on an estate that is two miles from the GP surgery. She finds it very hard to get to the surgery with three children, as it is a long way to walk and she cannot afford to take the bus.

Overcome by: having a mobile surgery to visit the estate twice each week so that mothers with young children and older people on the estate will not have to travel. This would also reduce the cost to the clients.

Ian works shifts. The GP surgery is not open when he is off work, so he can never go for his health checks.

Overcome by: holding some surgeries at the factory where Ian works or having early or late surgery appointments on one weekday or at weekends.

If service users were faced with the barriers given above, or any other barrier, this is likely to affect their self-esteem/self-concept. They are very likely not to feel good about themselves and consider that they might not be as good as other people. The effects will not be the same for everyone but some of the effects could be:

- not feeling valued
- feeling unimportant
- thinking that others do not care about their disability
- having a low self-esteem/self-concept
- being depressed
- feeling angry
- feeling unloved/unwanted
- becoming withdrawn
- feeling excluded.

Some of these reactions will be physical, others will be emotional, some will be intellectual and others will be social.

Group Activity

Work with another person. Think about a time when you or someone in your family was unable to access a service you/they needed. How did you/they feel?

ACTIVITY   Overcoming the barriers

1. For each of the case studies on the previous page, provide a **different way** in which the barrier could be overcome, describing how the suggestion would help.

2. For each case study, explain how the service user would feel when faced with the barrier. Explain how it might affect the service users physically, intellectually, emotionally and socially.

3. How would overcoming each barrier help to empower the service users?

The postcode lottery

Group Activity

Discuss the article below as a group. What are the likely effects if the treatment is a success? What effect will this have on the NHS? What effect could it have on service users?

Drugs and treatment are expensive. Decisions about which drugs and which treatments to provide in any area are made by the local Primary Care Trust or by a central organization called 'NICE' (the National Institute for Health and Clinical Excellence). This is an organization that decides whether a drug is too expensive for the health service to use.

On occasions, a certain drug is used or a treatment is made available in some areas, while it is not in other areas. This is known as the postcode lottery. This type of decision is considered to be unfair, particularly by those for whom a drug or treatment is not available. On other occasions, NICE will decide that no one can access the drug or treatment because it is not good value for money. In either situation, a service user's life could be affected, as their condition could get worse or they could even die.

CASE STUDY   New therapy could hold out hope for Britain's 400,000 Alzheimer's sufferers

New treatment for Alzheimer's disease

Doctors are calling for a clinical trial of an experimental drug treatment that it is claimed can reverse the symptoms of Alzheimer's disease 'in minutes'.

US researchers say the treatment allowed an 82-year-old sufferer to recognize his wife for the first time in years.

In the UK, specialists believe the claims should be properly tested, as only a few patients have been treated so far.

The treatment involves injecting a drug called Enbrel – which is normally used to treat arthritis – into the spine at the neck. Patients are then tilted to encourage blood flow into the brain, where the drug is designed to block a chemical responsible for inflammation. At least one Alzheimer's patient had his symptoms reversed 'in minutes' while others have shown some continuing improvement in problems such as forgetfulness and confusion after weekly injections.

They needed less help from carers during treatment, which appears to reach a plateau at three months.

Around 50 people are being treated by the Institute of Neurological Research, a private clinic in California, with some having had injections for three years.

In one case, the clinic has video evidence of Marvin Miller, 82, which showed he was unable to answer basic questions by a nurse, or identify everyday objects like a bracelet and a pencil. Shortly afterwards he is injected with the drug and it is claimed that five minutes later he could greet his shocked wife, who said he had not recognized her for years.

The experiment follows the discovery that levels of TNF (tumour necrosis factor) can be up to 25 times higher in the fluid surrounding the brain in sufferers of Alzheimer's disease.

Continued on next page

▶ *Continued from previous page*

Enbrel, a biologic treatment licensed for rheumatoid arthritis, binds to excess TNF in the body and makes it inactive.

When used by arthritis sufferers, the drug is self-administered by injection and researchers had to develop a way of injecting the drug into the spine in order to get an effect in brain cells.

Enbrel is not approved for treating Alzheimer's in the US or in the UK and is regarded at this stage as a highly experimental therapy.

Rebecca Wood, chief executive of the Alzheimer's Research Trust, said: 'It is too early to speak of a miracle cure and we need to do more research into this'.

New hope for Alzheimer's sufferers after new treatment 'restores memory in minutes', by Jenny Hope, Mail Online (last updated 11 April 2008).

Group Activity

Work with another person to find newspaper cuttings about individuals who have complained about not being able to access the drugs they need.

Make a summary of their protest.

Discuss your findings with the rest of the group.

Poor integration and rationing of services

Currently the government is trying to persuade organizations within health, social care and early years services to work together rather than to operate individually. By working together there is more likely to be 'a **seamlessness of service**' and **continuity** of care. The individual's needs will be viewed **holistically** by a small team rather than having to be seen in different places by different specialists. By working in this way, those involved will need to work together in a partnership and it is hoped that this approach will bring better results for an individual, as well as being more **economical** to run. More information about this type of approach was given earlier in the unit (see pages 127–128).

> ✓ **...WORD CHECK**
>
> **seamlessness of service** – continuous; without any breaks.
>
> **continuity** – without a break; continuous.
>
> **holistically** – looking at the whole (person).
>
> **economical** – costing lesss.

ASSESSMENT PRACTICE: PREPARATION

You must choose the same service user as selected for the earlier Assessment Practices.

For the service user you have chosen and the services that they are using, you need to:

1 Find out about any possible barriers that the service user found or that could have occurred when using the services. To do this, you may wish to produce a questionnaire so that you have primary evidence for your fact-finding exercise.

Alternatively, (with your tutor's permission) you could invite a small group of service users to your centre to ask them which services they use and what barriers might exist. You will still need to prepare a questionnaire in order to obtain the answers.

2 Write up the findings from the questionnaire and give a full report about the barriers to access of the services that could occur and the problems a service user may encounter in accessing provision.

Try to analyse your findings and present the answers using either a bar chart or pie chart as well as written analysis.

Include as many different types of barriers as you can, making sure you cover each group given within the specification.

Remember: Continue with a plan that shows the order in which you will work, giving the dates, actions and the reasons for the actions to be taken. Keep a bibliography that shows primary and secondary sources of evidence and any Internet or other material used.

Note: this is only preparation for the controlled assignment that will be issued by the examination board.

Workers in health, social care and early years

▶ Getting started

You will gain an understanding of:

a the main work roles of care practitioners and the skills and qualifications needed to deliver services effectively, including:

   i direct carers, to include doctors, nurses, community nurses, health visitors, midwives, health care assistants, portage workers, child development workers, early years practitioners, family support workers, occupational therapists, physiotherapists, teachers

   ii indirect carers, to include practice managers, medical receptionists, school reception staff, catering staff

   iii indirect services which are mostly outsourced to private companies, to include cleaners, catering services, security, portering, waste management.

DIRECT CARERS

...WORD CHECK

direct – straight to the person/openly; to be responsible for a person's care.

Jobs in health, social care and early years can be divided into direct and indirect roles. **Direct** care roles are jobs where the practitioner is in personal contact with the individual and caring for them is the main purpose of the role.

Examples of direct jobs in health care

Nurse   Physiotherapist   Health visitor   Community nurse
Midwife   GP/consultant   Health care assistant

Examples of direct jobs in social care

Social worker   Care assistant   Adoption/fostering officer   Home tutor
Occupational therapist   Family support worker

Examples of direct care jobs in early years

Nursery nurse   Care assistant   Play leader   Support assistant   Teacher

Some professionals work in the community, caring directly for individuals who need support. Such professionals come from all three sectors, for example, health, early years and social care. Examples are:

Professional	Job role
District nurse	Attends to health monitoring, changing dressings, health needs
Health visitor	Promotes good health through diet and exercise and gives advice
Care assistant	Works in the client's own home or in day care centres or residential settings. Assists with dressing/undressing, shopping, cleaning
Home tutor	Assists learners who are unable to attend education centres, for example, because of disability, pregnancy or illness
Childminder	Cares for children in the childminder's own home while parents are at work
Chiropodist	Visits individuals in their own home to help provide foot care
Health care assistant	Assists with health monitoring in the individual's own home and with bathing/showering
Occupational therapist	Will help the individual to decide what aids or adaptations are needed in the home
GP (doctor)	Will visit individuals who are over 70 in their own home to give medical help

Registered Nurse

A registered nurse could work in:

hospice

hospital

service user's own home

nursing home

residential home

clinic

health centre

day-care centre

A registered nurse would have a variety of different tasks to carry out. If the registered nurse was based in a hospital, examples of the main tasks could be:

- assisting with service users' medical treatment
- monitoring the individual's health, for example, temperature, pulse, blood pressure
- changing dressings
- supervising the distribution of drugs
- writing reports
- talking to service users and relatives
- looking after the general care of service users
- liaising with other agencies, for example, physiotherapist, social worker
- accompanying the doctor on their rounds of the ward.

A typical day for a registered nurse in a hospital could follow the one outlined below, but it must be remembered that no two days are ever the same as the individuals' needs will change!

Group Activity

Try to arrange for a registered nurse to visit your centre (with your tutor's permission).

Ask them to outline what they do in a typical day.

Remember to make lots of notes for your portfolio if it is needed.

I start work at the hospital at 8:00am and work through until 4:00pm. I get an hour for lunch and two coffee breaks. When I come on duty I have a meeting with the sister and the other nurses on the ward and we find out what has happened to the service users during the night. This is called our 'briefing'.

I greet all the patients in the ward and ask them how they are. I usually tell them what the weather is like outside. The patients will have had their breakfast, so my first job is to make sure all the breakfast things are removed and then to help the patients get washed. Some will be able to go to the bathroom by themselves but others will need help with washing.

Some patients will need bedpans and I have to help them to sit comfortably on these and empty them when the service user has finished.

I work with other nurses to do this as we are not allowed to lift patients on our own. We always have to do a risk assessment before doing this.

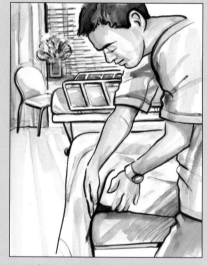

▲ Making sure the beds are made properly.

I then have to make sure that the beds are made properly and that each patient is comfortable.

The patients are left to sleep or to read or watch TV while I check their records and make sure these are in order for the doctor's round. The doctors do the rounds of the wards between 9:30 and 11:00am. I go round with them and answer their questions about the medication the patient has received and tell them about any changes in the patient's condition. The doctor will talk to them in person and ask them how they feel. The doctor will then decide whether there is to be any change in medication or treatment for that person.

◀ Doing the rounds of the wards with the doctor.

Continued on next page ▶

At around 11:00am the tea and coffee arrives and I help to make sure that everyone gets the drinks they want.

Some patients will need a dressing changed or will need to be prepared for physiotherapy or surgery.

Lunch arrives around 12:30 pm. I make sure the patients that have to remain in bed are in a comfortable position so they can eat their lunch.

Throughout the day I am talking with all the people in the ward and trying to brighten up their day. Some are worried about their condition or about the treatment they are to have and I try to support them by reassuring them and explaining exactly what is going to happen. I find people are not so afraid if they know the facts.

After lunch we monitor the patients' health by taking temperatures and pulse. Sometimes a health care assistant is available to do this. Whether I do the monitoring or the health care assistant does, the measurements are recorded on charts. Some patients will need medication and I accompany the sister who is giving out medication to check that the correct medication, in the right amount, is being given to the right person.

Visiting time starts at 2:00pm. At this time I make sure that all the records are up to date. I also chat with patients who do not have any visitors. Sometimes I have to change more dressings or give some help to patients who are feeling very unwell.

Before I go off duty I have a meeting with the staff who are coming on duty so that we can exchange information about the patients' health and the treatment and medication they have received.

▲ Monitoring the patient's health.

Snapshots of different direct job roles

Childminder

I care for children in my own home. Sometimes a child will come for half a day, some will stay for the whole day and some will come after school until their parent comes to collect them.

I try to make the time they spend with me interesting. If they are staying all day, we start with activities like playing with a variety of toys, for example, cars, dolls, building bricks.

Halfway through the morning the children have a drink and sit quietly. I then read them a story.

After lunch, if it's dry, I take them for a walk with our dog. We collect things like leaves, flowers or conkers.

Then they can watch TV, read or draw until they are collected by a parent.

Physiotherapist

I work at the local hospital where I design programmes of exercise for patients who have broken bones or muscle injuries to help strengthen the injured part. Sometimes I use heat and massage to help with the treatment. I have to keep very careful records of the exercises each patient does and of the effects these seem to be having on the injured part. I have to make sure that the patient understands how to do the exercises correctly, so communication skills and getting on with clients is a very important aspect of my work. I have a degree in Physiotherapy and also a qualification in Remedial Gymnastics.

Volunteer in a charity shop

I help in a charity shop that sells anything that people decide to give our collectors. The charity raises money for the local children's hospice so I do not get paid for the work I do. Sometimes I serve customers and help them to find something they may be looking for. On other occasions I work upstairs helping to sort the items that we have received and to freshen them up, such as ironing clothes or wiping off dust. I do enjoy my work.

Complementary approaches therapist

I own my business which is working with people who want to try alternative approaches to medicine. I specialise in aromatherapy, massage and acupuncture.

Many people are nervous about acupuncture but many find it very therapeutic. I know exactly where the needles should be placed to relieve pain.

Stephen: care assistant at a local day-care centre

Stephen has a job as a care assistant at a local day care centre. This is a typical day experienced by Stephen. It should be remembered that a care assistant working in a different setting could have an entirely different day.

◄ A care assistant must be prepared for anything.

'My day starts at 8:00am with a staff briefing where the manager talks to us about which individuals to expect for the day and about any special conditions or needs they may have. Our supervisor will also talk to us about the programme for the day and make sure that we know who is responsible for each activity.

At 10:00am the first people start to arrive in the social service buses. I help receive the individuals and help them off with their coats, making sure they are sitting comfortably and with their friends. I then fetch them a coffee or a tea. By 10:45 am all the service users have arrived and they are busily talking to one another.

I join each group and read them what is on the menu for lunch. I ask each one what they would like but I make sure they know what choices they have first. When all the lunch orders have been taken, one of the care assistants will start a quiz for the whole group. We take turns to do this.

At lunch time I help the service users to the meal table and make sure they all have the meals they ordered. One resident needs feeding. I ask her what she would like to eat first and tell her what I have on the spoon. The feeding takes some time, as the service user cannot swallow very quickly. I try to make sure the feeding maintains the service user's dignity, by not spilling food down her chin or on her clothes.

When the residents are settled in the community room again after lunch, they can do their own thing. Most read the papers or have 40 winks!

Later I help the people for whom I am responsible. Some want me to help them write a letter. One gentleman likes doing crosswords, so I help with this. Another person may just want to talk to me or may ask about a problem that is worrying them. We have tea at 2:45pm and then play bingo. At 3:30pm the transport comes to take them home. I then have to do my record keeping'.

Group Activity

Try to arrange for a care assistant from a different setting to visit your centre (with your tutor's permission). Ask them to outline what they do in a typical day. Remember to make lots of notes for your portfolio if it is needed.

A typical day in the life of a nursery nurse

There are a large number of jobs available working with children and young people. One of the most well-known jobs is that of a nursery nurse. Below is an example of a typical day in the life of a nursery nurse in a children's playgroup. However, it must be remembered that job roles as a nursery nurse will vary considerably according to the types of setting.

I arrive at work around 8:00am and work through until 4:00pm. Most of the children stay with us for the whole day, but some leave at lunch time. Our nursery is only open for these times whereas some are open from 7:00am until 9:00pm.

Most of the children's parents are at work and we look after the children while they are away. We have to be quite sure that we know what each individual child is allowed to do or eat. We also have to be sure that we have a contact number for the parents in case of an emergency.

The children's names and family records are kept on computer, but only two of us have access to the information.

There is a short staff meeting to check that we all know what is expected from us. The equipment is put out by the member of staff employed to do this but we are asked to check each section.

We greet each child in our group, individually and make sure we have asked the parent about any special things that have happened or they want us to do. As the children arrive a register is kept so that we know exactly which children are in the building. The parents know that they must actually hand the child to a member of staff and not just leave them to play.

▲ Checking the equipment in the playroom.

At 9:30am we all join together and we all greet one another. We have to make sure that the cultural needs of each child is observed when we are greeting one another, so we have different poems and short sayings read out each day during the greeting. This session usually lasts for ten minutes.

▲ Story time.

Activity time is next. Some children will paint, some will stick and glue, some will colour. Each helper or nursery nurse supervises an activity. We make sure there are lots of different materials, from a range of cultures, for the children to use.

At 11:00am there is a drinks break. The children sit in a circle and have a drink and a piece of fruit.

At 11:15am we have story time or singing. This is led by one of the staff but the children join in and take part in the actions or mime.

Before lunch we have 'large' equipment or 'outdoor activities', which means the slide and trampoline are brought out and all the large tractors and cars. The children can go outside if they wish. Sometimes we organize a walk to the park to find things for the 'interest table'.

Continued on next page ▶

Quiet music is played after lunch to help the children relax. Each day a tune from a different culture is played.

The children can choose which activity table they sit at in the afternoon. Some activities are different from those provided in the morning. Sometimes we have some finger painting, cooking, or paper mâché work for the older ones.

Around 3:30pm we have a sing along for five minutes before the free play at the end of the day. Staff try to talk with each parent of the child in their group as they arrive to give them information about how their child has got on.

I enjoy working with the children. It is very satisfying to watch them develop and become more independent and confident.

▲ Different activities are available for the children.

INDIRECT CARERS

Group Activity

Carry out research to find out about the work of:
- practice managers
- catering staff
- school receptionists.

Indirect care roles are jobs where the person is providing support to those who are personally or directly caring for service users. Examples of such jobs are:

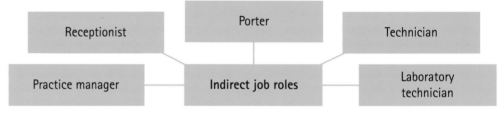

Receptionist		Porter		Technician
Practice manager		Indirect job roles		Laboratory technician

⊘ ...WORD CHECK

indirect – not directly responsible/ not obvious.

promote – to put forward; to support something.

Both direct and indirect job roles are important, as the service user will only receive the best care when both are working together to **promote** the interest of the service user. Individuals working as indirect care workers are very important, as without them the practitioners would not be able to do their jobs successfully. The receptionist, for example, may be the first person to greet a service user and the first impression a service user will get of the care setting and the people who work there. The receptionist will need to have good communication skills because greeting people, making them feel welcome and directing them to the care worker they need is an important aspect of their role.

Kieron (hospital porter)

I enjoy my work as each day is different. I sign in at 7:00am and finish at 3:45pm. I have a contact radio and when I am needed I get a call on my radio. Sometimes I have to collect a parcel or equipment or set up equipment ready for the specialist to use. At other times I will be asked to take a patient down in the lift to the x-ray department. I try to talk to the patient if they are well enough, as this cheers them up and stops them worrying about what is going to happen next. I meet some interesting people in my work.

◄ Making things as pleasant as possible.

JOBS THAT ARE OUTSOURCED

Some indirect jobs are **outsourced**, that is given to private companies. Examples of such jobs are:

Cleaner
- brushes/mops floors
- dusts surfaces
- talks to service users
- cleans basins/baths/ toilets.

Security
- checks buildings are safe
- makes sure packages that cannot be accounted for are not left in buildings
- helps to deal with issues relating to fights and arguments between service users and staff.

...WORD CHECK

outsourced – buying services from outside.

genetic – inherited, passed down from one member of the family to another.

Group Activity

Carry out research to find out about the job roles of a:
- porter
- security officer.

WHAT ARE QUALITIES?

Qualities are what we are like as a person. They are partly the result of our **genetic** make-up, inherited from our parents. Qualities are also the result of factors that have influenced our development, for example, family, education, income, social class and where we live.

Patience
Being prepared to spend time listening to an individual who finds it difficult to speak or think quickly.

Empathy
Being able to see things from the same perspective as the individual.

Understanding
Being able to see an individual's point of view even if it is different from our own.

Calmness
Not going into a panic when a difficult situation or problem arises.

Honesty
Speaking the truth and being open about situations.

Sense of humour
Being able to laugh and find a funny aspect to the situation.

Respect
Being able to make the person feel valued.

Willingness
Being helpful; nothing is too much trouble and wanting to do as much as possible.

Cheerfulness
Looking at things from a happy perspective.

No one thing has contributed to our **individuality**. We are the way we are because of inherited factors and the experiences that we have had. For example, a person brought up as an only child may be less likely to share things with others than a person who has several brothers and sisters. A person whose mother always panics in a crisis may have inherited the same **trait** from her.

Qualities contribute to the person that we are and often **reflect** the things that are important to us; the things that we value. They are things we do naturally because they are part of our make up or a **characteristic** that makes us so **unique**.

When providing practical care for service users, qualities that come naturally to us will help to improve the care that is provided.

CASE STUDY Mya

Mya is a care assistant who is trying to settle a dispute between two older adults in a day care centre who are quarrelling over words used in a game of Scrabble. Mya takes time to listen and to talk to both adults to find out exactly what the problem is and to suggest a solution. She does not rush away to find someone else to deal with the problem. While listening, she smiles and looks happy. She does make it clear to the adults that she is expecting them to listen to what each has to say, but while speaking she tells a joke that makes both adults smile. Once the difficulties are sorted Mya asks both adults if they would like a cup of tea and goes off to fetch one for them.

1 Find all the qualities shown by Mya in the case study. For each, give an example.

2 In pairs, write a case study of your own that shows a professional care worker demonstrating qualities. Do not **explicitly** give the quality.

On a separate sheet of paper write the answer, for example, willingness – being prepared to help over and above the call of duty.

Exchange the case study with another pair and find the qualities they have included, giving the example. Exchange answers and mark the answers given to your case study. Give oral feedback.

Skills

Skills can be learnt by individuals while they are carrying out their jobs. Individuals **acquire** some skills quite quickly as they seem to have a natural ability to be able to do them. Others have to be practised many times before a person feels comfortable doing them. Some skills are used in practical situations, for example, they are demonstrated in carrying out specific tasks in day-to-day work. Bed making, taking a pulse or giving an individual a bed bath are examples of practical skills carried out by nursing staff.

Other skills are more **academic**, in other words they involve thinking about a particular problem or issue. Such skills include accounting, reading, dealing with mathematical problems and finding solutions. These skills would not necessarily have to be carried out by doing practical tasks while working; they could be achieved by sitting at a desk.

Whether skills are practical or more academic, knowledge will be required in order to be able to demonstrate the skill. A nurse would be unable to take a pulse unless they had been taught the correct way to do it.

Other skills that are most likely to be used are:

- working as a member of a team
- interpersonal skills (customer/service user care)
- planning and organizing
- time management
- problem solving.

 16 In what situations would these skills be used?

A nursery nurse

A nursery nurse is concerned with the care, education and well-being of children and will take responsibility for the children in their care. The duties of a nursery nurse will depend on the age of the children for whom they care. For example, if they are caring for toddlers and pre-school children, they will focus on developing language skills and exploring through the world of play. Some nursery nurses will be required to organize and supervise outdoor play if they are caring for children who are aged between two and four-and-a-half years. If they are caring for babies, then quite a lot of practical and physical caring will be involved, for example, feeding, washing and changing nappies.

Nursery nurses may also be involved in keeping records for the children for whom they care and for observing and assessing children. Meeting and talking with parents, main carers and other professionals is likely to be part of their work. They will also be involved in organizing, planning and managing activities for the children.

Nursery nurses can be employed in:

- day nurseries, playgroups and crèches
- in schools – where they provide support for teachers
- in hospitals – where they will be involved in caring for infants, children and young people who are ill
- as nannies in private homes.

What tasks would be part of a nursery nurse's job role if they were working in a nursery that provided care and education for children between two and four-and-a-half years? What skills would be needed?

Some ideas are given in the table below:

Tasks carried out by a nursery nurse	Skills used by a nursery nurse
Greeting children and parents	Oral communication skills, listening skills
Putting up play equipment	Practical skills, problem solving skills
Planning activities with others	Interpersonal skills, communication skills, organizational skills
Story telling	Communication skills, interpersonal skills
Preparing practical activities, for example, dough, paint	Scientific skills, creative skills, practical skills, mathematical skills
Talking with children and answering questions	Oral communication skills, listening skills, problem solving skills
Keeping records	Written communication
Comforting children	Interpersonal skills, oral communication skills
Giving basic first aid	Scientific skills, interpersonal skills, practical skills, oral communication

Group Activity

Work with another person to divide the skills listed below into **two** main groups, for example, mainly practical skills and mainly academic skills:

- cooking
- cleaning a ward
- measuring out drugs
- reading instructions
- planning care for an individual
- talking to a service user
- making a time plan
- solving a problem
- keeping records.

Share your list with another group and compare the similarities and differences.

From the list of tasks it is possible to see that a large number of skills would be needed. Some of these skills would be learnt while actually doing the job or would have been learnt while training. Others would probably be present in the nursery nurse already, as we often choose jobs that we 'are good at' and for which we already have shown some **aptitude**.

From the table it can be seen that the main skills needed by the nursery nurse are:
- communication skills, for example, the ability to speak clearly and listen carefully
- interpersonal skills, for example, when relating to children and parents
- practical skills, for example, in providing help with activities
- scientific skills, for example, an awareness of health and safety, first aid.

The nursery nurse will also need additional skills such as:
- being able to work well in a team
- organizing, presentation and management skills
- problem solving skills, for example, how to cope in difficult situations and find solutions.

A Registered General Nurse

How do the skills required by a nursery nurse compare with the skills of a Registered General Nurse (adults) who is working in the recovery ward of a hospital?

Such nurses care for service users who are over the age of 16. They do a lot of practical nursing such as checking temperatures, blood pressure and respiration rates. They often assist doctors with physical examinations as well as giving drugs, injections, cleaning and dressing wounds. Taking the **clinical history** and helping to draw up a care plan in consultation with doctors and others is part of the role of a Registered General Nurse and frequently they are required to counsel service users and relatives, providing emotional support to help them cope with their current situation. Sometimes a nurse in a hospital will be responsible for supervising health care assistants.

What would be the day-to-day tasks and skills needed by a Registered General Nurse (RGN)?

Day-to-day tasks of a Registered General Nurse	Skills required to carry out the tasks
Greeting clients and talking with them	Communication skills, interpersonal skills
Taking temperature, pulse and monitoring blood pressure	Scientific skills
Recording the health measurements taken	Communication skills
Hygiene routines	Practical skills, communication skills
Cleaning a wound, changing a dressing	Practical skills, scientific skills
Admitting new clients to the ward	Communication skills, interpersonal skills
Helping with the physical examination of a client	Practical skills, scientific skills
Working with others, for example, nurses, doctors, physiotherapists	Interpersonal skills, communication skills
Planning care for service users	Organizational skills, communication skills

Some of the skills used by the nurse are very similar to those used by the nursery nurse. Both will use communication, interpersonal, practical and scientific skills. It is likely that the RGN nurse will use more scientific skills than the nursery nurse because of the tasks being carried out.

ACTIVITY

1 Copy and complete the table below to show which skills would be needed by a physiotherapist when completing each task.

Task	Skills needed
Greeting service user	
Making notes about the service user's needs	
Showing the service user how to do the suggested exercise	
Observing the exercise being carried out by the service user	
Keeping records	

2 Explain, using examples, which skills could be used by a care assistant when carrying out tasks in a service user's own home. Choose **one** task that the care assistant will carry out.

3 Explain, by using examples, which qualities would help a nurse who had to give distressing news to a service user.

4 How would a care worker show empathy?

Qualifications

A qualification is proof that the person to whom it is awarded has achieved a certain standard of knowledge or a recognized standard of skills. Most qualifications involve both skills and knowledge but occasionally they are weighted towards a skills base or a knowledge base. The table below gives information about some qualifications that can be achieved by individuals who wish to obtain work in the health, social care or early years sectors:

...WORD CHECK

relevant – appropriate to.

Qualification	Type
NVQs	Based in the workplace and involve learning skills relevant to the particular sector, for example, health or child care. Slightly more skills based but knowledge of the subject also included.
OCR Nationals	Based in a school, college or with a training provider. Having a slight emphasis on theory but knowledge must be applied through work experience or simulation to practical situations in the workplace, for example, bed making, taking temperatures, activities with children and young people.
AS and A2	Based in schools, college or with training providers. Theory based with some practical knowledge and application of knowledge to practical situations.
EDEXCEL Diplomas and Certificates	Some of these are focused particularly on specialist pathways, for example, childcare. While similar to the OCR Nationals, they are more general preparation for working in health, social care or early years settings.
CACHE	Specific childcare courses to prepare individuals for working with children and young people, for example, childminding, pre-school leader, nursery nurse.
Diploma in Society, Health and Development	A new qualification that incorporates the principal learning related to health, social care, early years and justice sectors as well as functional skills (English, Maths and ICT) and an Extended Project, besides requiring some additional learning, for example, a GCSE.

These are only examples of qualifications that are available but are some of the most common. Smaller qualifications can be in subjects such as First Aid or Food Hygiene, for example. Each qualification obtained by an individual, no matter how large or how small, will contribute to an individual's ability to carry out a role in that particular area effectively. When all qualifications are put together, they show the employer that the person who has achieved them has been successful in following a particular course of study to an agreed national standard.

ACTIVITY — Becoming qualified

Sanjay wishes to become a nurse.

Marcus would like to be a nursery nurse.

Telfer would like to be a social worker.

1. Investigate the qualifications, skills and qualities required for **one** of these job roles.
2. Identify and discuss at least **two** different ways of achieving the qualifications, skills and qualities for the job role.
3. Discuss the advantages and disadvantages of each way of obtaining the qualifications, skills and qualities.

Changes in service provision can affect job roles

Service provision is changing rapidly as the development of highly technical treatment and medicine means that many service users require an 'integrated service'. This in turn means that professionals will require a range of different skills and will need to be 'multi-skilled'. Specialists will work together in groups based on the disease or condition that is being treated and clinical teams will be system based, which will cut across traditional professional boundaries.

This will allow:

- early diagnosis of conditions/diseases
- quality and safety systems to be in place
- accessibility to services
- integration of care
- teaching and research
- continuity in long-term management.

As a result jobs will change in order to meet these needs and requirements.

ASSESSMENT PRACTICE: PREPARATION

For the service user that you have chosen for the earlier Assessment Practices, select **two direct** job roles. For the roles selected, carry out research to find out:

1 What is involved in the job role – their role within the service.

2 The qualifications, skills and qualities required, giving a wide range of examples to show how these would be used in the job role.

3 About the day-to-day tasks carried out by the professional chosen, making sure you know how they meet the health and social care needs of the individual service users as part of the tasks they perform.

If possible, try to interview an individual who has this job role.

When you have completed your research, write up the investigation to give a comprehensive and detailed explanation of the role, making sure you include all the above points.

Remember

Continue with the plan that shows the order in which you will work, giving the dates, actions and the reasons for the actions to be taken.

Keep a bibliography that shows primary and secondary sources of evidence and any Internet or other material used.

Note: this is only preparation for the controlled assignment that will be issued by the examination board.

Care values which underpin service provider interaction

▶ Getting started

You will gain an understanding of:

a the care values which underpin care practice with service users, including:
   i   promoting anti-discriminatory practice
   ii promoting and supporting individual rights to dignity, independence, health and safety
   iii promoting effective communication and relationships
   iv maintaining confidentiality of information
   v   acknowledging individual personal beliefs and identity

b how these care values are reflected in the behaviour, attitudes and work of care practitioners.

CARE VALUES

The care values, or principles, are statements that underpin all practical caring. In order to meet the needs of individuals, the professional care worker will need to establish a good relationship with the service user. The 'principles' or 'values' of care have their foundations in human rights and mean treating others as you would wish to be treated yourself, if you were in the same position as the service user.

In health, social care and early years organizations the main components of the care values or principles are:

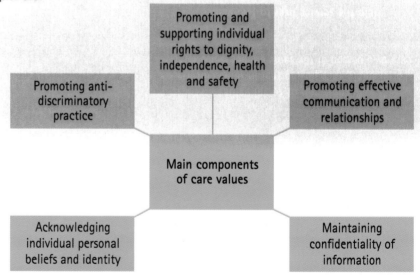

Promoting and supporting individual rights to dignity, independence, health and safety

Promoting anti-discriminatory practice

Promoting effective communication and relationships

Main components of care values

Acknowledging individual personal beliefs and identity

Maintaining confidentiality of information

This will involve:

Trust
The individual must feel that they can discuss issues without the professional care worker ridiculing them.

Confidence
Knowing only information that is on a 'need to know' basis will be passed to others and all else will be kept confidential.

Positive attitude
The individual will be provided with non-judgemental support by the care professional which does not label, stereotype or show prejudice.

Communication
Speaking in a way that does not patronize the individual and that presents the facts, allowing the individual to make decisions and choices.

Recognition of culture
Allowing the individual to express their views and to follow the traditions of their own religion or beliefs, for example, providing a place for prayer.

Recognition of social values
For example, recognizing that in some cultures, care by a person of the same gender is preferred.

Competency in knowledge and skills
Carrying out tasks and skills with confidence.

Help the service user to feel valued
Promoting positive self-esteem by not putting a person down or ignoring them.

Help the service user to feel fulfilled
By giving mental stimulation and encouraging participation.

Promoting anti-discriminatory practice

This includes:

- not showing prejudice, stereotyping and labelling
- understanding and valuing the benefits of **diversity**
- having knowledge of the bases of discrimination, such as gender, race, age, sexuality, disability or social class
- having an understanding of your own beliefs and assumptions.

What does this mean in practice?

Professional care workers must treat individuals with respect, for example, calling a person by their preferred name and not calling them 'love' or 'dear'. Each of us has a name and the correct name should be used to address a person. If their nickname is their preferred name, and the service user has consented to its use, this is acceptable.

Allowing an individual to give their views and opinions is also a way of encouraging respect. For example, a professional carer should give their full attention when communicating and employ 'active listening skills'. An individual should not be cut off in mid-sentence, nor should a sentence be completed for them, unless there is a medical or psychological reason for doing so.

> **...WORD CHECK**
>
> **diversity** – being different from others.
>
> **active listening** – to make sure all concentration is on the speaker; concentrating the mind on what is being said.

When carrying out tasks, the professional care worker should do so to the highest quality possible. Just because an individual is from a different culture to the care worker does not mean that they should receive sub-standard care. Professional care workers should have thought about any views or opinions they may have that could affect the quality of care that they may be giving. Sometimes our **prejudices** can influence the way in which we respond to others. For example, if we think that everyone should be dressed in a particular way and then we are asked to attend to a service user who is dressed quite differently, our prejudice could be shown through speaking roughly to the individual or not giving them the care to which they are entitled.

All individuals should feel that they are valued as a person and that they have the care worker's respect.

ACTIVITY   Care values in practice

a A care assistant at a day care centre leaves the toilet door open while a service user is using the toilet. She also shouts, 'Are you ready love?'

b The nursery nurse tells Graham that he cannot play in the kitchen because the girls want to play there and it's more suitable for them to do so.

c Maureen keeps wandering around moving other service users' belongings from one place to another. She thinks she is being helpful but a care assistant shouts at her and tells her she will lock her in the cleaning cupboard if she does not stop.

1 Ask the group to say which of these actions are wrong and why.

Promoting and supporting individual rights to dignity, independence, health and safety

Group Activity

Work with another person and prepare a role play for one of the scenarios in the above activity. You should:

- demonstrate the wrong way to deal with each situation AND
- role play the correct way of dealing with the situation.

This includes:

- choice, for example, to be able to make one's own decisions and to be consulted about possible treatment needed
- dignity, for example, to be treated with respect
- safety and security, for example, to be protected from harm
- privacy, for example, having one's own space that is not invaded by others without consent.

All individuals have the right to use their own GP (doctor), rather than being told that they 'must have the same GP as all the other residents in a residential home'. Making choices about what is worn, what we have to eat, who we sit next to and at what time we go to bed are all examples of decisions that adults have the right to make.

Individuals who are receiving health, social care or early years services also have the right to be part of the decision-making process and to contribute to discussions when the subject for discussion affects them.

Safety and security is an important feature of all care settings. Each setting must have a policy relating to health and safety and must make sure that all staff follow the requirements of the policy and have staff training based on the subject. Service users have the right to know that they are safe.

Promoting effective communication and relationships

Communication is an important part of all our lives as we use it every day for a variety of reasons. Oral conversation is such a common, everyday event that we often think it does not require any special skills.

However, in informal conversations with friends or family members, or in more formal exchanges with a teacher or employer, you will use a range of skills such as words, body language, gestures and active listening.

A major part of a care worker's day-to-day tasks is to make sure their communication is effective. People who use health, social care and early years services are often dependent on professional care workers for obtaining and giving information and they may also want to express their feelings and emotions. Individuals will want to know that they can rely on the care worker to value them as a person and that the information shared will be kept confidential.

Effective communication is at the heart of any relationship. This means that professional care workers need to be aware of the skills required to communicate effectively with service users. Inappropriate communication can have the effect of lowering a service user's self-esteem and could in extreme cases cause the service user to become emotionally upset. For example, older people can become upset or aggressive if they think they have not been understood. Similarly, a child in a playgroup may misunderstand something that has been said by the nursery nurse and may be upset and cry as a result.

> **Group Activity**
>
> Work with another person to think about the number of conversations you have had already today. Were they formal or informal conversations? Make a list and see which could be put under the headings 'formal' and 'informal'.

Using communication skills to interact with service users

When communicating we do so in order to:

- obtain information, for example, about the service users' history
- give information to others, for example, which services are available
- exchange ideas and opinions.

Communication is the interaction between two or more people, that is, two or more people talking with, or having a conversation with, one another. Effective communication is dependent on the use of appropriate skills.

When talking to people, individuals often use non-verbal signals as well as speech, such as gestures or smiles. This is known as 'body language' and is a form of giving messages to those with whom we are speaking, for example, smiling will convey friendliness. Some methods of communication used in care settings are:

▼ Effective communication is at the heart of any relationship.

Body language, for example, smiling

Verbal communication, for example, speaking and listening

Written communication, for example, care plans

Different ways of communicating

Electronic communication, for example, emails

Special methods of communication, for example, Braille, sign language

Having a meaningful conversation with someone requires the development of skills and social coordination. It means:

- being interested in the person and the topic
- having the skills to maintain the conversation
- being able to start and end conversations.

Skills that are involved when communicating could include any from the list below:

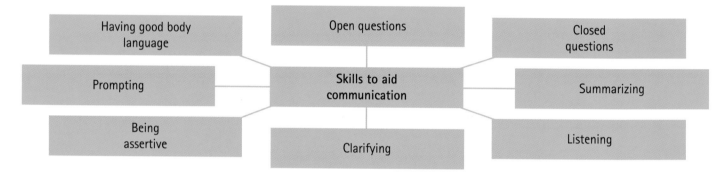

Having good body language

Open questions

Closed questions

Prompting

Skills to aid communication

Summarizing

Being assertive

Clarifying

Listening

Effective communication requires professional care workers to:

- **analyse** their thoughts and to think about what they are going to say
- use skills to help to **interpret** the language
- understand and **draw conclusions**
- present the ideas for continuing the conversation.

Communication in health, social care and early years settings are is likely to be of a **complex** nature and may have several purposes. Care workers will need to be aware that each individual will have their own way of interpreting messages. Effective communication means more than just passing on information. It means involving or engaging the other person. The process of communicating involves various stages within a cycle:

The communication cycle

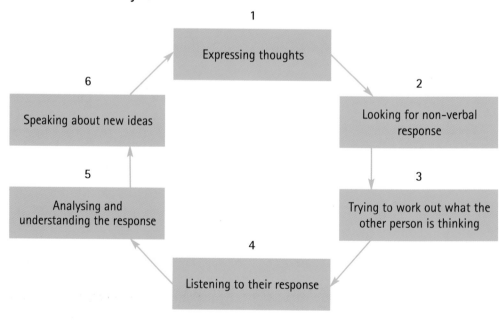

1 Expressing thoughts

2 Looking for non-verbal response

3 Trying to work out what the other person is thinking

4 Listening to their response

5 Analysing and understanding the response

6 Speaking about new ideas

Communicating has to be a two-way process, where each person is trying to make sense of what the other person is saying. Often it is easier to understand people who are similar to ourselves, for example, a person who has the same accent, or a person who is in a similar situation to ourselves. Our decoding equipment in the brain tunes in, breaks down the message, analyses the message, understands it and interprets its meaning and then creates a response or answer. This is all helped by the body language or signals, such as smiles or gestures, that have been given by the person who is sending the message. When a care worker is speaking with a service user he or she is forming a mental picture about what they are being told.

Other forms of communication used in settings

Written communication

The rules that govern writing are very different from those rules that are followed for spoken language. In all health, social care and early years settings accuracy of the written word is extremely important. If inaccuracies occur in the keeping of formal records, a service user could have the wrong treatment or be given incorrect information with disastrous results.

In many care settings written communication is used to record personal history. Communicating in writing helps care settings to keep in contact with service users and other professionals.

Types of written information kept by a setting could include:

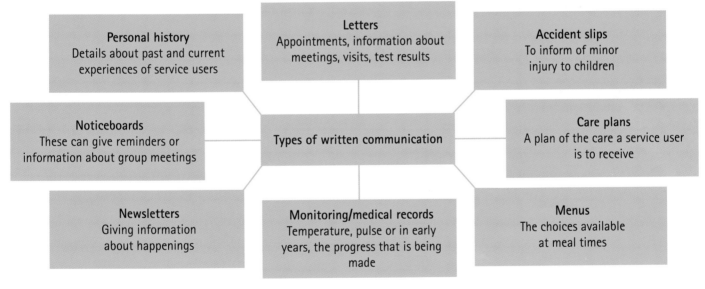

Personal history
Details about past and current experiences of service users

Letters
Appointments, information about meetings, visits, test results

Accident slips
To inform of minor injury to children

Noticeboards
These can give reminders or information about group meetings

Types of written communication

Care plans
A plan of the care a service user is to receive

Newsletters
Giving information about happenings

Monitoring/medical records
Temperature, pulse or in early years, the progress that is being made

Menus
The choices available at meal times

Computerized communication

In recent years, electronic mail (email) has proved to be quite a significant form of communication. Emails can be both formal and informal depending on their purpose.

An advantage of the email is that it provides a very quick way of interacting with another person or organization, as answers can be received in a matter of minutes, rather than having to wait for several days. However, care has to be taken to ensure that confidentiality is maintained and 'secure' systems are necessary before personal confidential information can be exchanged.

The Internet, too, is more often being used as a source of information for a variety of purposes.

▶ Email can be a convenient way of communicating.

▲ Some service users need special methods of communication.

Special methods of communicating

All health, social care and early years settings need to be prepared to provide for service users who have special needs where communication is concerned. Special needs could include:

- difficulty in hearing or deafness
- poor eye sight or blindness
- language difficulty, for example, not speaking English as a first language.

Special methods of communicating could involve:

- Braille
- Makaton
- sign language.

Using communication to support relationships

The needs of human beings are complex and care workers often work with service users who may be afraid or who may not understand what is going to happen to them. The service user could feel threatened by the situation that they find themselves in. At each stage of development communication plays a major part of meeting these needs. It is essential that support is provided when communicating by:

- being patient
- using a tone of voice that conveys empathy
- not speaking down to the individual
- explaining the situation in a way that can be understood.

Such action will prevent misunderstandings and will contribute to positive and effective supportive relationships.

Positive communication factors that can influence relationships are:

Group Activity

Carry out research to find out more about each of these methods of communicating.

Produce a handout on each method.

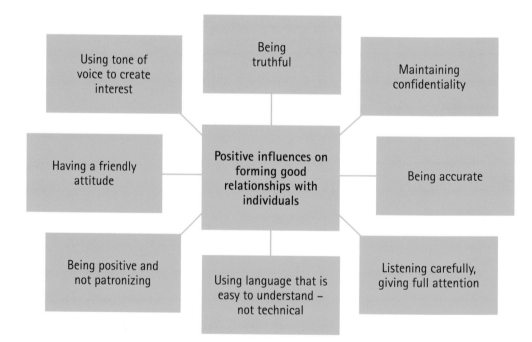

Using tone of voice to create interest

Being truthful

Maintaining confidentiality

Having a friendly attitude

Positive influences on forming good relationships with individuals

Being accurate

Being positive and not patronizing

Using language that is easy to understand – not technical

Listening carefully, giving full attention

When these factors are the focus of any communication, whether oral, written or in the content of an email, the result is more likely to meet the needs of the individual, particularly their emotional, social and intellectual needs.

Communication in a multicultural society

For service users for whom English is not a preferred or first language, **interpreters** can help with communication. In the past, some interpreters have been people who are were members of the service user's own family but this has now been discontinued as far as is possible. It was considered that using family members was not a very good idea, as they were then privy to information that the service user may want to keep confidential. For example, a mother whose daughter was interpreting for her may not want her daughter to know that she had an incurable disease.

In many health, social care and early years services, leaflets concerning health topics or health facilities are not only produced in English but also in several other languages so that many people in our multicultural society can access the information.

> **...WORD CHECK**
>
> **interpreters** – change words into something that can be recognized by a person, for example, a language or simplified words being used.
>
> **disclosed** – passing on confidential information.

ACTIVITY — Parkside Residential Home

Parkside caters for residents who are over 60 years of age. Many of the residents have special needs when communicating.

1. Kathy has very poor vision. Suggest how her communication needs could be met by the staff at Parkside.

2. Marcus has severe hearing impairment. How could the staff provide for Marcus' communication needs?

3. Ji-Sung has difficulty with English as it is not his first or preferred language. He needs to have information about the different health and social care services in the area. Explain **two** ways in which the staff could help Ji-Sung.

Maintaining confidentiality of information

Confidentiality means keeping the information given to oneself, that is, not sharing it with anyone who does not 'need to know'. It means making sure personal and private information cannot be accessed by others. Any information given by the service user should not be **disclosed** without the service user's permission. Personal information can include:

- information being discussed orally, for example, care workers discussing proposed treatment with the service user
- written information, for example, a care plan being stored safely
- electronic records, for example, a person's medical history being stored securely, with only authorized personnel having access.

> **Disclosure** is passing on personal information given by a service user in confidence, which was considered to be a secret between the service user and the care worker.

Care workers should never promise not to pass on personal information. They should explain to the service user that they will not pass on personal information unless there is a very good reason to do so.

Disclosure of information can be necessary in special circumstances. For example:

- if a service user intends to harm themselves
- if a service user intends to harm others
- if a service user is involved in a criminal activity.

Maintaining confidentiality means:

- Keeping personal information secure and away from people who do not need to know.
- Preventing access to files containing personal information by keeping them in locked filing cabinets.
- Having passwords that must be used for accessing electronic records.
- Not gossiping about service users or speaking about them by name in front of others so that they can be identified.

▲ Maintaining confidentiality.

Group Activity

GROUP ACTIVITY

A neighbour of a service user who has been admitted to hospital asks the nurse 'What is wrong with Nellie?'

What should be the response? Why?

Acknowledging individual personal beliefs and identity

...WORD CHECK

disclosure – passing on confidential information.

age of consent – the age at which something is permitted by law, for example, having sex.

These include:

- the right to be different, for example, in terms of sexual orientation, beliefs
- freedom from discrimination, for example, not to be singled out and treated differently
- to be able to worship freely and to practice your beliefs
- the right to promote your own customs.

We are all different. We like different books, different music, different films and different food. Some individuals may be different in their beliefs, customs or sexual practices; therefore, professional care workers need to make sure that they do not discriminate against those that do not conform to their own values. Having a same-sex partner, for example, is acceptable, providing the two people concerned are of the age of consent.

CASE STUDY   Joy and Margaret

Joy and Margaret have been partners for over 15 years. They are now in their late sixties and Joy has been admitted to hospital because she has had a mild stroke.

Margaret visits Joy each day and when she greets Margaret she kisses her fully on the lips and gives her a cuddle.

On seeing this, one of the nurses rushes to the sister in charge of the ward to complain about Margaret's behaviour. Some of the other visitors are a little taken by surprise by this behaviour.

1. As a group, discuss why the behaviour of Joy and Margaret has caused concern.

2. How should this situation be dealt with in your opinion? Give reasons why.

CASE STUDY   Acknowledging personal identity

Bob and Patrick tell the social worker that they want to share a bed when they move into a residential home. The social worker becomes very angry.

Treatment is being planned by staff at a meeting following an assessment of Helana's needs. Helana attends the meeting but is not asked what she would like.

Tom, Justin and Betty are watching a TV programme in the lounge of a residential home. Seb enters the room, looks at the programme and goes over and switches the programme over to something he wants to see. The care assistant takes Seb's side as he says, 'The programme being watched by Tom, Justin and Betty has nearly finished'.

1. As a group discuss which of the actions are wrong and why.

2. Work with another person and prepare a role play for **one** of the scenarios, showing the correct way to deal with the situation.

HOW CAN PROFESSIONAL CARE WORKERS APPLY THE CARE VALUES?

A practice nurse in a GP surgery

A practice nurse who is changing a dressing needs to find out how the service user is feeling and whether they have taken their medication regularly, as well as changing the dressing on the service user's leg. How can they do this and apply the care values? This could be achieved by:

- Drawing the curtains around the service user when changing the dressing, to help maintain dignity.

- Calling the service user by their correct name. This promotes respect between the service user and the practice nurse and promotes the service user's rights.

- Explaining to the service user the need to find out what medication has been taken. Using effective communication they will ask open questions to encourage the service user to talk and closed questions to obtain specific answers. They will use the correct tone of voice, vocabulary that is not too difficult and allow the service user to ask questions besides listening carefully.

- The practice nurse will keep their voice low in order to maintain confidentiality.

- The practice nurse will make sure that any cultural requirements or beliefs are met, for example, having a female nurse if the service user is female and if it is traditional within the culture to have a same-sex nurse in attendance.

- Not talking about the service user to others in a way that they can be identified, in order to maintain confidentiality.

▲ Correctly applying the care values.

Other care workers will endeavour to apply the care values in a similar way. The table below gives examples of how each of the professional care workers listed could achieve this:

Professional care worker	How the care values would be applied
Health care assistant	• Explaining to the service user what they are going to do when taking temperature or a pulse (effective communication) • Asking the service user when they would like a bath (rights) • Talking quietly to a service user about their treatment (equality and confidentiality)
Occupational therapist	• Explaining how aids could be used and adaptations of the home made (effective communication) • Talking with the service user about needs that are required and their availability (rights and equal opportunities) • Recognizing that the service user has a different sexual orientation from their own and accepting the arrangements in the service user's home (accepting diversity)
GP or consultant	• Diagnosing illness and active listening (equal opportunity and effective communication) • Providing information about the range of services available (choice and rights)
Social worker	• Actively listening to the personal problems experienced by the service user (confidentiality and communication) • Making an assessment of need (rights and equal opportunities) • Talking with the service user about the range of services available (choices and effective communication)
Nursery nurse	• Organizing different cultural events to be celebrated (promoting personal beliefs) • Asking a child what they would like to do out of the activities being offered (choice) • Talking to the child using language they can understand (effective communication) • Finding out from parents about their requirements, for example, who to contact in an emergency (rights and choice)

CASE STUDY   Ray and Asif

Ray and Asif have been together for 15 years, but Ray is now in need of an assessment as he has mobility problems and some loss of short-term memory. Asif has a nasty ulcer on his leg that will not heal. A social worker has arranged to meet both Ray and Asif in order to discuss this.

1. Explain how the social worker can apply the care values when making an assessment of Ray's needs and when talking to both Ray and Asif about the situation.

2. The social worker agrees with Ray and Asif that they will require a health care assistant to help with monitoring health, giving each a bath, and changing dressings on Asif's leg. Explain how the health care assistant will apply the care values while helping Ray and Asif to cope.

3. It is agreed that an occupational therapist will visit Ray and Asif at home to talk to them about aids and adaptations. Explain how the occupational therapist will apply the care values when talking with both of them.

4. Both Ray and Asif need to visit the physiotherapist for treatment. Explain how the physiotherapist would apply **all** of the care values/principles while making an assessment and carrying out treatment.

5. Evaluate how clients may feel if the care values are not applied.

6. Two years later, Ray and Asif decide that they should move into residential care. Analyse how the professional care workers at the residential home could apply the care values for Ray and Asif.

Early years care values

The welfare of the child is paramount	The welfare of the child is the most important. They should be listened to and their views taken into account.
Keeping children safe and maintaining a safe environment	Safe working practices must exist.
Working in partnership with parents and families	Sharing openly information about children's development and progress. Respect must be shown for family traditions.
Children's learning and development	Children should be offered a range of experiences and activities that support all aspects of development: physical, intellectual, emotional and social.
Valuing diversity	Information relating to traditions should be presented in a positive manner.
Equal opportunity	Each child should be offered equality of access to opportunities to learn and develop, and so work towards their potential.
Anti-discrimination	Expressions of prejudice by children or adults should be challenged.
Confidentiality	Information about children and adults should never be shared with others without consent. Secure storage of records is legally required.
Working with other professionals	Liaison with other care professionals should only take place with prior permission.
The reflective practitioner	Early years workers need to reflect on their practices and plan for developing and extending practice.

...WORD CHECK

non-judgemental – considering something without already having made a decision or judgement.

Care workers must behave in a **non-judgemental** way, working to the principles of good practice by valuing service users for their individuality and diversity, enabling them to direct their own lives. All individuals, whether service users of health, social care or early years, must be accepted for who they are. They must not be judged by standards that govern the professional care worker's life. Personal values have to be put aside so that individuals are given the best possible treatment and care.

ACTIVITY Applying the care values to achieve quality care

...ACTIVITY

Usha is working as a nursery nurse in a local playgroup.

Fawzia is working as a care assistant in a day care centre.

1. Compare how Usha and Fawzia will apply the care values in the workplace. You should consider similarities and differences.
2. Fawzia is going to take an older person to the toilet. How will she:
   - maintain dignity?
   - use effective communication?
   - provide choice?
3. Usha is responsible for providing a healthy and safe working environment for the children who attend the playgroup. What will this involve?
4. How can applying the 'care values' and 'principles' of care contribute to helping clients to improve the quality of their lives?
5. Explain how a professional care worker could apply the principle of 'being a reflective practitioner' in their work at the playgroup.

 **ASSESSMENT PRACTICE: PREPARATION**

Choose **two** of the short scenarios given below. The scenario chosen should match with the two professional care workers chosen for the Assessment Practice on page 153.

Scenario 1
Britany works as a nurse in the local foundation hospital.

Scenario 2
Banazir is a social worker in the local community.

Scenario 3
Selina is a nursery nurse in a playgroup in the local area.

1. Which care values will influence the day-to-day work of your chosen practitioner?

2. Explain how the care values will be applied by the practitioner in their day-to-day work.

3. How will the application of the care values help to empower service users?

4. What are the likely effects on service users if the care values are not applied?

Remember

Continue with the plan that shows the order in which you will work, giving the dates, actions and the reasons for the actions to be taken.

Keep a bibliography that shows primary and secondary sources of evidence and any Internet or other material used.

Note: this is only preparation for the controlled assignment that will be issued by the examination board.

You must also remember to:

Evaluate the work you have done and make realistic suggestions for improvement to all aspects of your work.

Try to make sure that you have clearly presented and organized your work using accurate spellings, punctuation and grammar.

3 Promoting Health and Well-being

Contents

About this unit

Health, social care and early years practitioners aim to promote the health and well-being of service users. In this unit you will develop knowledge and understanding of:

- definitions of health and well-being
- factors that affect health and well-being
- the effects of factors affecting health and well-being
- methods used to measure individual's physical health
- ways of promoting and supporting health improvement.

The unit will be assessed internally by the staff in your centre and externally by Edexcel.

The exam board will provide pre-release material about an individual or group of individuals, which will include information about their health and well-being, and the factors currently affecting their health and well-being. You will be expected to produce a health and well-being plan for this individual or group.

Evidence required for the controlled assessment will be related to service users and settings. This may be drawn from any of the following:

- health
- early years
- care of older people
- individuals with specific needs.

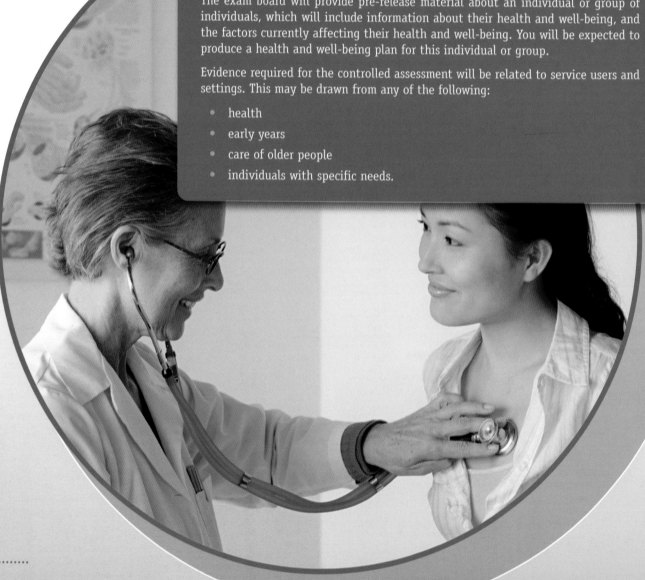

▸ Introducing this unit

Think about what being healthy means to you. Is it just not having to go to see your doctor very often? Perhaps being healthy is more than just that. It might also involve living in an area where there is very little crime or pollution, and having a good school to go to. Also consider what things affect your health that might explain why some people are healthier than others. This might also be linked to where you live, the relationships you have with other people, the lifestyle you lead or possibly an illness you might have inherited from your parents.

When you do see your doctor, he/she might test your health by measuring your height and weight to see if you are overweight or not. They may also check your cholesterol levels to see if you are eating a healthy diet and your blood glucose levels to see if you are at risk from diabetes.

It is likely that you will have come across attempts by the government to improve your health in your school and on television. Your school or college is likely to have a healthy eating policy. If you smoke you will be aware of the risks because the government has spent millions of pounds showing you the dangers by what they put on the cigarette packets and on posters all around where you live. If you wanted to give up smoking there is a lot of help available both in your school and the community. Promoting health and well-being involves you thinking about all of these issues.

Think about your own health.

List **three** areas of your health which you know are strong points.

List **three** areas of your health where you know improvements could be made.

Share your thoughts with another person. How would you and the other person improve each of the three areas identified?

How do you know which are the strong points about your own health?

Have a whole group discussion about the strong points and the improvements that could be made.

Understanding health and well-being

Getting started

In this section you will gain an understanding of:

a how practitioners define health and well-being

b the different methods used by practitioners and individuals to define health and well-being, including:

   i   holistic definitions of health – assessment of health based on a combination of physical, intellectual, emotional and social factors

   ii positive definitions of health – assessment of health based on achievement and maintenance of physical fitness and mental stability

   iii negative definitions of health – assessment of health based on the absence of physical illness, disease and mental distress

c health and well-being as a socially constructed concept relative to an individual's life stage and cultural setting.

HOW PRACTITIONERS DEFINE HEALTH AND WELL-BEING

Holistic definitions of health

A practice nurse, a GP (general practitioner), a social worker and a care assistant, when interviewed, did not look for a single cause for good health but described health as being:

> 'The ability for an individual to live to their full potential, making sure that all aspects of an individual's life are as effective as possible, to include:
>
> - physical health
> - social health
> - mental health
> - spiritual health
> - emotional health
> - societal health.'

In other words, the professionals are considering an **holistic approach** rather than considering one aspect of health. For example, a person who has a lung infection should not just be treated for the physical illness. All other needs, as listed above, must be taken into account. The individual may also suffer from depression as a result of the illness. This may lead to them losing their job, resulting in social isolation from their work colleagues and friends. In order to help, the care professional would need to treat all aspects of the individual's health and well-being (P.I.E.S.).

> **...WORD CHECK**
>
> **holistic approach** – treating a service user as a whole individual by providing care to meet all needs, linking the care provided together to ensure all aspects are looked at.

Good health includes all aspects of an individual's lifestyle.

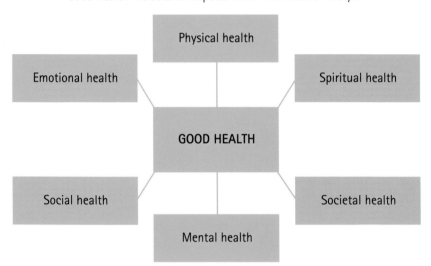

Physical health

Emotional health

Spiritual health

GOOD HEALTH

Social health

Societal health

Mental health

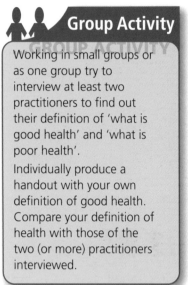

Group Activity

Working in small groups or as one group try to interview at least two practitioners to find out their definition of 'what is good health' and 'what is poor health'.

Individually produce a handout with your own definition of good health. Compare your definition of health with those of the two (or more) practitioners interviewed.

What are each of these features of health? The table below briefly answers this question.

Features of health	What do they involve?
Physical health	Making sure that each part of the body can function effectively and is not impaired in any way. Eating healthily, taking sufficient exercise, and having a balance between work and recreation are some of the ways that physical health can be maintained.
Mental health	Having the ability to reason through situations and to think clearly and reach conclusions is part of the way to maintain good intellectual health. Having friends with whom an individual can talk through problems or ideas and listening to the opinions of others can contribute to good mental support. Lack of worry about different situations, such as work, income or safety, can also help to prevent poor mental health.
Emotional health	Emotion is to do with how we feel, for example, happy, sad, angry. Emotions are sometimes determined by the effect others have on us or how we see ourselves. Having good relationships with others and truly knowing ourselves can contribute to good emotional health as we will feel valued and loved.
Social health	Getting on with others, whether at work or in leisure activities, makes a positive contribution to social health. Meeting with individuals who have the same interests and who enjoy going to the same places as we do can help to stimulate our intellect and our emotions, which helps our ability to interact with others.
Spiritual health	Following our own beliefs and views can promote a feeling of well-being. This could involve our religious beliefs or our political beliefs or the standards we think we should follow. When we take part in activities that go against our principles, we do not feel happy and can feel very uncomfortable about what we have done.
Societal health	All of us are influenced by our location, that is, where we live. If we are in harmony with others in our community, we are more likely to enjoy life but if we disagree with others or if we are being persecuted, our societal health could be damaged.

The professionals recognized that several factors and not just one single factor could contribute to an individual's state of health. Alternative medical approaches such as homeopathy try to cure the whole person rather than just curing the immediate problem.

...WORD CHECK

not impaired – weakened or diminished.

determined – a way of making a decision that's usually based on evidence.

harmony – when events or actions work together well.

homeopathy – an alternative therapy that uses substances that cause dysfunction in small amounts, to treat or cure the dysfunction.

Positive definitions of health

There are a number of ways to describe health. The Health Promotion Agency supports the view of the World Health Organization (WHO) whose **definition** is that health is:

'a state of complete physical, mental and social well-being and not merely the absence of disease or infirmity'.

Health is a fundamental human right and the highest possible level of health is of worldwide importance. Those working to promote health view it as being a resource that is needed to support everyone in their day-to-day life.

Health is important to everyone at every life stage, be it infancy, adolescence or later adulthood. Money cannot buy health, but lifestyle choices can affect it. Although health education campaigns can be costly, they can save the NHS billions of pounds in the long term. This is because health campaigns can **empower** service users by giving them information to help them decide to make life-changing choices, which could improve their health and well-being.

Achieving good health has many positive benefits; however, what is considered to be good health can change as people age. As people get older they will understand that their level of health is often limited by:

- the physical condition of their body
- the understanding of their health
- their emotions and their state of mind
- their social situation.

World Health Organization

▲ Health is a fundamental human right.

The positive definition of health sees a healthy person as someone who achieves and maintains physical fitness and mental stability. An individual who sets targets for him/herself, such as exercising regularly and learning new skills throughout life, is adopting a positive view of health. Such individuals are likely to suffer less illness and disease as they are monitoring their body and brain on a regular basis. If more people adopted a positive view of health then the strain on the health and social care services would be reduced.

Group Activity

Look up the World Health Organization at www.who.int. Find out about their six point agenda to improve public health.

Negative definitions of health

This definition of health is very different. Some individuals think that good health is just based upon not being ill or suffering from disease, therefore, as long as they feel well they will continue the lifestyle they currently have, even if this is not particularly healthy. They expect a care practitioner to make them better when they have an illness. If a more positive view was adopted, an illness might not occur in the first place. This definition possibly explains why some people ignore health advice and campaigns, such as eating your five-a-day and drinking alcohol within acceptable limits.

HEALTH AND WELL-BEING AS A SOCIALLY CONSTRUCTED CONCEPT RELATIVE TO AN INDIVIDUAL'S LIFE STAGE AND CULTURAL SETTING

Some individuals are healthier because they live in a society that has high levels of good hygiene and diet. Even within the same society there are huge differences in life expectancy. For example, women live longer than men and middle-class people live longer than working-class individuals (on average).

ACTIVITY — Life expectancy

Using census data at www.statistics.gov.uk, look up life expectancy figures for men, women and different social classes.

1 Try to explain why, at the moment, women live longer than men.

2 Why might this not necessarily be true in the future?

'Cultural setting' refers to the area or society a person lives in. In the developing world the majority of the population have a poor level of health compared to more wealthy countries such as the UK.

Health is also linked to the life stage an individual is in. At the moment, many young people are suffering from poor health as a result of obesity linked to poor diet. Increasing numbers of young women are likely to suffer from alcohol-related diseases in adulthood as a result of dangerous levels of drinking in their teens and twenties. As people today are living longer, more people are suffering from a range of age-related illnesses, such as dementia. These type of problems hardly existed in the past because most people died before they reached the age when such illnesses occur.

Group Activity

Do some research into health-related problems linked to life stages. Choose two life stages and look at the illnesses and diseases most commonly found during those life stages.

Group Activity

Discuss the reasons why individuals in continents such as Africa experience poor levels of physical, intellectual and social health. (Look back at Maslow's pyramid of needs on page 104).

Look at the World Health Organization's website at www.who.int and find out the life expectancy figures for different countries.

CASE STUDY — Pradeep and Angelina

Pradeep

Pradeep is 25 years old and works as a financial assistant for a bank. He is studying for his examinations while he is working. At lunch time he has a takeaway bread roll and a drink and collects his evening meal from different takeaway shops on his way home. He watches TV most nights but goes clubbing on a Friday evening with his friends.

Angelina

Angelina is overweight and does very little exercise. She thinks she eats very little and cannot understand why she is putting on weight. She does drink quite a lot of alcohol each evening, but takes the dog for a short walk before she settles down to TV and a drink.

1 What advice would you give each individual in the case studies regarding their health?

2 What type of health promotion campaign might help each of them?

3 Which professional care workers could assist each of them?

ASSESSMENT PRACTICE: PREPARATION

You have been asked to conduct a survey to find out how an individual maintains their health and to investigate any improvements needed.

1 Give a comprehensive explanation of what are meant by the terms 'good health and well-being' and 'poor health and well-being'. Try to give examples to explain the points made.

2 For the **one** person chosen, prepare detailed interview questions and/or a questionnaire that will help you collect the information required. Trial the questionnaire with others to make sure the questions are clear and unambiguous.

3 Draw up an appropriate recording document which groups the questions in order within the topic and which gives a space to record the answers given. Group the questions under physical, intellectual, emotional and social factors.

4 Write a letter to the chosen person asking if it is possible to conduct the survey. Give them a copy of the questions that you will ask during your visit.

5 Analyse the results of the survey and present them in the form of a report, drawing conclusions that make accurate reference to interpreting the information correctly.

To complete these tasks you may prefer to use a case study to practise your skills ready for the controlled assignment.

PRACTICE CASE STUDY – Faith Hirst

Faith is a married woman who is 41 years of age. She has two children who have left home and one child who is just finishing her examinations in the hope of being able to go on to university. Faith spends a lot of time on her own, as she does not work, and so she is often lonely, and smokes heavily, as her husband spends quite a lot of time travelling, as he is a manager of several chain stores.

Faith often comfort eats and has consequently put on quite a lot of weight. She used to attend a fitness club but gave up as she was never very successful in getting rid of the excess weight. Faith often drinks alone when she is home and goes out with her friends two evenings a week clubbing. She often ends up drunk and has to get a taxi home.

After such a night out Faith will sit and watch television for most of the day, continuing to drink and smoke throughout the day. She never does any exercise, not even very much shopping as she has it delivered to her house after ordering it on-line.

One morning Faith decides that she cannot go on as she is. She must make some changes to her life. How could she do this?

Factors affecting health and well-being

▶ Getting started

You will gain an understanding of:

a factors which can affect an individuals health and well-being

b how a range of factors can affect health and well-being in either a positive or negative way, including:
   i physical factors such as genetic inheritance, illness, disease, diet, exercise, alcohol and smoking
   ii social, cultural and emotional factors – such as family, friends, educational experiences, employment/unemployment, community involvement, religion, gender, ethnicity, sexual orientation, culture and relationship formation including marriage and divorce
   iii economic factors – such as income, wealth, employment status, occupation, social class, poverty and material possessions
   iv physical environment factors – such as pollution, noise, housing conditions and rural/urban lifestyles
   v psychological factors – such as stress, relationships within the family, friends and partners
   vi health monitoring and illness prevention services (such as screening and vaccination).

FACTORS WHICH CAN AFFECT AN INDIVIDUAL'S HEALTH AND WELL-BEING

Many factors combine together to affect the health and well-being of individuals and communities. Whether individuals are healthy or not is determined by their circumstances, lifestyle and environment. To a large extent, factors such as the food we eat, where we live, the state of the environment, genetics, income, educational experiences, and our relationships with friends and family have considerable impact on health and well-being. Also, other factors such as sexual orientation and illness can often have a major impact. The way people run their lives determines their health! This also means that individuals have a responsibility to themselves to remain healthy. Individuals are unlikely to be able to control all of the **determinants** of health directly but have to accept responsibility for those that they can.

> ✅ **...WORD CHECK**
> **determinants** – to cause to come to a conclusion or decision.

Group Activity

Work in a small group to discuss why some risks to health can be affected, whilst others are more difficult to influence. Which risks would be easier to affect than others? Why?

Share the group's ideas with the whole group.

Some factors will have a positive **impact** on the lives of individuals while others could pose a risk. Some examples are shown below:

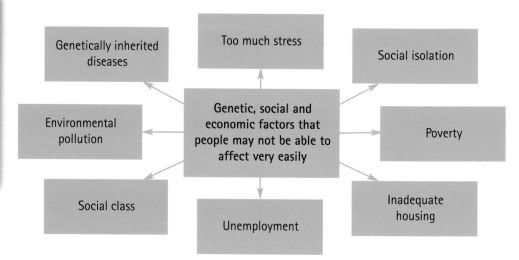

Health is a very individual term and means different things to many people. There are a number of factors that can have a positive impact on health, which can be built on to improve the individual as a whole.

Group Activity

Decide which three factors from diet, exercise, supportive relationships, location and stress have the most positive influence on your development. Why?

Share your findings with another person.

Work with another person to find out if any factors in either of your lives are negative.

Write down **three** and suggest ways in which these aspects could be strengthened.

Share how the items could be improved with others in the group.

PHYSICAL FACTORS

Genetics

Genetic inheritance is having a mixture of **genes** from our parents, which acts as a plan of what we will be like when we grow. Genes are tiny pieces of information inside every cell in the body. They are the instructions that the body uses to build itself. The human body is very complicated and it needs a lot of instructions to do this.

See page 31 for more information about genetics.

⊘ ...WORD CHECK

impact – the effect or action on an event or person.

genetic – a gene passed from parents or grandparents down through the generations.

genes – part of a chromosome that controls a particular characteristic, for example, eye colour.

Genetically inherited diseases and conditions

There are many diseases and physical problems that can be inherited genetically. The following are some of the main types:

- autism
- Down's syndrome
- cystic fibrosis
- Asperger's syndrome
- diabetes
- heart condition.

Genes influence individual differences such as gender, hair and eye colour, height, and skin colour. Some medical conditions, such as Tourette's syndrome do 'run in families'. Autism, a condition that is associated with the development of the nervous system, is also influenced by genes.

Genetic disorders are likely to have serious physical, intellectual, social and emotional effects on the individual's health and well-being. For example, an individual suffering from autism is likely to have communication difficulties, such as not being able to express themselves. Their behaviour will be erratic with rapid mood swings and often displays of anger. The parents of an autistic child may feel guilty or responsible for their child's condition. People in society may also find it difficult to relate to autistic children and the health and social care services will need to provide a considerable amount of long-term care and support.

In a health promotion plan for an individual with a genetically inherited condition or disease, it is important to set realistic targets for any health improvement. This will need to be resourced both in terms of finance and care workers.

It is interesting that a documentary on Channel 4 'Born with Down's syndrome' found that more mothers are now choosing to keep their Down's syndrome babies than have an abortion. Many parents found that life and society had improved for people affected by this condition. Some parents also said that their decision was influenced by the fact that they knew people with the condition. This suggests that the wider society is much more understanding and supportive than in the past when most people were very ignorant of such conditions and those suffering from the condition would often be isolated and **institutionalized**. Cara Boys, the Chief Executive of the Down's Syndrome Association, said, 'Now there is much greater **inclusion** and acceptance, with **mainstream education** having a huge role. We think this plays a part in the decisions parents make – there's been a baby with Down's syndrome on Eastenders.'

Diabetes is a condition that is increasing rapidly in society today, partly because of the increase in obesity and poor diet. There are two main types of diabetes. Type 1 occurs when the body stops making insulin, which is necessary to break down sugar. Treatment to control the blood glucose level comes from **insulin** injections and a healthy diet. There is a genetic factor with this condition. A first degree relative (sister, brother, son, daughter) of someone with Type 1 diabetes has about a 6 per cent chance of developing the condition. This is higher than the chance of the general population, which is about one in 250. This is probably because certain people are more prone to develop auto-immune diseases such as diabetes and this is due to their genetic make-up, which is inherited. Type 2 diabetes is caused by the body not producing enough insulin or not using what it produces effectively. It's the most common form and accounts for around 90 per cent of all those with diabetes. This form can often be controlled by improved diet and/or the use of tablets. This type of diabetes usually occurs in people over the age of 40.

▲ Pete Bennett, winner of Big Brother series 7, has Tourette's syndrome.

Group Activity

Look up autism and the effect it will have on an individual's behaviour at www.nas.org.uk/autism. Have a whole-group discussion about the effects autism could have on an individual.

...WORD CHECK

institutionalized – to become conditioned to work and live in a way designed by a large organization, for example, a psychiatric institution.

inclusion – to be a part of or to be included in an event.

mainstream education – normal education accessed by all.

insulin – a body hormone that helps the body to use glucose (sugar).

CASE STUDY   Jane and Jack

Jane became diabetic when she was 23 years of age. Three years later she went to her doctor to see about the possibility of having children. Her doctor said that it should be fine but there was an above average risk that the child would also be diabetic. Jane became pregnant and gave birth to Jack. Unfortunately at the age of three he started to be thirsty all the time, passing a lot of urine and always feeling tired. When his blood sugar level was tested, he had high levels and, like his mother, was put on to insulin. Jane now has to inject both herself and Jack with insulin three times a day. This is the only way they can both survive.

1. How would diabetes impact upon Jane and Jack physically, emotionally, intellectually and socially?

2. Look up diabetes on www.diabetes.org.uk and find out what a health promotion plan would involve for diabetics. You will need to consider diet, weight, exercise, smoking and alcohol.

3. What health risks are diabetics more likely to suffer from?

Illness and disease

Physical illness and disease can also affect our emotional, intellectual and social development. For example, if a child misses a lot of school, they miss learning opportunities as well as the opportunity to mix and socialize with other children.

Serious illness in adulthood may mean that an individual cannot work, so they lose social contacts. This may also have emotional effects, and people may experience depression and lowered self-esteem if they are unable to work.

In later adulthood, many people have **degenerative** illnesses such as arthritis and rheumatism. These have the physical effect of making it difficult for them to care for themselves. Other illnesses, such as Alzheimer's disease, have intellectual effects, including confusion and memory loss. Having to rely on others for everyday care tasks may have emotional effects. People who are unable to care for themselves may also become depressed. This is likely to happen if their carers are not careful to offer them choices. If illness makes people less mobile, they may find it difficult to leave their homes. Again this will have social effects and they could become isolated.

It should be remembered that happy and contented people are less likely to be ill and that a balanced diet and sufficient exercise can contribute to good health.

> ⊘ **...WORD CHECK**
>
> **degenerative** – where a body organ or system slowly begins to break down.
>
> **balanced** – an even distribution or equal amounts.
>
> **essential components** – parts of an object or activity that cannot be done without.

Balanced diet

A **balanced** diet is essential if overall good health is to be achieved, but which are the best foods to include on a daily basis and which ones are best avoided? What is a balanced diet? A balanced diet is made up of the following seven **essential components**.

Vitamins

The vitamins needed are found in a variety of foods. If any of the vitamins are absent from a person's diet, deficiencies occur that can cause health problems. In Britain in the seventeenth and eighteenth centuries, sailors constantly suffered from a disease called scurvy.

Scurvy was caused by a lack of vitamin C, which resulted in skin problems. It also led to bleeding gums, causing teeth to fall out. The disease was eventually stopped when it was noticed that Spanish sailors did not have this problem because they ate oranges as part of their diet when onboard ship. However, the best the British navy could offer was limes, which were also high in vitamin C.

Vitamins fit into two categories by the way that they are absorbed by the body. Vitamins in the first category are soluble in water and needed by the body on a regular basis. The regular need is because they are easily excreted in urine and need to be replaced. Vitamins B and C fit into this category, as they are water-soluble. The remaining vitamins, A, D, E and K, are all fat-soluble and form the second category. As these vitamins are fat-soluble they can remain in body fat for months and sometimes years.

◀ Oranges are a good source of vitamin C.

Group Activity

Work in pairs to find out which foods are a source of:

vitamin A, vitamin B, vitamin C and vitamin D.

What is their purpose in the body?

What are the effects of not having each vitamin in the correct amount each day?

Complete the following table.

Vitamin	What it does	Which foods contain it	Effect on body function of not having the vitamin each day
A			
B			
C			
D			

Minerals

These are simple elements such as iron, calcium and potassium. They are found in most of the foods that are eaten, some foods being higher in some minerals than others. Minerals are needed by the body in small quantities so that it can function correctly. There are 22 minerals that are essential in remaining healthy. Minerals such as calcium help to build strong bones and teeth, and iron helps in the formation of red blood cells. Minerals are divided into two main groups, minerals that are needed in relatively large amounts, major minerals or elements, and minerals that are needed in much smaller amounts, trace minerals or elements.

A deficiency of minerals in the diet can lead to disease; for example, a lack of iron in the diet may lead to anaemia (low red blood cell count).

Group Activity

Work in pairs to find out which foods are a source of iron and calcium.

What is their purpose in the body?

What are the effects of not having each vitamin in the correct amount each day?

▲ Essential for body building.

Group Activity

Work with another person to find out the difference between saturated and unsaturated fat. What is their role in the body?

▼ Fats are found in many forms.

Protein

From hair to fingernails, protein is a major functional and structural component of all our cells. Protein provides the body with roughly 10–15 per cent of its dietary energy, and is needed for growth and repair.

For adults and children, proteins are very important for building the brain, muscle, skin, blood and other tissues. Proteins also provide the materials needed to repair the cells in our body.

Proteins are made up of complex chemicals called **amino acids**. To function properly the body needs 21 different amino acids. The body can make 12 of these itself through complex chemical processes. The other nine are found in different foods that people consume.

There are two types of protein:

- animal protein
- vegetable protein.

Animal proteins are found in products such as meat, fish, eggs, milk and cheese. These products contain all of the remaining nine amino acids that the body requires.

Vegetable proteins come from plant products such as peas, beans, lentils and nuts. They are a very good source of protein, especially for vegetarians. The remaining nine amino acids that the body needs can also be found in vegetable proteins.

Health professionals recommend that protein makes up 10–15 per cent of our diet. They suggest that adult men eat 55.5g of protein every day and adult women eat 45g every day. Eating a moderate amount of protein – in one or two meals every day – should give all the protein that a person needs. Everyone needs to eat the correct amount of protein daily because the body can not store protein. It is not possible to stock up on it by binging. Simply eating a variety of foods every day is all that is needed.

Water

Water is essential for the body's growth and maintenance, as it is involved in a number of processes. For example, it helps get rid of waste and regulate temperature, and it provides a medium for biological reactions to occur in the body. A person can go without food for weeks and still survive. However, if their supply of drinkable water is cut off, they will die in a matter of days.

Water can be found in fruit juices, teas, sparkling water and other fizzy drinks. Drinking pure water allows the body to wash out toxins without having to put stress on the digestive system. Water consumption is one of the single most important daily tasks a person performs in order to live a long and healthy life.

1 ▶ How much water should you drink a day?

Fats

Fats are very good at providing energy to the body and are found in both animal and vegetable products. There are two main types of fat.

- **Saturated** – found in both animal and vegetable products. Meat, milk and eggs are high in saturated fats.
- **Unsaturated** – found in vegetable products and some fish. Vegetable oils, sunflower oil, olive oil, herring and cod liver oil are valuable sources of unsaturated fat.

Carbohydrates

Carbohydrates also provide the body with energy but their energy value is not as high as fat. Most carbohydrates come from sugars, starches and fibre. Foods such as biscuits, chocolate, cakes, honey and jams are high in carbohydrates. A second source of carbohydrates is foods such as pasta, rice and potatoes. These also provide a high energy source and at least 30 per cent of our diet should be made up of carbohydrates. It is possible to measure the energy in both fat and carbohydrates in units known as **kilojoules** or **calories**. These are the same calories that people count when they monitor their diet.

Fibre

It is recommended that fruit and vegetables form the basis of everyone's diet, with a minimum intake of five portions each day – about a third of the daily food consumption. Many of our vitamins and minerals are gained this way. They also provide the bulk of our daily intake of fibre that helps regulate our bowel habits.

Fibre in our diet adds bulk to the food that we eat. This helps our digestive system to move the food through the bowel. Without these muscular movements it would be easy to become constipated.

Fibre is found in a variety of different foods:

- bran
- cereals
- fruit
- rice
- vegetables (peas, beans, greens)
- wholemeal bread.

Without fibre in our diet we could also suffer from poor digestion of our food, which could lead to **constipation**.

A healthy diet contains all of the **nutrients** needed by the body. Scientific studies have shown that people who eat a lot of fruit and vegetables are usually healthier. They may have a lower risk of getting illnesses, such as heart disease and some cancers. For this reason, it is recommended that people eat at least five portions of fruit and vegetables every day. It doesn't matter whether they are fresh, tinned, frozen, cooked, juiced or dried.

Portion is a word for a measure of food eaten. In everyday eating, the portion would be:

- One piece of medium-sized fruit, for example, an apple, peach, banana or orange.
- One slice of large fruit, such as melon, mango or pineapple.
- A few handfuls of grapes, or berry fruits.
- A glass (100ml) of fruit or vegetable juice.
- The vegetables (100g) served in a portion of vegetable curry, lasagne, stir fry or casserole.
- A side salad.
- A small handful of dried fruit, for example, small pack of dried apricots.
- A small tin (200g) of fruit.
- Peas, beans or carrots, served with main meal.

Group Activity

Make a list of what you had to eat yesterday. What dietary components did it contain?

Share your list with another person in the group.

How could your diets be improved?

...WORD CHECK

kilojoules – a unit of work or energy expended.

calories – the unit of heat according to the French standard; the amount of heat required to raise the temperature of one kilogram (sometimes, one gram) of water 1°C, or from 0 to 1°C.

constipation – the intestines become filled with hardened faeces.

nutrients – substances that provide nourishment.

portion – a part of, or an amount of.

Group Activity

Work with another person to find out how much an individual should take in each day of:

- vitamin C
- calcium
- iron
- vitamin A.

2 How many portions of fruit and vegetables do you need each day?

It is recommended that an individual eats:

- Carbohydrates sourced from bread, cereals, pasta and potatoes. This should be roughly 30 per cent of each day's meals.

- Sugary foods, but individuals should eat less of them. It is possible to cut down on sugary foods by snacking on fresh or dried fruit rather than biscuits and chocolate.

- Government guidelines recommend that fat makes up no more than 35 per cent of the diet. For the average woman, this means about 76g of fat per day and, for a man, this means roughly 100g of fat per day. In reality, though, most of us have higher fat intakes than this.

- Everyone requires vitamins and minerals in their daily diet.

What is the role of calories, kilojoules and joules?

Calories and joules are units used to measure the amount of energy the body uses. They can also be used as terms for measuring energy values of food. They are used to measure the energy we burn off in exercise.

Look at the calorie table (see Appendix 1, pages 288–289). Use this table to create healthy diets for the person you chose when carrying out the assignments. It will also help to make sure that you, too, are eating the right foods.

ACTIVITY   Finding out about diet

1 Keep a diary of every thing that you eat and drink in a week. Calculate the following:
- How many portions of fruit and vegetables have you eaten?
- How many bags of crisps or similar have you eaten?
- How many calories were in the crisps? (The packet will tell you how many calories are in a bag.)

2 Copy and complete the sentences:

Protein helps to _____ _____ and _____.

Protein foods can be found in _____ , _____ and _____

There are _____ main types of protein.

3 Maxine, aged 16, has the following for her evening meal: beefburger, chips, tomato and chocolate.

Give the main nutrients that are in the meal and explain how Maxine could make the meal well balanced.

4 Plan a meal for Maxine that is well balanced. Explain why it is well balanced, making reference to nutritional values.

Exercise

Physical exercise is any bodily activity that **enhances** or maintains physical fitness and overall health. It is performed for many different reasons. These include:

- strengthening muscles
- strengthening the cardiovascular system
- weight loss or maintenance.

Frequent and regular physical exercise boosts the immune system, and helps prevent diseases of **affluence** such as heart disease, cardiovascular disease, Type 2 diabetes and obesity. It also improves mental health and helps prevent depression. Childhood obesity is a growing global concern and physical exercise may help decrease the effects of childhood obesity in developed countries. Lack of exercise can lead to:

- cardiovascular problems
- coronary heart disease
- muscle and joint problems
- obesity
- osteoporosis.

Exercise helps to maintain fitness. It strengthens the body and helps to control weight, whilst burning off extra energy. It has a great many other health benefits, too, because it:

- helps in building up **immunity**
- helps the heart work more efficiently
- improves **circulation**
- improves **mobility**
- improves **stamina**
- improves the strength in muscles
- reduces the risk of a heart attack.

Not having any exercise can put a person's health at risk.

Exercise has other positive effects on health and well-being such as psychological effects; for example:

- building confidence
- giving a general feeling of well-being
- helping relieve stress
- improving **self-esteem**
- it is a great way to socialize.

Babies, from the moment that they are born, begin to exercise their muscles. Children exercise in all of their activities, and sport is a major part of growing up. Exercise protects physical as well as emotional well-being. It also helps protect against diseases in later life such as **osteoporosis**.

3 Why is exercise important?

Aerobic exercise

Aerobic exercises include walking, jogging and swimming. They involve muscles moving through their full range over set time periods (15–20 minutes). These activities are an addition to the normal daily routines. During these activities, the heart and respiration rates will increase. This type of exercise is used to improve cardiovascular fitness. It also increases blood flow to the muscles and benefits the whole body.

Aerobic exercises are planned to increase the heart rate to 70 per cent of its maximum. This is 220 beats per minute (bpm), minus the person's age.

> **...WORD CHECK**
>
> **enhances** – something that makes an item or activity better or stronger.
>
> **affluence** – abundance of property; wealth.
>
> **immunity** – the way the body produces resistance against disease.
>
> **circulation** – the movement of the blood in the blood-vascular system.
>
> **mobility** – to be able to move around.
>
> **stamina** – a person's continued strength during an activity.
>
> **self-esteem** – how a person feels about themselves.
>
> **osteoporosis** – a condition of brittle and fragile bones caused by loss of bony tissue.
>
> **aerobic** – with the use of oxygen.

▼ Swimming is one type of aerobic exercise.

Anaerobic exercise

Anaerobic exercise is the bodybuilder's method of building muscle. It involves **high intensity** activity aimed at developing the muscles. It is only done for short periods of time.

Weightlifting is a good example of an anaerobic exercise. Anaerobic activities increase the amount of muscle and strength. Benefits to the heart and the lungs are limited by using this method.

 What is the difference between aerobic and anaerobic exercise?

How can safety be maintained when exercising?

When starting exercise, beginners should ideally be supervised and should be made aware of the dangers of over-exercising, especially the strain that they can put on their heart and circulation. Making muscles work to the point of exhaustion is dangerous. If the person's health and heart are poor, this could bring on a collapse or a heart attack.

Exercise should always be moderate and not excessive. It should also be regular. This allows the body to build up stamina and reduces the risk of injury.

Which exercises are best?

Just as certain foods are better for us than others, so are certain exercises. Exercise should start off at an easy pace. Eventually an individual should be doing 30 minutes of exercise at least five times a week. Remember exercise should not make an individual exceed 70 per cent of their maximum heart rate.

Whether a person is young or old, fit, unfit or disabled, they can always find some form of exercise to suit their age or condition. Being fit is becoming very fashionable, which fits in with the government's health plans, as it encourages individuals to take responsibility for their own health.

Remember:

- To lose one kilogram in weight you have to burn off 8000 calories or 33,600 kilojoules (3500 calories per pound in weight).

ACTIVITY   Learning about exercise

1 Carry out some research to find out about **two** other types of aerobic and **two** types of anaerobic exercise.

2 Keep a diary of how much exercise you have done during the week. What did you do? How much did you do? Make a plan to show the exercise done during the week. Draw some conclusions about how the exercise contributed to your health status. What could you do to improve your exercise programme?

3 Create a plan of regular exercise for a friend who needs to improve the amount and type of exercise taken. This plan should be for one week. Make sure the exercises can be done safely. Explain how the exercises will help to improve or maintain fitness.

4 If someone takes regular exercise and becomes fit, how will the improvements affect their health, well-being and self-esteem?

Alcohol

Most health promotion plans for all age groups, apart from very young children and babies, will have to analyse the use of alcohol by the individual. Alcohol is the most widely used and accepted drug in our **culture**. It is widely available and is a way of life for many people. Most soap operas on television have a pub as an essential part of the community.

For many individuals, drinking alcohol is not a major risk to their health if they stick to the recommended limits:

- For men, no more than three to four units a day with at least two alcohol free days a week.
- For women, no more than two to three units a day with at least two alcohol free days a week.

The biggest risk to health at the moment is the culture of binge drinking. A study of people held at a police station in Plymouth revealed that many were not hardened criminals but ust ordinary people who had had too much to drink. Two-thirds of people arrested were drinking at 'hazardous' levels. The biggest drinkers were young men aged 17–24, in which group more than 1000 drank more than 10 units of alcohol a day and many admitted to drinking with the express intention of getting drunk. This behaviour is increasingly being copied by young women.

High levels of drinking has a widespread effect upon many aspects of society:

▲ On Coronation Street a lot of the drama happens in the local pub.

Violent crime

Long-term hospital care

Domestic violence

Heavy drinking

Days off work with hangovers

Heavy use of Accident and Emergency departments in hospitals

Anti-social behaviour on the streets

Group Activity

Carry out some research and find out what one unit of alcohol is for beer, wines and spirits.

A health plan would need to point out the short- and long-term physical, emotional, social and intellectual health risks attached to high levels of alcohol consumption. In particular, the message would need to get across to young men and women:

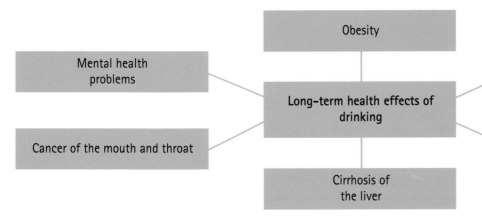

Obesity

Mental health problems

High blood pressure

Long-term health effects of drinking

Cancer of the mouth and throat

Coronary heart disease

Cirrhosis of the liver

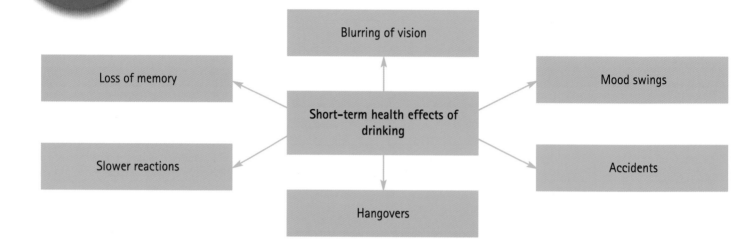

Smoking and substance misuse

Any health promotion plan for individuals over the age of 16 is likely to involve a discussion of the use of legal, and possibly illegal, substances such as tobacco. The diagrams below show some legal substances and others that are illegal:

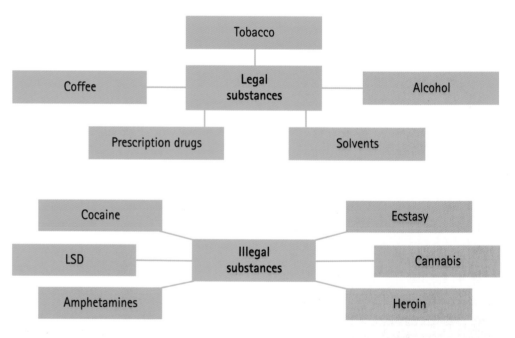

Most people are aware of the health risks linked to smoking such as:

- bronchitis and emphysema
- coronary heart disease
- high blood pressure
- kidney and bladder cancer
- lung cancer
- throat and larynx cancer.

Half of all teenagers who currently smoke will die from diseases caused by tobacco if they continue to smoke. It has been estimated that in England 364,000 patients are admitted to NHS hospitals each year due to smoking-related illnesses. This is equivalent to 7000 hospital admissions a week, or 1000 a day!

The government has tried health promotion campaigns to reduce smoking, such as banning smoking in public places and recently putting dramatic, shocking pictures of diseased lungs, and so on, on cigarette packets. Despite this, approximately 400 children start to smoke each day! One in seven 15 year olds is already a smoker.

If the individual health plan involves pregnant women, then the advice has to be to stop smoking immediately. For other people, the plan should involve strategies to reduce and eventually give up smoking altogether. Such strategies could include:

- deciding when to quit
- keeping a smoking diary
- talking to a doctor for advice
- planning a coping strategy – use nicotine replacements, chew gum
- getting rid of all your cigarettes, lighters, tobacco and ashtrays on the day you give up
- trying to stay away from people who smoke in the first few weeks.

According to the anti-smoking group, ASH, the economic cost to society of smoking is huge. In 2008, it is estimated that smokers cost the NHS in England £2.7 billion a year compared with £1.7 billion ten years ago.

Smoking
causes fatal lung cancer

 ▲ Shock tactics to try to stop people smoking.

Group Activity

Look up ASH on www.ash.org.uk and find out how they campaign to stop people smoking. Their ideas might be useful if your individual health plan involves a smoker.

SOCIAL, CULTURAL AND EMOTIONAL FACTORS

Look back to Unit 1 to find out about the effect that these factors can have on health and well-being, as all the main topics in this section are covered on pages 38–47.

Family, friends and relationship formation

Most humans like mixing with other people. A person's health and well-being can be affected by the relationships that are made. Having supportive relationships at home gives security and provides a level of happiness. Therefore, feeling happy and secure is a major factor in feeling good. When a person feels good, they have pride in themselves. They then look after themselves and this helps them to remain healthy.

Supportive relationships are, therefore, very important. They can lift self-esteem and make people feel positive about themselves. This feeling of good 'self-concept' is needed to stay healthy. The mind is a powerful force and people will act according to how they feel about themselves. If they wake up in the morning and everything around them is good, then they might feel good all day. If they wake up and, for example, think their relationships are not working, they are more likely to have a bad day. Everyone has days when they do not feel very good about themselves. If this lasts for a long period of time, they can become depressed and this can affect their health. Their **immune system** can also be affected and they then become more **prone** to illness.

...WORD CHECK

self-concept – the image we have of ourselves.

immune system – a body system that prevents infection in that body.

prone – when a person has a problem that can happen on a regular basis.

5 ▶ Why do we need to socialize with other people?

Educational experiences

Education plays an important part in health and well-being. It allows everyone to have greater control of their lives and hopefully to make better decisions. It can affect all decisions whether they are intellectual, emotional or social.

A willingness to learn makes an individual **inquisitive** and this in turn helps the individual to make the best choices. These choices could include choosing a job, whether to go to university or which parts of the world to see. Life is full of choices and it is not always possible to make the best ones. People have to use their **intellect** to make decisions if they are going to make the correct ones.

An individual who does not use their intellect will become bored and this could lead to unacceptable behaviour or crime.

Intellectual activities can include:

▲ Learning can help to stimulate the mind.

* reading
* word puzzles/crosswords
* taking part in a quiz
* solving a crime
* helping to make decisions.

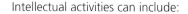

> ⊘ **...WORD CHECK**
>
> **inquisitive** – to be very interested and enquire.
>
> **intellect** – the mind; the brain's activity.

Employment/unemployment

For an adult, not having a job usually leads to serious risks to their health. The Samaritans believe that unemployment triples the risk of suicide. They believe that this is partly linked to social isolation. Possible emotional sources of support for an unemployed person, such as work colleagues, are no longer there. A person's self-esteem is badly damaged through losing their job.

According to Professor Aylward, of the Wales Centre for Health, the damage of being unemployed for more than six months to a person's health is the same as smoking 200 cigarettes a day!

Unemployment causes:

* depression
* social exclusion
* loss of self-respect
* loss of identity.

All of these have a big impact upon a person's physical health and well-being. In some parts of the UK several generations of the same family have not worked because of the lack of jobs in those areas. More and more, doctors are seeing clients with health problems brought about by loss of jobs and all the worries that go with that.

Being able to work and earn money can be linked to health and well-being because it will influence the social activities that are possible. By earning money it is possible to buy important items that are needed and less important personal items that are desired. Money will also allow people to socialize, so they can go out to the cinema or a nightclub and meet people.

It is possible to get a lot of social enjoyment from working and the relationships developed with work colleagues. This can have a very positive effect on health and well-being. Working gives a person's life **structure**. This is a **framework** that they can build everything else around. If an individual is working, they are more likely to have more confidence and self-respect. The big psychological boost is that it can give them status and make them feel important.

Employment can have a large effect on people and their families. If someone is actively employed they may well feel:

- empowered
- happy
- financially secure.

They may also have:

- high self-worth
- high self-confidence
- high self-esteem.

6 How does being employed affect emotional well-being?

Group Activity

Work in small groups to discuss how, in a health plan, if the individual is unemployed, it is important that they should try and keep themselves busy. In what ways would you encourage them to keep occupied?

Share your ideas as a whole group.

...WORD CHECK

structure – a pattern or routine.

framework – the frame or constructional part of anything; as in, the framework of society.

ACTIVITY — Money and work

1 In pairs or small groups, produce questions to find out how people feel when:
- they are in a safe job that they like
- they are in a job that they do not like
- they have been out of work for more than 6 weeks.

2 Draw some conclusions from the answers received.

3 How is the self-concept of each group of people likely to be affected?

4 Use the words given below to discuss, in writing, the effect of each on personal development:
- debt
- material possessions
- need to make regular payments.

Community involvement

An individual can become involved in the community, for example, they could become involved in organizing a club for adolescents or become a member of an art group taking part in creative art. Whether as a leader or a participant, skills will be used that stimulate the intellect, and social interaction will take place.

Other social, cultural and emotional factors that can affect development are:

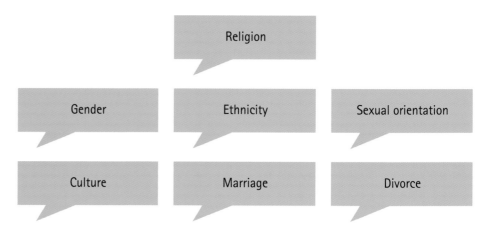

Look back at Unit 1 as details of each are given.

ECONOMIC FACTORS

Look back at Unit 1 for the details relating to economic factors. The table below summarizes the meaning of each topic in this section:

Factor	Explanation	Effect on development
Income	The amount of money coming in through earnings, pensions, savings or benefits	Contributes to a feeling of self-worth and gives safety and security
Employment status	Actually being employed or obtaining a higher position when working (through promotion)	Improves self-concept and helps an individual to feel valued
Occupation	What we do while we are at work – our job role	Helps us to feel fulfilled
Social class	Our social class is often based on economic factors and the job we do. The economic status of the person enables them to have opportunities that others may not get. In Britain, the system is known as the 'class system'. The differences between the classes being in terms of educational success, the type of work that is being undertaken and the money earnt. These differences are recorded in scales; for example, the Registrar-General's Scale.	Where we are in terms of social class will contribute to self-esteem. If we are considered to be high on the scale we are more likely to have high self-esteem but being lower on the social scale could contribute to an individual feeling worthless and having little to contribute.
Material possessions	The items we buy when we have money to spend, for example, a flat or a house, a car, clothes, food, and so on	Gives us confidence and makes us proud to own items

Wealth and poverty

As mentioned in Unit 1, wealth is very important for human growth and development.

Someone with a high income can borrow money from a bank or building society to buy a house, or can afford a high rent. They have a choice about what type of home they live in and where it is. A person with a low income or no income at all may not be able to buy their own home,

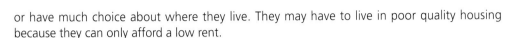
or have much choice about where they live. They may have to live in poor quality housing because they can only afford a low rent.

Someone with a reasonable amount of income will probably have a car and be able to get to supermarkets where they can afford good quality food. People on low incomes often have to rely on public transport, which may not be convenient. They may have to buy food locally from small shops, and sometimes this will mean paying more.

People with a high income can afford good quality clothing, and will not have to worry about fuel bills. This means that they can meet their own physical needs and the needs of the people dependent on them.

Poverty is a key factor affecting health and well-being. In Britain today very few people suffer from absolute poverty, which is the condition found in many developing countries where individuals are literally starving to death and are unable to meet the lowest level of Maslow's hierarchy. Poverty in this country is relative poverty, where an individual is unable to reach a level that is seen as acceptable for a relatively rich society. This could include not having three meals a day, not being able to afford one basic holiday a year or not being able to pay monthly heating bills.

A health plan would need to look at the financial situation of the individual and possibly suggest ways that would help overcome debt and all that it leads to. A weekly budget plan would be one possible suggestion to identify where the individual is spending their money and how they could put money aside for savings.

According to a report published by 'End Child Poverty', an organization of children's charities and church groups, 'poverty is the UK's hidden child killer'. They show that:

- children from poor families are at ten times the risk of sudden infant death as children from better-off homes
- babies from disadvantaged families are more likely to be born underweight
- poorer children are two-and-a-half times more likely to suffer chronic illness when toddlers and twice as likely to have cerebral palsy.

'From the day they are born, children's health and very survival are threatened by family poverty', according to Donald Hirsch, co-author of the report.

Fact: according to the Department of Work and Pensions, 2.9 million children were living in poverty in the UK in 2008.

Group Activity

Look up this report and find out how poverty is still a problem affecting growing numbers of children in the UK (www.endchildpoverty.org.uk).

PHYSICAL ENVIRONMENT FACTORS

Housing conditions and rural/urban lifestyles

Where people live can strongly influence the development of individuals, particularly children. For example, if a person lives in a rural area, this could determine the number of health, social care and early years services they are able to access, and the recreational activities they can join could be limited. Visiting friends and extended family members may be more difficult and they may have to travel to receive their education. However, living in a rural area could provide easier access to natural environments, which can enhance learning and development, and provide the opportunity for walking or community activities.

Group Activity

You have been given the opportunity to decide where you will live, for example, a rural or urban area. Which would you choose? Give advantages and disadvantages. What are the likely effects on development?

Children and people living in an **urban** area could experience **social deprivation** as they could be exposed to higher crime rates and vandalism, and may be fearful of going out. Access to services may be easier when living in a town or city and there may be more activities in which to participate.

Housing in inner cities and towns may take the form of flats with no gardens, whereas in rural areas houses are more likely to be detached, semi-detached or terraced, having their own gardens. There is likely to be less traffic in a rural area and consequently pollution is likely to be less of a problem.

Cold and damp conditions within the home can aggravate chest conditions and other conditions such as arthritis and rheumatism. Overcrowded housing can also affect the spread of illness and disease, as where people live closely together, infection can spread more quickly. Illnesses such as the common cold can easily be spread through families and, in the past, tuberculosis (TB) and cholera often reached epidemic proportions.

What are the effects on development likely to be?

Effects of living in a rural area	Effects of living in an urban area
Promotes good health because of natural open areas	Illness treated quickly because services are easier to access
May be reserved as social activities may be restricted	Could be more comfortable in social situations and with people
May be physically fitter as open countryside enables walking, cycling and so on	Could be less fit as there are fewer open spaces or these may be more difficult to reach
May be more economically aware as money is needed to reach urban areas for shopping, leisure activities and so on	May be able to spend more money on wants as travelling costs do not have to be taken into account

CASE STUDY   Herbie

Herbie, who is 13 years old, lives in an urban area where there are very few green spaces and not a lot to do. In the evenings and weekends he hangs around with some older boys who are not interested in improving their lives as no one seems to encourage them or really take an interest in them.

The group go round the estate where they live using bad language, shouting names at people and bullying individuals into giving them money, which they spend on alcohol.

Sometimes, when they have drunk a lot of alcohol, they go round the estate pulling the mirrors off cars and letting down tyres.

1. What factors are influencing Herbie's development?

2. Explain how one factor could link with another and how they could affect Herbie's development. Use theory to help explain your answer.

3. Discuss your answers as a whole group.

CASE STUDY   Elaine and family

Elaine is a lone parent with three children, Olivia, aged one, Rebekh, aged four, and Benjamin, aged six. They live in an upstairs flat in an old house with no access to the garden. The flat has been badly converted, has poor heating and the windows don't fit properly. The cooker is not working as only one ring heats and the oven tends to burn food if put on the recommended temperature, so the family often eat takeaway food.

The house is on a busy road, and the nearest play area is some distance away. Elaine has put up with these conditions for a long time because she has no alternative solution and has become frustrated, angry and depressed. The children are boisterous and she is always yelling and shouting at them. Sometimes she hits them. Benjamin has missed a lot of school through illness. When he goes, his teacher often complains that he is unable to concentrate.

1. Think about Elaine. How is her physical, intellectual, emotional and social development being affected by the environment her family lives in?

2. What would be the advantages and disadvantages to Elaine and the family if they lived in a rural area?

3. How might Benjamin's development be affected if he is being physically punished?

4. How is Olivia's development likely to be affected by the living conditions?

5. Suggest ways in which the family could have support to help them in their present living conditions.

Good quality housing will usually have a positive effect on people and poor quality housing is more likely to have a negative effect. For instance, a high-rise flat may suit a single person, a couple/partners without children or adults who do not want a garden. It would not be suitable for a single parent, two people with young children or for older people who could find access difficult.

Inadequate housing is a good example of how the risk factors are closely linked together. Individuals who live in poverty are almost certainly living in housing that is unhealthy, badly heated, too small for their needs and possibly unsafe.

The charity Shelter tries to campaign to improve the living conditions for millions of people in the UK. They have found that children who live in overcrowded and damp housing are:

- at higher risk of viral or bacterial infections, including meningitis
- at greater risk of tuberculosis and respiratory problems, including wheezing and asthma
- more likely to suffer mental health problems.

The British Medical Association, which represents doctors, found that children who live in temporary housing such as bed and breakfast accommodation have increased risk of:

- behavioural problems
- stress
- poor sleep
- infections
- gastric (stomach) problems.

▶ Poor housing can have long-term health effects according to Shelter.

Group Activity

Ask your tutor if it is possible to get a visit from a Shelter representative.

CASE STUDY

Real life case study from Shelter: 'Amanda's story'

'When I was 16 I found that my mother's alcoholism was too unbearable to be around. She was constantly asking me to leave the house, slapping me and getting rid of my belongings. Eventually she threw me out for good and I went to stay on my friend's bedroom floor for 11 months. My friend lived there with her three siblings and her parents, so eventually I had to move to a local homeless youth hostel. It was a dangerous place to live and I found it quite hard to manage my college work. Eventually my college raised funds to help me move into a small bed-sit. It was quite a dangerous area and after being a victim of violent crime, I had to move out and stay with another friend's family. Eventually a Connexions personal advisor helped me to get a job and to move to a different area.'

1   Discuss, with other members of your group, the risks to Amanda's physical, intellectual, social and emotional development of having no permanent, safe accommodation.

How can pollution affect development?

Group Activity

Carry out research to find out more about radiation and the illnesses and conditions it can cause.

There are three types of pollution that can affect development that people are most concerned about. These are:

Chemicals

Noise

Radiation

Chemicals

There are strict laws about the use of chemicals. Agriculture uses large quantities of fertilizers and pesticides, and some of these are washed by rain into the water supply. Some may remain on the food we eat, which is why it is sensible to wash fruit and vegetables. Some people eat organic foods to avoid these chemicals.

A form of pollution that affects a lot of people is the exhaust emissions from cars, buses and lorries. Engines release chemicals and tiny particles that cause respiratory problems. People who live in built up areas where there is a lot of traffic will be most affected.

   How can chemicals harm us?

Radiation

Radiation can affect development if it should leak from a nuclear power station so that people who live nearby or who are working within the building are affected by it. There are strict rules that govern the building and maintenance of such power stations. Leukaemia is one illness that results.

Noise

Noise is not often thought of as a type of pollution, but it can be very harmful. Exposure to loud noise can cause deafness, and there are laws about how much noise a person can be exposed to in the workplace. Noise is produced by industry, transport and people going about their everyday lives. People who live near airports often complain about the noise of aircraft taking off. Busy roads and railway lines can also be very noisy for people who live near them.

Noise can be caused by inconsiderate neighbours playing loud music or having late-night parties. People may be particularly harmed by noise in their homes. It causes stress and may prevent them sleeping properly.

 8 Why can noise be harmful?

PSYCHOLOGICAL FACTORS
Stress

Many individuals suffer from stress for a number of reasons:

- financial worries
- pressure at work
- relationship problems
- unemployment.

It is well known that stress can cause immune system changes that make a person more prone to infections and other illnesses. There is now evidence that parents with stressful lives may be making their children, as well as themselves, vulnerable to illness. A University of Rochester study found sickness levels were higher in children of anxious or depressed parents. Long-term stress related illnesses include:

- heart attacks
- ulcers
- depression
- stomach and bowel disorders.

- strokes
- anxiety
- high blood pressure

As well as causing health problems, it is estimated that one in five workers suffers from stress at some time in their life and it costs industry an estimated £3.7 billion each year through stress-related absence from work (source: www.amian.co.uk).

If the individual in your health plan is in a stressful job then you will need to try and assess the level of stress and put forward recommendations for reducing this stress. This could include looking at the work–life balance, which will be considered later in this unit.

Other factors such as family, friends and partners have already been dealt with in Unit 1. Look back at pages 38–40 and remind yourself what was included in these topics.

HEALTH MONITORING AND ILLNESS PREVENTION SERVICES
Screening and vaccination

Preventing disease is a way of helping individuals to stay healthy for longer. Some diseases are not always visible and can be difficult to detect. It is possible for a person to have a disease and not know that they have got it. Diseases like tuberculosis may not show any symptoms for up to six months. For this reason, many different methods of **detection** and prevention have been developed.

Health care professionals can use tests such as chest x-rays and blood tests to help detect illness

> **...WORD CHECK**
> **detection** – the act of detecting; the laying open what was concealed or hidden; discovery.

and disease. These will show any changes in the person caused by the disease. The x-ray will provide a visible picture of any infection in the chest. The blood test may show chemical changes in the body. Where these tests are done on a large scale, they are known as **screening programmes**. Screening allows doctors to examine many people and to select those that need treatment because a disease has been found.

Screening can include:

- breast screening
- chest x-rays
- cervical smear tests
- blood tests.

These tests are all done for the purpose of finding out if a problem exists.

9 Why do we need to test people for diseases?

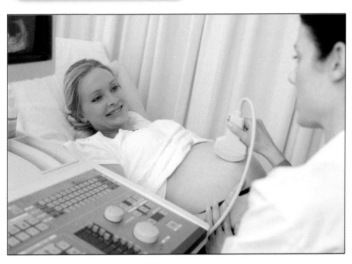

▲ Checking that the baby is healthy.

The government currently runs **vaccination** programmes. This is where people who have a high risk of catching certain illnesses can have medical help to prevent them from catching the disease. Some diseases are so dangerous that a method had to be found to prevent them from occurring. This is often done by giving vaccinations through an injection.

Vaccination programmes have been running in the UK for over 50 years. The killer disease called smallpox was totally **eradicated** by vaccinating everyone to prevent it. More recently, vaccinations against measles, mumps and rubella (MMR) and influenza (flu) have become available. These have been introduced because these diseases can be killers of children and older adults.

10 Why do we vaccinate small children?

CASE STUDY   Jana

Jana is 25 years old. She has always lived in a rural area on the outskirts of a small market town. She has one older brother and a younger sister. Jana's father is the manager of a small company and her mother works part time at the local infant school.

When she was small, Jana went to nursery school and made friends with children who lived in the area. As she grew up she joined a gymnastic club and an athletics group. The equipment needed was quite expensive but her parents bought it so that Jana could learn the skills needed to achieve.

Jana also had a laptop as a present for one of her birthdays, so she was able to look things up on the Internet as well as chat to her friends. Her father used to spend time teaching her how to use the computer. She enjoyed these occasions and was able to use her skills in the schoolwork she was doing.

Jana went to college after she finished school and followed a computer course. Now she has a job working with computers and still meets her friends for a pub meal or for leisure activities. They all talk a lot together and listen to each other's problems.

1 What factors have influenced Jana's development?

2 Explain how one factor could link with another and how they could affect Jana's development. Use theory to help explain your answer.

3 Discuss your answers as a whole group.

ACTIVITY   Vaccinations and screening

1. Helen is expecting her first child. Carry out research to find out which tests Helen could have to make sure that her unborn child is not going to be born with a health problem.

2. Produce a leaflet or a handout that gives Helen information and advice about vaccinations available for young children. Explain why screening tests are important.

3. Explain how health monitoring and vaccinations could contribute positively to an individual's development.

▶ ▶ ▶ ▶   ASSESSMENT PRACTICE: PREPARATION

For the individual chosen for the previous Assessment Practices:

1. Select factors that have positively affected the development of the individual. Include at least **three** factors. Describe each factor chosen.

2. Analyse how each factor has positively affected the health and well-being of the individual, using theory to help explain the positive effects.

3. Explain how the factors have inter-related (worked together) to positively affect the health and well-being of the individual.

Remember

- update the bibliography
- make sure your plan has covered all of the topics above and includes dates, actions and reasons for the actions taken.

Indicators of physical health

▶ Getting started

You will gain an understanding of:

a indicators used by health practitioners to assess health and well-being

b how these indicators are used as health assessment measures, such as:
  i   blood pressure
  ii   peak flow
  iii body mass index
  iv hip/waist ratio
  v   body fat composition
  vi cholesterol levels
  vii blood glucose tests
  viii liver function tests
  ix resting pulse and recovery pulse rates after exercise

c how to present conclusions from health and well-being assessments and make reasoned judgements

d how results of assessments will be used to develop realistic health improvement plans for an individual or group of individuals.

INDICATORS OF PHYSICAL HEALTH

...WORD CHECK

SI units – scientific units of measurement, for example, kilograms, kilojoules.

physical – relating to the body as distinguished from the mind or spirit.

physiological – actions or events relating to body function and chemical processes.

range – a differing collection of results.

functions – different activities.

There are a variety of factors that influence an individual's health and well-being, which means there must be a variety of ways to measure health. When visiting the health clinic, GP or hospital, there are a range of tests available to measure health. It is not only professionals that can measure. Anyone can monitor their own health but some are best done by professional care workers.

When health workers carry out these tasks, they refer to them as clinical tests. When carrying out such tests they use conventional **SI units** to calculate results. Health professionals will take **physical** and **physiological** measurements. The word physical indicates basic measurements like weight and temperature.

Physical health is often measured using charts. These can be graphs or tables that provide information. Various types of chart have been produced over the years by the different health care professions. Their purpose is to show the **range** of normal readings, which helps highlight abnormal readings when they occur. These include body mass index and height-weight charts. They measure an individual and then compare the measurement to the measurement that is commonly considered to be the 'norm' across the population. One of the best examples of this is a height-weight ratio chart. This compares the height of a person against their weight. This chart can be used by both health care professionals and ourselves to monitor whether people are the correct weight for their height.

Physiological measurements show how the body **functions** and measures these functions. Examples of this are blood pressure and peak flow, which will be looked at later on.

Blood pressure

Blood pressure is made up of more than one measurement. It will vary in different people due to age, weight or illness.

Blood pressure is the measurable force in the vessels that is created when the heart pumps blood around the body. The two letters BP are often used to represent blood pressure. Two measurements are taken to measure blood pressure. They are known as the **systolic** pressure and the **diastolic** pressure.

The force of the blood pumping out of the heart creates the systolic pressure. The diastolic pressure is a measurement of the continuous pressure put upon the arteries as the heart relaxes.

To measure these pressures a **sphygmomanometer** is used. It is easier to say, 'sphyg' for short.

A sphygmomanometer consists of an inflatable rubber cuff that is wrapped around the upper arm. This is connected by two tubes to a pressure gauge that has a column of mercury. There are also new sphygmomanometers with digital displays. These are often referred to as **digital osimeters**.

With a **stethoscope** the operator listens to the brachial artery in the bend of the elbow. The cuff is then pumped up until the operator can no longer hear the pulse. At this point the pressure outside equals the pressure of blood inside the artery and this is the systolic pressure. The cuff is then slowly released and the column of mercury begins to fall and the pulse returns. As the sound of the last beat disappears the operator looks at the column of mercury or display; they now take a reading. This gives them the second reading, the diastolic pressure. Electronic blood pressure meters take the pressures in a similar way but automatically.

It must be remembered that blood pressure should only be taken by a trained person. If it is done incorrectly it can be painful and sometimes dangerous.

The average blood pressure of a young fit person is expected to be in the region of:

120/80 (120 = systolic, 80 = diastolic).

Doctors take into account factors that include height, weight and age when diagnosing high blood pressure. Stress can also cause blood pressure to rise. If an individual's systolic pressure is higher than 160 and/or their diastolic is over 100, then they are clinically at risk from high blood pressure. This is also known as **hypertension**. Persistent high blood pressure can lead to problems such as a **stroke (cerebro-vascular incident)**. This is when a small blood vessel in the brain bursts. This causes damage to that area of the brain. If this happens, a person can lose the ability to speak and move. A stroke can sometimes cause death.

11 What does a sphygmomanometer measure? Describe how to take a person's blood pressure.

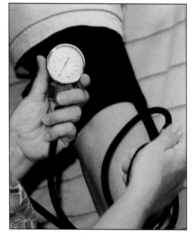

▲ A sphygmomanometer is used to measure blood pressure.

✔ ...WORD CHECK

systolic – the force created in blood pressure.

diastolic – the rhythmical expansion or dilatation of the heart and arteries.

sphygmomanometer – a device for measuring blood pressure that is strapped to the arm.

digital osimeters – a digital blood pressure measuring device.

stethoscope – an acoustic device for listening to a person's breathing.

hypertension – high blood pressure.

stroke (cerebro-vascular incident) – a blood clot or a burst blood vessel in the brain.

average respiration – the normal rate at which a person breathes.

Peak flow

The body is made up from cells, which all need oxygen to function. The blood absorbs oxygen in the lungs during the action of breathing. At rest, breathing is usually at a rate of 15–20 breaths in every minute. This is the **average respiration** rate. As activity increases, so does respiration rate. This is because activity in the body uses up extra oxygen, so you have to breathe faster to replace it.

Illness and disease can also affect respiration rate. Asthma causes a reduction in air flow to the little air sacs (alveoli) in the lungs. This will reduce the amount of air getting in and reduce the amount of oxygen being absorbed. It then causes an increase in the rate of respiration. The

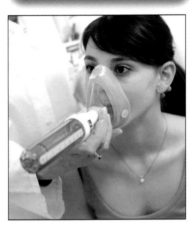

▲ Measuring breathing rate with a peak flow meter.

wheeze that can be heard when a person has a chest infection is the air being forced along narrowed airways.

These air sacs (alveoli) can also become too big because of a disease known as emphysema. This is not an advantage because the surface area that absorbs the oxygen decreases as they become bigger. This is because bigger air sacs take up more space, so there are less of them. This causes continuous gasping for air and often the only solution is an oxygen mask or nasal cannula.

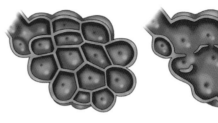

▲ Normal alveoli.   ▲ Dilated alveoli.

Watching someone breathe will only give basic information. To be more accurate, the measurement of the amount of air breathed out and force by which it happens is required. This can be done by using a **peak flow meter**.

This simple machine measures the maximum rate at which a person blows out (expels) air from the lungs in one second. To do this, they just breathe out hard into the peak flow meter. The scale on the side will give the reading in millilitres per second. This can be compared to a table of expected scores.

People with chronic lung disease or bad asthma will normally score below 350, whereas a fit person will score in the region of 500–600 on the scale. Very fit athletes can almost blow the needle off the scale.

CASE STUDY   Brad

Brad has smoked a lot since he was 15 years old and he is now 35. He is having difficulty breathing, particularly when he tries to walk anywhere. As a result he takes little exercise. He is still able to work part time as he is a telephone operator, which means he is sitting down. Brad visits his GP for some advice.

The GP advises Brad that he urgently needs to stop smoking and to adapt his lifestyle. The GP also takes some health measurements so that he can help Brad in more detail.

1   The GP does a peak flow test for Brad. Explain how this would be done and the results it would show.

2   The GP is interested to know what Brad's blood pressure is. Explain how the GP would take Brad's blood pressure and how it would be calculated.

3   What is the norm for blood pressure? How are norms calculated?

Body mass index

The relationships between height and weight can be a good indicator of the state of an adult's health. As a rule, a person's weight should be **proportional** to their height. By looking at the whole population, scientists have worked out the weight a person should be for their height. A person will be considered to be obese when their weight is 20 per cent or more above the average weight for people of the same height. To make this as accurate as possible, scientists base this on individuals with similar personal and cultural characteristics. From this, they have produced a general chart that gives a range of comparisons of height against weight.

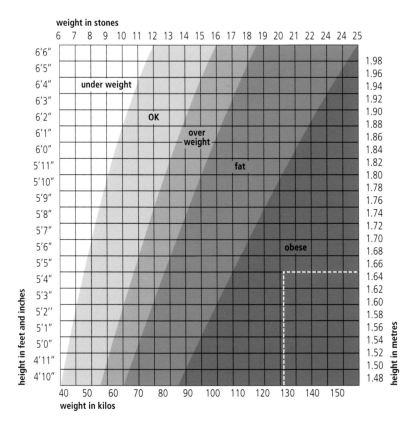

◀ A height–weight chart.

The chart provides us with information about categories that go from underweight to obese. By reading the two measurements (height and weight) for the person from the chart and looking at the point where the two meet, it is possible to see exactly what 'category' a person will fit, for example, obese.

ACTIVITY   Weighing and measuring

1 Weigh and measure **four** other people who have given you their permission. Plot the measurements on the chart provided. What 'categories' do they fall into?

2 How can knowing the height and weight measurements help when working out a health plan for a person?

3 Use the height and weight of a famous person who is overweight and draw up a diet plan for one day for this person.

It has to remembered that this is a **generalized** system and this does not always provide an accurate result.

Let us think about an Olympic weightlifter weighing in at 100kg and 1.80m. Our chart would make him fat. He needs to be muscular for the work he is doing and this makes him heavy. So there are **exceptions**, this means that we cannot use a single method in **isolation**, as it can be inaccurate.

Height and weight are also used to calculate body mass index (BMI). When looking at the height–weight chart, the weightlifter appears to be fat. How does he measure up using the BMI test? A BMI is a straightforward calculation that will give an index number. Again, scientists have worked out, by using statistics, what the healthy normal range is.

The calculation looks like this.

$$BMI = \frac{\text{body weight (kg)}}{\text{height (m}^2)}$$

In the weightlifter's case he still does not fit into the scientists' category of 'normal', even though he is a picture of health.

12 ▶ Work out the weightlifter's BMI.

For a weightlifter the balance of his body tissues is different to that of the average man in the street. He has very little body fat and much more muscle than normal.

With his weight being 100kg and his height being 1.80m, the calculation will look like this.

$$BMI = \frac{100 \text{ (kg)}}{1.80 \text{ (m}^2)} = 30.9$$

His index number of 30.9 is above the normal range of 20–24 for men (19–24 for women). Having a number over 30 puts him in the obese range, which is obviously incorrect.

His body is made up of more muscle than fat, which has confused the calculation. This is because most people do not normally have such a large amount of muscle tissue.

For most people this system works well. This is because the extra weight that is carried by many people is usually fat. The super-fit weightlifter is an exception.

ACTIVITY — Calculating BMI

1 Try calculating your own BMI and compare the results with the table below:

Weight group	BMI (kg/m²)	Obesity class
Underweight	<18.5	
Normal	18.5–24.9	
Overweight	25.0–29.9	
Obesity	30.0–34.9	I
	35.0–39.9	II
Extreme obesity	40.0+	III

2 Now try calculating the BMI for another person in the group.

3 Explain how knowing a person's BMI would help the development of a plan of exercise for a person.

Hip/waist ratio

Hip/waist or waist to hip ratio is one of the predictors of risk for heart disease and diabetes. So what does their shape say about that person? Waist-to-hip ratio (WHR) is the ratio of the circumference of the waist to that of the hips. It is calculated by measuring the waist circumference (located just above the upper hip bone at the joint). That measurement is then divided by the hip circumference at its widest part (waist). WHR has been found to be a more efficient predictor of mortality in older people but is not considered totally accurate when used on its own.

Are you an apple or a pear?

To determine if the person has a healthy waist to hip ratio, use a measuring tape to measure the circumference of their hips at the widest part of their buttocks. Then measure their waist at the smaller circumference of their natural waist, usually just above the belly button.

To determine the ratio, divide their waist measurement by their hip measurement.

For a female, a waist measurement of 75cm (30 inches) divided by a hip measurement of 90cm (36 inches) equals a WHR of 0.83.

This appears to indicate that they are close to being at an increased risk for heart disease and diabetes.

However:

Waist measurement of 70cm (28 inches) divided by hip measurement of 90cm (36 inches) equals a WHR of 0.77.

This appears to be within a healthy range.

A ratio of more than 0.95 for men and 0.85 for women may mean they have a predisposition to heart disease, and should be extra careful with their diet and lifestyle.

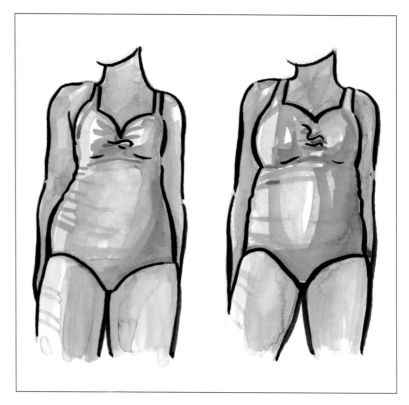

Research shows that people with 'apple-shaped' bodies (with more weight around the waist) face more health risks than those with 'pear-shaped' bodies, who carry more weight around the hips. It's all related to the distribution of fat in the body. 'Apple-shaped' people predominantly store fat in the abdominal area and are more likely to have health-related risks than those who are 'pear-shaped'.

ACTIVITY   Calculating waist to hip ratio

1   Try calculating your own WHR and compare it to the guideline previously mentioned.

2   Now try calculating the WHR for another person in the group.

3   Explain how knowing a person's WHR would help in developing a plan of exercise and diet changes for a person.

Body fat composition

A person's total body fat percentage is the total weight of the person's fat divided by the person's weight, and reflects both essential fat and storage fat. Essential fat is that amount necessary for maintenance of life and reproductive functions. The fat percentage for women is greater than that for men, due to the demands of childbearing and other hormonal functions. Essential fat is 2–5 per cent in men, and 10–13 per cent in women. Storage fat consists of fat accumulation in adipose tissue, part of which protects internal organs in the chest and abdomen.

Some body fat percentage levels are more culturally valued than others, and some are related to better health or improved athletic performance. Ideal percentages are also based on age categories as well.

...WORD CHECK

predisposition – when an event is more likely to happen to a person.

adipose tissue – tissue used for the storage of fat.

Body fat percentage is categorized as follows:

Description	Women	Men
Recommended amount	20–25%	8–14%
Adult average	22–25%	15–19%
Obese	30%+	25%+

Categorized ranges of body fat percentages as follows:

Description	Women	Men
Essential fat	12–15%	2–5%
Athletes	16–20%	6–13%
Fitness	21–24%	14–17%
Acceptable	25–31%	18–25%
Obese	32%+	25%+

▲ Body fat calipers measure skinfolds to assess body fat.

Note that the essential fat values in the chart above are lower than the recommended minimum body fat percentage levels. A small amount of storage fat is required to be available as fuel for the body in times of need. It is unclear whether falling in a particular category of these body fat percentages is better for one's health than any other.

Cholesterol levels

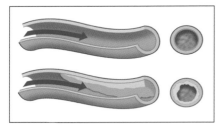

▲ High levels of cholesterol in the blood can lead to fatty deposits in the arteries, which can cause strokes or heart attacks.

Cholesterol forms part of the outer membrane that surrounds every cell. It is used to insulate nerve fibres (and so make nerve signals travel properly) and make hormones, which carry chemical signals around the body.

Without cholesterol, your body wouldn't work and it is vital to ensure the body's normal function. Too much cholesterol in the blood, however, increases the risk of coronary heart disease and disease of the arteries (see diagram).

One of the biggest misconceptions people have is that food is packed with cholesterol. In fact, very little cholesterol is found in foods. The main culprits are eggs, offal and shellfish. What is important is the type of fat in the food you choose, especially saturated fat. Once inside the body, the liver turns this fat into cholesterol.

Knowing your cholesterol level isn't, on its own, enough to tell you your personal risk of heart disease. You also need to know about lipoproteins. These are special molecules that carry or transport cholesterol around the body.

There are two main types:

- Low-density lipoprotein (LDL), often known as bad cholesterol, carries cholesterol from the liver to the cells. If supply exceeds demand, it can cause a harmful build-up of cholesterol.
- High-density lipoprotein (HDL), or good cholesterol, takes cholesterol away from the cells and back to the liver where it's either broken down or excreted.

The greatest danger is when someone has high levels of LDL cholesterol and low levels of HDL cholesterol. High levels of cholesterol in the blood can lead to fatty deposits in the arteries, which can cause stroke or heart attacks.

The average total cholesterol level in the UK is 5.5 millimoles per litre (mmol/l) for men and 5.6mmol/l for women, which is above a normal level. To decide whether an individual's cholesterol levels are dangerous, the levels need to be considered in light of the person's overall risk of heart disease.

This overall risk is determined by a combination of factors, including age, gender and family history of heart disease. Also, whether someone smokes, is overweight, or has high blood pressure or diabetes can affect their risk. The higher the risk of heart disease (for example, a male smoker with high blood pressure and diabetes), the greater the need to get cholesterol levels down.

But what constitutes a healthy cholesterol level is controversial, even among doctors. So the National Institute for Health and Clinical Excellence (NICE) and the Department of Health have produced cholesterol guidelines for doctors to follow. They say that a person's cholesterol should be:

- total cholesterol – less than 5.0mmol/l
- LDL cholesterol – less than 3.0mmol/l.

However, the Joint British Societies (a group of the main UK expert societies involved in cardiovascular disease) recommend different cholesterol limits for people who have, or are at risk of, coronary heart disease:

- total cholesterol – less than 4.0mmol/l
- LDL cholesterol – less than 2.0mmol/l.

These guidelines match the more stringent recommendations used in Europe. NICE is currently reviewing its national policy guidelines.

Many believe the lower the cholesterol level, the better in terms of preventing heart disease. One in 500 people has high cholesterol because of an inherited problem, called familial hyperlipidaemia. The first steps in treating high cholesterol levels are:

- regular physical activity
- healthy eating.

Also cutting down on fats and eating foods that may help to lower cholesterol levels can help. These include:

- garlic
- soya
- oats
- corn
- selenium-enriched cereals.

Blood glucose tests

Blood sugar concentration, or glucose level, is tightly regulated in the human body. Normally, the blood glucose level is maintained at between about 4 and 6mmol/l. The normal blood glucose level is about 90mg/100ml, which works out to 5mmol/l. Glucose levels rise by a few grams for an hour or two after meals and are usually lowest in the morning, before the first meal of the day.

Diabetes occurs because the body can't use glucose properly, either owing to a lack of the hormone insulin, or because the insulin available doesn't work effectively.

According to the charity Diabetes UK, more than 2 million people in the UK have the condition, and up to 750,000 more are believed to have it without realizing they do.

Different types of diabetes are:

- Type 1, where the body is unable to produce any insulin. This usually starts in childhood or adolescence.
- Type 2, where not enough insulin is produced or the insulin that is made by the body doesn't work properly. This tends to affect people as they get older, and usually appears after the age of 40. Refer to page 177 for more information on these different types of diabetes.

Normal blood sugar control

The body converts glucose from food into energy. Glucose comes ready-made in sweet foods such as sweets and cakes, or from starchy foods such as potatoes, pasta or bread once they're digested. The liver is also able to manufacture glucose.

Under normal circumstances, the hormone insulin, which is made by the pancreas, carefully regulates how much glucose is in the blood. Insulin stimulates cells to absorb enough glucose from the blood for the energy, or fuel, that they need. Insulin also stimulates the liver to absorb and store any glucose that's left over.

After a meal, the amount of glucose in the blood rises, and this triggers the release of insulin. When blood glucose levels fall, during exercise, for example, insulin levels fall too.

A second hormone manufactured by the pancreas is called glucagon. It stimulates the liver to release glucose when it's needed, and this raises the level of glucose in the blood.

Types of glucose test

For blood testing, a syringe with a fine needle is used to remove a small amount of blood from a vein in your arm. It will then be sent to a laboratory to be tested. Blood sugar tests measure how well your body processes sugar (glucose). Some blood sugar tests are used to diagnose prediabetes or diabetes. Others determine how well you are managing your diabetes.

▲ Patient having a blood test.

Fasting blood sugar test

Measures the amount of sugar (glucose) in the blood after you fast for at least eight hours or overnight. A normal range is 70 to 100 milligrams of glucose per decilitre of blood (mg/dl) or 3.9 to 5.6 millimoles per litre (mmol/l). A level of 100 to 125mg/dl (5.6 to 6.9mmol/l) indicates impaired fasting glucose and is commonly known as prediabetes. To confirm the diagnosis, the doctor may repeat the fasting blood sugar test several days to a week later.

Random blood sugar test

Measures the blood sugar at any point in time, not necessarily a certain amount of time after a meal. A normal random blood sugar level hasn't been clearly defined but even if the person has recently eaten, their blood sugar level shouldn't be higher than 200mg/dl (11.1mmol/l).

Oral glucose tolerance test

An oral glucose tolerance test measures the body's response to sugar. First the fasting blood sugar level is measured. Then:

- the person drinks a sugary solution
- their blood sugar level is measured after one hour and again after two hours.

If their blood sugar level rises more than expected – to 200mg/dl (11.1mmol/l) or more – they may have diabetes. A modified version of the oral glucose tolerance test, known as a glucose challenge test, is often used to screen pregnant women for gestational diabetes.

Liver function tests

As the liver performs its various functions, it makes a number of chemicals that pass into the bloodstream and bile. Various liver disorders alter the blood levels of these chemicals. Some of these can be measured in a blood sample. Certain liver dysfunctions can be caused by excessive consumption of the following:

- alcoholic drinks
- fatty food
- recreational drugs.

A blood sample can be taken by your GP or a nurse at a local clinic, or by hospital staff. It will then be sent to a laboratory to be tested. The laboratory provides a 'normal value' or 'reference value' to the test, which shows the doctor, nurse or specialist whether your test is within the normal range. Abnormal functions are shown by how much they are below or above the normal range.

So what are liver function tests used for?

- To help diagnose liver disorders if you have suggestive symptoms (such as jaundice). The pattern of the blood results may help to say which disorder is causing the problem. For example, depending on which enzyme is highest, it may point to a particular disorder.
- To monitor the activity and severity of liver disorders, for example, alcohol poisoning (cirrhosis).
- As a routine precaution after starting certain medicines, to check that they are not causing liver damage as a side-effect.

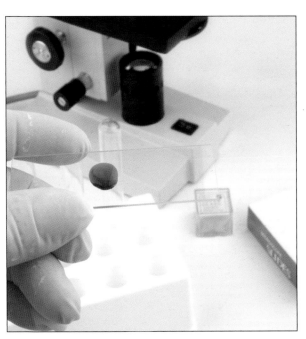

▲ Lab staff testing blood.

Some tests that are commonly done on a blood sample are called 'LFTs' (liver function tests). Usually the liver function test gives an indication of how much the liver is inflamed and possibly either damaged or changed in its ability to work properly. Different diseases of the liver will cause different types of damage and will affect liver function tests accordingly. It is possible to suggest which disease may be present from a liver function test but these tests are not the conclusive way of diagnosing liver disease. They are helpful, but only show part of the picture. They are also useful for monitoring someone with liver disease, but are not always accurate. Other tests, such as a liver biopsy, ultrasound scan, other types of scan and so on, may be needed to clarify the cause of a liver disorder and/or to monitor its progress.

Resting pulse rates and recovery pulse rates after exercise

Pulse and respiration can provide important information, as these can give a good overview of a person's health and fitness. A person's pulse can be felt at many different points on their body, for example, the wrist and neck.

When nurses and doctors are observed taking a patient's pulse, they usually press on the patient's wrist or neck to get the reading. What they are actually doing is pressing a blood vessel, called an artery, against something solid like a muscle or bone. The carotid artery in the neck and the radial artery in the wrist are commonly used. The force of the heart pumping blood around the arteries can be felt as a pulsing sensation. This is measured in 'beats per minute' and the only equipment needed is a watch with a second hand.

ACTIVITY   Taking your pulse

Try taking your own pulse:

1 Place your first and second finger of your right hand on the edge of your left wrist just below your left thumb (see picture).

2 Press gently until you feel the artery begin to pulse.

You are now feeling the force of the blood being pumped around the body. People who are very fit can have a slow pulse with a strong force when resting. People who are less fit may have a faster pulse when resting.

Trick of the trade

To save time, they don't measure your pulse for one minute. This is because the heart has a very regular beat. So they measure it for 15 seconds and then multiply the number by four. This is how professionals take pulse measurements. This is what can be found:

Pulse is 18 beats in 15 seconds; now multiply both by 4.

18 beats x 4 = 72 and 15 seconds x 4 = 60 seconds (one minute).

This gives 72 beats per minute.

This is an accurate way of measuring pulse. Now try this method on another person.

ACTIVITY   Taking a pulse measurement – short method

1 Measure a person's pulse for 15 seconds at the point of the wrist. Calculate what the pulse will be for one minute.

2 Now measure their pulse over one minute; compare the two results. Are there any differences? If the difference is within five beats, the reading is reasonably accurate.

3 How would a pulse measurement be used to help plan an exercise programme for a person?

By using this method, 45 seconds are saved. This may not sound a lot but if a nurse has to check a whole ward of patients, the saving soon mounts up. The average adult pulse rate while they are resting is between 70 and 80 beats per minute. If an adult is very fit, it can be as low as 60 beats per minute. A newborn baby's pulse rate can be anything from 120 to as high as 180 beats per minute.

During exercise a person's pulse rate increases; it then returns to normal when at rest. Other events will also cause a pulse rate to increase. For example, when people are afraid, the brain orders an increase in a chemical called adrenalin. This increases the heart rate, which delivers more blood to your body to allow the person to act more quickly or run from danger. When the danger is over, the brain orders noradrenaline to be released, this slows the heart down again.

Pulse rate can also be affected by heart disease and lung disease, which can reduce the oxygen in the blood. An increase in the rate can occur because the body is not getting enough oxygen. The brain will sense this and cause the heart to pump the oxygen-containing blood around the body much faster.

The time it takes for the pulse rate to return to normal is known as the **recovery rate**. It will vary between different people and is related to how fit they are. The fitter they are, the shorter the recovery time. Recovery time can be improved by regular exercise. The fitter a person is the better it becomes.

✅ **...WORD CHECK**

recovery rate – the time it takes for the pulse rate to return to normal after exercise.

ACTIVITY   **Recovery rate exercise**

1. Get someone in the group to take your pulse and the number of breaths you take in for one minute while you are resting. Write them down so that the readings are not forgotten.

2. Exercise for one minute, for example, walk up and down stairs quickly.

3. Get your partner to check your pulse and number of breaths again immediately after finishing the exercise. Write down the results.

4. Now check your pulse every minute until your pulse rate returns to the resting rate.

5. Record your results on a table that looks like this:

	Pulse beats/min	Breaths	Recovery rate
Before exercise	84	15	
Exercise finished	120	30	Time starts here
One minute	110	25	
Two minutes	95	20	
Five minutes	84	15	Time stops here 5 mins

HOW TO PRESENT CONCLUSIONS FROM HEALTH AND WELL-BEING ASSESSMENTS AND MAKE REASONED JUDGEMENTS

There are many different ways of presenting data. These include:

- charts
- graphs.

Charts

The two most popular charts used for presenting information are:

- bar charts
- pie charts.

Bar charts

Bar charts are a popular choice for presenting simple data, as they are easy to draw and to understand. Bar charts can be used as an alternative to pie charts for displaying percentages or whole numbers, where there are too many groups for a pie chart. They are especially useful when you have a lot of categories to display.

▸ Example of bar chart for an individual's blood pressure.

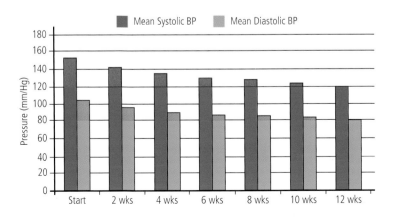

When presenting information in a bar chart, ensure:

- the chart has an appropriate title
- the bars should be the same width
- the vertical axis is clearly labelled
- the units of measure must be identified.

Pie charts

A pie chart is a circular chart, which resembles a pie that has been cut into slices. Each slice represents a proportion/percentage of the whole.

When presenting a pie chart, remember to have:

- a clear appropriate title
- each slice labelled
- each slice shaded/coloured to differentiate.

Pie charts are best avoided when there are less than three or more than nine categories of data to display.

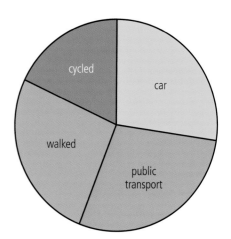

▲ Example of a pie chart showing the method of transport used to travel to school for a Year 10 class.

Graphs

Line graphs are a good way of showing trends, especially over time, for example, temperature and pulse. They are the most popular type of chart when the researcher has a lot of data to display. Although more than one line may be displayed, it is important to avoid having too many different lines on the graph, as it can be messy and difficult to read.

When presenting line graphs, remember to have:

- a clear appropriate title
- vertical and horizontal axes clearly labelled
- units of measurements clearly indicated.

▼ Examples of line graphs for temperature and heart rate.

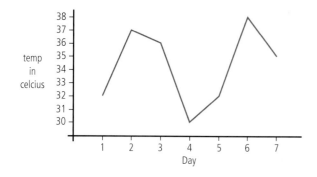

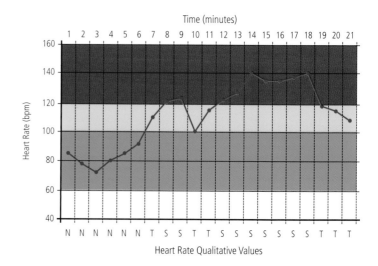

Making judgements

Making judgements about assessments involves:

- reflection – reviewing all areas of your assessments from the beginning of the planning stage to the end
- analysis – all aspects of your performance need to be examined in detail to find out what needs are a priority and which areas could be introduced at a later stage
- making informed decisions – this is using your understanding and knowledge to help make a judgement
- planning for improvement – how to build the plan so that the individual will be motivated to follow it and how support could be provided.

HOW RESULTS OF ASSESSMENTS WILL BE USED TO DEVELOP REALISTIC HEALTH IMPROVEMENT PLANS FOR AN INDIVIDUAL OR GROUP OF INDIVIDUALS

Taking physical measurements and making decisions about them are very important. The assessment must be accurate and the individual's current lifestyle must be taken into consideration before drawing up a plan. Their personal preferences must also be considered, as they are unlikely to succeed if they are asked to follow activities for which they have an extreme dislike. The format of the plan will also be of vital importance as if it is eye catching, it is more likely to motivate the individual.

The measurements taken and analysed will be the focus for developing the health and well-being plan. They cannot be considered by themselves, however. Cost will be an important factor to think about, as if the activities planned are too expensive, the individual will not be able to afford to participate.

The plan must be tailored to bring about change to the individual's lifestyle that will result in making future test results better. When short- and long-term targets are being reviewed, the physical assessments should show a positive improvement, for example, BMI should be nearer to the norm, and blood pressure should be nearer to the norm for the person's age, gender and lifestyle.

Both the person who is developing the health and well-being plan and the individual the plan is for must agree how best to make it effective and what should be included. They must decide, for example:

- Which measurements showed where a change is most needed?
- What are the long- and short-term targets?
- What do they hope to change through following the plan?
- When and how will the planner be able to re-assess the physical measurements in order to review the plan?
- What is the best way to achieve the desired outcome?

In other words, will the individual feel satisfied with the results of the plan and will the quality of their life be improved?

ASSESSMENT PRACTICE: PREPARATION

Practise your skills on the following case study.

Gina is 19 years of age and lives on her own. She has been unemployed since leaving college and has very low self-esteem as she thinks she is not wanted by anyone. When she first left college she applied for many jobs as a health care assistant but didn't get any of them, so she has now given up trying.

Gina sits on the settee all day watching TV and during the evenings she drinks several glasses of wine. Gina knows she has put on some weight as she has to use safety pins to do up her skirts and trousers.

Gina's friend Kim has talked to her and as a result Gina thinks she could benefit from a health plan to improve her health and well-being. She has given Kim permission to take the following measurements:

Height: 160cm   Weight: 68kg
BMI: 26.5   Waist to hip ratio: 0.86
Peak flow: 380   Blood pressure: 130/88
Resulting pulse rate: 78   Recovery rate: 24.5 mins

1. Analyse the findings, comparing Gina's measurements to the norms taking into account Gina's age, gender and lifestyle.

2. From the results, identify two physical needs to help Gina that are to be the focus of the health plan. Explain why you have chosen these needs for her.

3. Identify two targets that will meet Gina's needs for each measurement that is to be the focus of the health plan.

4. Present the results of the physical assessments and analyse them, drawing conclusions.

5. Describe the possible impact on Gina's health if she meets these targets.

Promoting and supporting health improvements

▸ Getting started

You will be assessed on your ability to:

a   apply knowledge and understanding about the factors affecting health and well-being and measures of health

b   design a health and well-being improvement plan for an individual or group of individuals. The plan will include:

  i   the assessment of present health status through the use of physical measures of health and well-being and the factors presently influencing health and well-being

  ii   use of appropriate health promotion materials to motivate and support people in improving health and well-being

  iii design of a health and well-being improvement plan

  iv   setting realistic short- and long-term targets

  v   assessment of the difficulties which may be experienced in implementing a health and well-being improvement plan

  vi   support available in the implementation of a health and well-being improvement plan.

UNDERSTANDING FACTORS AFFECTING HEALTH AND WELL-BEING

How can individuals be motivated and supported to improve their health? In this section you will learn about the need for realistic assessment, advice and the need for targets in planning for health and well-being. You will also consider how appropriate health promotion material can motivate and support an individual and how this can affect their level of target achievement.

Many people believe that:

- too many people suffer from poor health
- too many people are ill for much of their lives
- too many people die too young from illnesses that are preventable.

At the same time, many people realize the value of better health and already take exercise, eat properly, and don't smoke.

When trying to make a positive change in order to improve health and well-being, it is important to compare the individual's needs with what is considered to be good health and well-being. For example, when formulating diet plans, it is important to use physical measures of health such as height and weight ratios and food tables. Organizations such as 'The National Advisory Committee on Nutrition and Education' (NACNE) produce a comprehensive range of information that can assist in the management of improvements to people's health.

Health in Britain: The facts
- 1 in 5 adults is obese.
- 1 million children will be obese by 2012.
- 1 in 4 men and 1 in 6 women drink more alcohol than the recommended levels.
- The majority of adults do not do enough exercise.
- Only 1 in 4 eat the recommended five portions of fruit and vegetables a day.

This is why the government have introduced on 2 January 2009 a health and well-being campaign to reduce the number of people who are overweight or obese. As a nation we all need to be more aware of health issues.

DESIGNING A HEALTH AND WELL-BEING IMPROVEMENT PLAN

Group Activity

...GROUP ACTIVITY

Look back at the questionnaire you produced earlier in this unit to decide which factors the plan is going to cover and why. Try to choose at least three factors for the health plan.

When creating the health and well-being plan for an individual or group it is important that it is in a form that is usable by the person for whom it is intended. It is also important to be aware of the health risks that different groups of people are influenced by and how promotional material can be used to support them. You should also consider the factors that are currently influencing the health and well-being of the individual or group that you have chosen. You will already have examined these aspects in different parts of this unit. You will now have to decide which aspects of their health and well-being will be addressed in the health plan. For example, will it be:

- their diet?
- the amount of exercise they should take?
- their stress levels?
- the amount of intellectual stimulation they are getting?
- the relationships they are experiencing?
- the environment in which they live?
- any other factors?

Assessment of present health status

▲ A physical health assessment.

It is important to **assess** the person before the plan is designed. This is done to maintain the person's personal safety. There are a number of areas that need to be assessed including the activities that they already take part in. Ask them if you can measure their health. With their agreement, obtain the following measurements and information:

- height
- pulse rate
- respiration rate
- how often they exercise

- weight
- body mass index
- diet habits (what they eat and drink)
- type of exercise they do.

The information gathered earlier in this unit will help to show the current health status of the individual or group. You will have to determine which aspects of their health and well-being need attention and what activities, such as exercise and diet, they will be able to cope with.

There will also be other considerations to be made about the person before they start any plan. These will be done so that risk is kept to an absolute minimum. Before they take on any new sports or exercise, it is important to find out if they have a health problem or past injury. It is also important to ask if they:

- have been previously inactive
- are significantly overweight
- have a history of heart problems
- have a chronic medical condition, such as diabetes
- are over the age of 40.

By considering the above, **accessible** activities can be created that are achievable. This will have the added bonus of not **demotivating** the person. They will then be one step closer to achieving their goal.

Identifying the person's needs

When assessing an individual, everyone's needs are different. Many different factors will affect a person's abilities to take part in health improvement plans. The following factors should be taken into account:

- Age, diet and activity have to be suitable. Asking someone who is 70 to start cross-country running is neither safe nor suitable.

- Gender – many women do not have the physical strength that men have but they could easily have more **agility** than men.

- Physical condition – if an individual has not exercised for a long time, it will be necessary to start off safely; gentle exercise to start with, building up as the individual gets fitter.

- Health condition – care must be taken not to ask an individual to take part in health plans that might make their condition worse. If someone is recovering from illness, they may need their doctor's advice before starting on a health improvement plan.

- Social position – many people may not have the time or money to go to a gymnasium. The exercise part of a health plan need only take up a maximum of 30 minutes a day. Special equipment does not need to be purchased to get fit. A set of stairs may be enough. People often have to put their family commitments first. They should not be put under pressure to make unacceptable commitments.

> **...WORD CHECK**
>
> **agility** – the ability to move quickly and flexibly.
>
> **intervention** – stepping in to help.

ACTIVITY — The health visitor

Take the following measurements for an individual:

- BMI
- resting pulse and recovery rate after exercise
- hip/waist ratio.

Make an assessment of the individual's health and well-being using the results from these tests.

Using appropriate health promotion materials

Health promotion materials are important because they motivate people to act positively to reach their goal of improved levels of health and well-being. Everyone can play a key role in helping to maximize their potential for good health. It is important to help people understand the value of health and freedom from disease, and to understand the known causes of diseases, both physical and psychological. With this knowledge individuals can reduce the risk of certain diseases and develop a healthy lifestyle – health is a shared responsibility, involving prevention as well as treatment when things go wrong. Activities that promote health can either be passive or active. With passive strategies individuals obtain benefit through the **intervention** of others. Normally this is through government intervention, for example, the provision of services such as:

- monitoring of food and food outlets
- infection control in primary health care settings
- vaccination programmes and advice on parenting
- advice on alcohol consumption
- air quality
- advice on diet
- advice on smoking
- advice on safe sex.

By contrast, active strategies are those that individuals actively seek out and adopt for themselves, for example, regular exercise and keep-fit activities (either alone or as a group member), **cessation** of smoking, weight watching, stress reduction and of course keeping the mind active.

Health promotion material is available in a variety of different formats. This is to appeal to as many people in as many different ways as possible. As individual likes and dislikes can be **incorporated**, this means that the more methods used to pass on information, the greater the chance of success.

The importance of having good health has led to health promotion becoming a very active area. It is a good way of providing accurate and helpful information to large numbers of people. It has shown that health promotion can make a real difference to people's health and well-being.

We have probably all seen information from health promotion **campaigns**. These will have been on TV and radio, and in newspapers, magazines and pamphlets. These campaigns will have covered many topics from alcohol and smoking to exercise and obesity. Advertising the ways to achieve good health is all around us. It is found in health centres, leisure centres, schools, colleges and supermarkets.

Advertising is targeted at various groups of individuals, for example:

- smokers
- drinkers
- young people
- pregnant mothers
- the homeless
- older people.

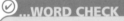

...WORD CHECK

cessation – to stop or to end.

incorporated – included in.

campaigns – political operations preceding an election.

There are other campaigns aimed at every age group. All campaigns are designed to appeal to the audience and to be eye catching. It often takes a great deal of money, expertise and effort to make them work.

There are many methods of providing information to people and they are shown below:

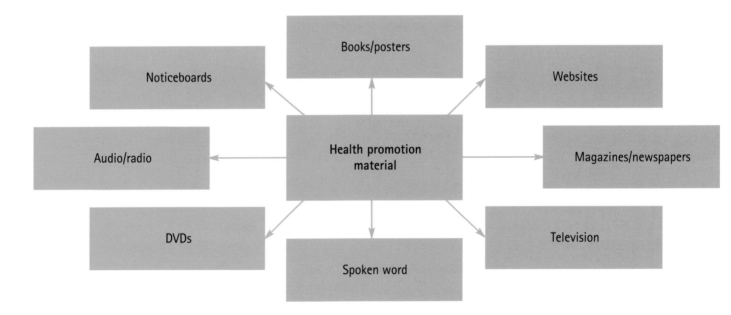

The diagram on the previous page shows the main methods used to convey information. All of these are used to great effect because they allow many people to see or hear the information. They can be targeted at different groups of people, in different languages, anywhere in the country. They are very effective methods of reaching large numbers of people. They can also be designed to reach different areas of the community by delivering in ways that appeal and are appropriate to specific groups.

They can, however, be **anonymous** and **impersonal** in that they do not always convey feeling or emotional warmth. This often means that although people will have seen or heard the information, it may be easily **dismissed**. If its **impact** is not strong enough, then people often take no notice. This is why information delivered in this way has to be dramatic, colourful and have that 'Wow' factor.

The diagram also shows us the wide range of availability of information. Many of these methods can be focused on people in their homes. This means that they will receive the information without stepping outside of their front door.

Personal delivery is another method that is used to convey information to individuals and groups. The diagram below shows how this can be achieved:

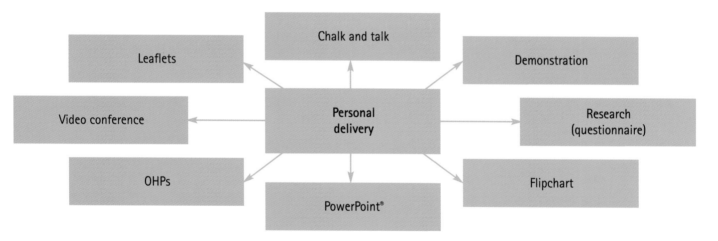

ACTIVITY   Health promotion materials

1. Look at a selection of **four** health promotion materials. These can be leaflets, advertisements or any other form of information. Briefly explain the aim of the each item.

2. List the audiences that each campaign is targeting.

3. Explain why you think the best ones are effective. What catches your eye? Are they easy to read? Is there a balance between the number of illustrations and the number of words used?

4. Select one piece of health promotion material. In no more than 50 words, explain how it would provide support for a person who is trying to improve their health.

Health promotion resources can be obtained from a variety of places that are accessible to the public. Leaflets and publications giving advice will be found in many locations that include:

- doctors
- dentists
- hospitals
- clinics
- schools
- libraries.

Health promotion resource centres provide health promotion, public health materials and resources to keep and to loan. They are usually free of charge to anyone with a role in health promotion. This service is also available to anyone who works or lives within the boundaries of the area that they serve. All new users complete a registration form and they can then use the services. So there is no reason why people should not access these resources. However, they may not always know exactly where to go to find them.

ACTIVITY   Success or failure?

Think of an example of health promotion material that made an impact on you.

1 Why do you think it was successful?

Now think of a material that did not impress you.

2 Why was this?

3 What would have made it more successful?

...ACTIVITY

✅ ...WORD CHECK

medium – a method or way in which information is delivered.

primary – the first.

emphasizing – highlighting or drawing attention to.

detrimental – causing detriment; injurious; hurtful.

Group Activity

Look at a range of health promotion materials that could be useful to the person for whom you are producing a health and well-being plan.

Select **four** that could be useful to the individual or group.

Explain to another person why they could be helpful.

Ask the person with whom you are sharing to tell you which health promotion materials they are going to use and to explain why.

In this modern technological age there are a variety of ways of getting the message across to the public. Health information does not only come in written form. Everywhere you look there are pieces of information designed to make individuals notice them.

Television is the strongest **medium** available because almost everyone watches TV. This makes it a **primary** force for providing health messages in the form of adverts and public information films. Radio is a less popular medium as fewer people listen to radio than in previous years. As it has no visual component, it tends not to have the impact that TV has, but may appeal to older adults. Whatever format the information is presented in, it will be creatively designed to have the maximum impact. The idea is to make individuals notice and remember the message.

Health promotion resources must also motivate, as they will not be successful if they don't! This can be done in two main ways:

1. Fear – by vividly describing the damaging effects an activity like smoking will have, people automatically take notice. Those who are most keen either to give up or extend their life will be affected most and benefit from the message.

The positive message can be given by demonstrating how much better an individual's lifestyle could become. This can be done by **emphasizing** improvements to the person and also how this could have a beneficial effect on friends, family and loved ones. A good example of this is the work that has been done to show smokers how they can have a **detrimental** effect on those around them. The fear of harming a loved one by causing them to become a passive smoker is often enough to make them give up.

2. Support – often the information provided in health promotion resources will have an element of **support**. This can include help lines where a person can ring up and obtain advice. The materials can explain where to go to get help and the type of help that is available. It can also provide information about like-minded individuals who have got together to help each other. These are known as self-help groups and are one of the most effective ways of changing negative activities like drinking and smoking. So health promotion resources can be a powerful weapon in helping to improve an individual's health and lifestyle.

Designing a health and well-being improvement plan

During the planning, attention should be paid to the current publications and legislation that help support and guide those wishing to improve their health. This is because they can provide a good foundation for understanding how health and well-being can be supported.

One of the main ways the government is trying to support individuals is to encourage them to take action for themselves and their families. Communities are now working together and can offer real help. This means that the government can continue addressing the bigger issues that affect health, such as housing, jobs and education, whilst at the same time supporting the key health issues that have already been mentioned.

During 1999, the government published '*Saving Lives: Our Healthier Nation*'. This was an action plan to:

- improve the health of everyone
- improve the health of those socially less fortunate.

This meant that the government could target the main killers.

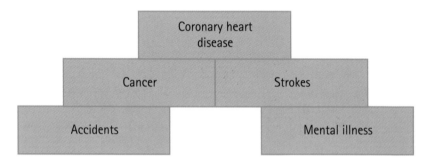

In order to achieve better health for everyone, especially those who were disadvantaged, the government decided to:

- put an extra £21 billion in the NHS to help secure a healthier population
- tackle smoking as the biggest preventable cause of ill health
- integrate government and local government, working to improve health
- stress health improvement as a key role for the NHS
- press for high health standards for everyone.

The race to achieve effective health and well-being was now on!

In 2004 the Department of Health produced its first ever White Paper on Public Health – '*Choosing Health: Making Healthier Choices Easier*'. '*Choosing Health*' set out a wide range of proposed actions to address major public health problems, placing population health and health **inequalities** at the centre of the government's health policy **agenda**. '*Choosing Health*' identified the following priorities for action:

- reducing smoking rates
- reducing obesity and improving diet and nutrition
- increasing exercise
- encouraging and supporting sensible drinking
- improving sexual health
- improving mental health.

> **...WORD CHECK**
>
> **inequalities** – the things that divide people such as money, housing and social class.
>
> **agenda** – list of intended actions.

ACTIVITY

The Health Promotion Team

…ACTIVITY

With your tutor's permission, contact the local Health Promotion Team to find out:

1. What their local health improvement priorities are.
2. How their choice of health promotion campaigns match the government health improvement targets.
3. Who is the main targeted audience in your area and why?

In July 2004 these targets were all confirmed in the 'National Standards, Local Action' document produced by the government. The core of the plan was to:

* Improve the health of the population. By 2010, increase life expectancy at birth in England to 78.6 years for men and to 82.5 years for women.
* Substantially reduce mortality rates by 2010 (from the 'Our Healthier Nation' baseline, 1995–97).
* Reduce coronary heart disease and stroke and related diseases by at least 40 per cent in people under 75.
* Reduce cancer by at least 20 per cent in people under 75.
* Reduce suicide and undetermined injury by at least 20 per cent.
* Reduce health inequalities by 2010, by 10 per cent as measured by infant mortality and life expectancy at birth (from a 1995–97 baseline), with reduction in the inequalities gap in areas worst hit by deprivation in the population as a whole.

The government also decided to tackle important causes of ill health and health inequalities by:

* Reducing adult smoking rates (from 26 per cent in 2002) to 21 per cent or less by 2010, with a reduction in prevalence among routine and manual groups (from 31 per cent in 2002) to 26 per cent or less.
* Halting the year-on-year rise in obesity among children under 11 by 2010 (from the 2002–04 baseline) in the context of a broader strategy to tackle obesity in the population as a whole.
* Reducing the under-18 conception rate by 50 per cent by 2010 (from the 1998 baseline), as part of a broader strategy to improve sexual health.

This paper supported the benefits of agencies working together to improve public health. It also highlighted the government's intention to tackle social inequality. From this, three core principles emerged to help support the new plan and they were:

1. Informed choice – in that people needed and wanted to make their own decisions but needed reliable and accurate information to enable them to make the right choices.
2. Personalization – for health inequalities to be improved, the support had to fit the individual's needs with services and support personalized in a flexible and sensitive way.
3. Working together – there had to be a partnership across all communities that included:
   * local government
   * business
   * retailers
   * communities
   * faith organizations and others.
   * the NHS
   * advertisers
   * the voluntary sector
   * the media

Only then would the actions help make the desired improvements.

Along with the major schemes set up by the government, a number of smaller campaigns were started. These were focused on various activities that could support health. These campaigns have been extensively advertised and the areas covered included:

- five-a-day programme – a scheme that aims to improve people's access to, and awareness of, fruit and vegetables
- local exercise action pilots – designed to identify and test the best ways of getting people more active
- teenage pregnancy – a national strategy designed to halve the under-18 conception rate and increase the participation of teenage mothers in education, training or work
- providing coordinated and **comprehensive** regional approaches to tobacco control to reduce smoking rates and the associated burden of tobacco-related illness.

'*Healthy Weight, Healthy Lives*' highlighted the effects of doing nothing, with a predicted 60 per cent of the population being obese by 2050 and potential costs of £45.5 billion to the NHS and wider society.

ACTIVITY   Legislation and policy

Legislation and policy are very important in supporting good health.

1. Why is it important that the country has legislation that supports good health?
2. How do the government's policies help the individuals to improve their lifestyle and health?
3. Identify two pieces of legislation and outline their purpose in supporting good health.
4. For one service user, identify and explain how a government target could assist them to improve their health.

Providing people with an effective plan to improve their health and well-being is very important. When planning, it should always be remembered the plan should be:

- drawn up with the person so that they feel in control
- **accessible** – they should be able to do the activities included
- **achievable** – the goals that are set should match the goals of the person and the plan should include short- and long-term targets
- **accurate** – if you say something or plan something, it must be correct
- the goals must be clear – what is the aim?

If there is failure in any of these areas then the plan may fail to work. The biggest **motivation** for a person is to see results. Even the smallest change for the better can be motivating. This means we should aim for small goals to start with, bigger ones to follow, making it *accessible*, *achievable* and *accurate*.

When presenting a plan to help improve a person's health it must be in a form that they can use. For example:

- if the plan is for a child, it should have more pictures than words
- if the plan is for an older person, it may need to be in larger print.

For some people, this will mean preparing a plan so that it can be placed on a wall where it can be accessed easily. Other people would prefer to have the plan in a booklet. Whichever way it is used, the plan needs to look attractive to the user.

⊘ ...WORD CHECK

comprehensive – complete and containing a high level of information.

accessible – easy to access or approach; approachable.

achievable – capable of being achieved.

accurate – precise, exact or careful conformity to truth.

motivation – encouragement to continue with an action or event.

Before any progress can be made, there has to be an overall picture of what is going to happen. All planning should be carried out with the following approaches in mind. It is important that all objectives are:

SMART

This means that the plan must be:

Specific	all aspects of the plan must be clear
Measurable	there must be a measurable outcome
Achievable	all targets must be achievable and realistic
Relevant	activities must be suitable and help the person achieve the final outcome
Timed	everything must happen in a realistic time frame

The diagram below gives an overview of how all of the main events could occur in improving a person's health and well-being. This seven point plan gives a framework to base all of the activities around. The main idea is to create an overall plan that is SMART and achievable.

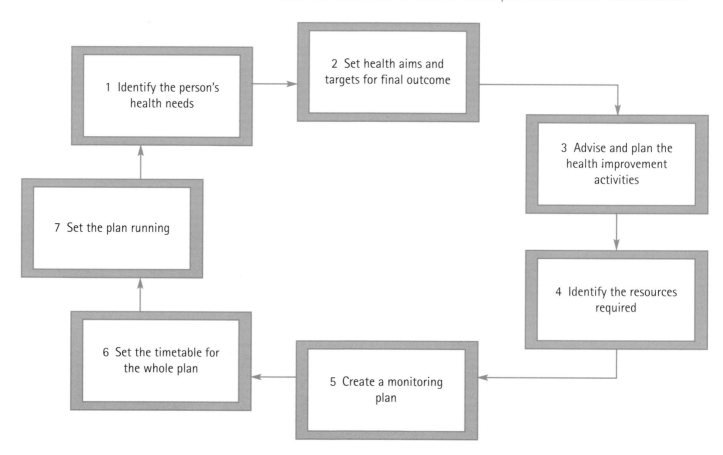

The advice given in the plan must always be based on the assessment. If this is not so, the advice could lead to inappropriate action or prove dangerous. Always remember the person producing the plan may not know all of the answers and so they should always be prepared to ask for advice. It is not a failing to ask; health care professionals do this all the time. When advising an individual, it is important to make sure that:

- they understand the plan
- it is written down (as a plan or description)
- it is suitable (to their age, gender and condition)
- it is accurate
- it is not dangerous and is within their ability to do.

Being able to motivate and support is a vital part of producing the plan:

- to motivate – help the individual to find a good reason 'why' they want to improve their health
- to support – decide with the individual who could provide help to achieve the plan, for example a friend or an organization such as 'WeightWatchers'.

13 Why does assessment and advice have to be accurate?

14 What factors affect the assessment and advice that is given to people?

> ...WORD CHECK
>
> **targets** – goals; points that must be achieved.
>
> **unrealistic** – something that is not possible to do or sensible to undertake.
>
> **review** – to look at an event in detail again.
>
> **accurate** – precise, exact or careful conformity to truth.
>
> **modify** – to make changes to an object or event.

ACTIVITY   Producing a plan

Isobella wants to lose 10 pounds (4.5kg) in weight. You know that she is not a healthy eater and she takes very little exercise. Your friend's only other problem is that she has mild asthma.

1 Design a two-day plan for diet and exercise to help Isobella.

2 Explain how you will make sure that the plan does not affect her asthmatic condition.

3 How do you think a person will feel physically, intellectually, emotionally and socially if they succeed in achieving their plan?

Setting realistic short- and long-term targets

Setting **targets** is important. These must be achievable for the person for whom the plan is intended. **Unrealistic** targets are the biggest reason why health improvement plans fail. The target that is set can reach the goal in step-by-step stages. It does not have to be achieved all at once. For example, if Isobella were overweight, one short-term target could be to lose three pounds in the first month. Her long-term target could be to lose a stone in weight in five months. Targets should not be so large that they are dangerous. Often a little at a time is best. If the targets are not working, **review** them. They may not have been correct in the first place!

By keeping **accurate** records during the health plan, it is possible to monitor what is happening. If a plan begins to fail, there has to be a reason. Investigate the reason and see if the problem can be repaired; you may need to **modify** the plan. This will help the person to get back on track and to succeed.

Group Activity

Work with another person in the group and select two targets that you could each work towards to maintain or improve your own health and well-being.

What action could you take to meet these targets?

Assessment of the difficulties which may be experienced in implementing a health and well-being improvement plan

In order to succeed in improving health and well-being, an individual must be motivated. Not being motivated is a difficulty that could prevent an individual or group from achieving their targets. The less motivated an individual is, the more they have to rely on willpower. Good willpower may work for a little while but it does not always last. It is unlikely to result in long-term successful results. To succeed we must have good motivation. This applies to anyone we are trying to help and especially to ourselves. We must really want to achieve the targets set.

So what is motivation? Basically, motivation is what makes an individual succeed. Everyone has to have a really good reason; it needs to be a genuine reason. People who are only doing something because they have been told to do it are less likely to succeed, unless it has a big impact. One reason for not improving health could be:

▲ If I swim three times each week, in a month I will start to look slimmer.

- 'My doctor told me to stop smoking; he does not understand.'

In this case the individual is not ready to stop smoking themselves and so they are less likely to succeed. If they wanted to improve their breathing, to be able to take part in physical activities or to save money for a holiday, they might be better motivated.

A reason for a man to take action to improve their health and well-being could be:

- 'My girlfriend said she would leave me if I did not lose weight.'

The individual may desperately want to keep his girlfriend and consequently has a motive to help him succeed. Other motives might include:

- I want to look good for me.
- Being fit will be great and improve my social life.
- My health will improve and I will be able to do so much more with my family.

There must be **motivation** – this means that the individual for whom the plan is intended really wants to improve their health, therefore, a genuine reason will need to be found to motivate them, for example being able to get into a size 12 dress rather than one that is size 14!

Assessments need to look at the whole person. This is known as an **holistic approach**. It has to take account of the person's physical, intellectual, emotional and social circumstances (P.I.E.S.). This way a better picture of the person is often achieved. If their lifestyle can be understood, the assessment is more likely to be successful.

It is important to keep in mind that maintaining a positive attitude is essential to success. When motivating and supporting someone else, we have to keep reminding them:

- how well they are doing
- how good they will feel and look when they reach their target
- how much more active they will be.

Although some people like to exercise alone, others prefer to be in groups. For these, group activity may be the incentive they need to succeed. Community-based fitness groups often provide the positive support and company that is needed. A little competition from others in the same position can also sometimes help.

Whatever an individual is trying to do, motivation and support are essential. Being positive can make a major difference to achieving goals.

15 ▶ Describe three different ways of motivating a person to succeed with a health plan.

> **✓ ...WORD CHECK**
>
> **motivation** – encouragement to continue with an action or event.
>
> **holistic approach** – treating a service user as a whole individual by providing care to meet all needs, linking the care provided together to ensure all aspects are looked at.

CASE STUDY — Bill

Bill is 47 years old and believes he is 22 pounds (10kg) overweight. He smokes 20 cigarettes a day and drinks five bottles of red wine a week.

He has discovered that light physical exercise now makes him out of breath; this has worried him. He has turned to you to help him get back to a normal size and weight. He also wants to become fitter.

He is 70 inches tall and weighs 14 stone (he does not use metric measurements).

1. Produce a plan to help Bill stop smoking.
2. Why is it important to assess his capabilities before he starts any plan?
3. Design and present the plan.
4. Describe ways that you could motivate him.
5. What health promotion materials could you use to help him?

Support available to implement a health and well-being improvement plan

▸ Working with a friend or attending a club can provide effective support.

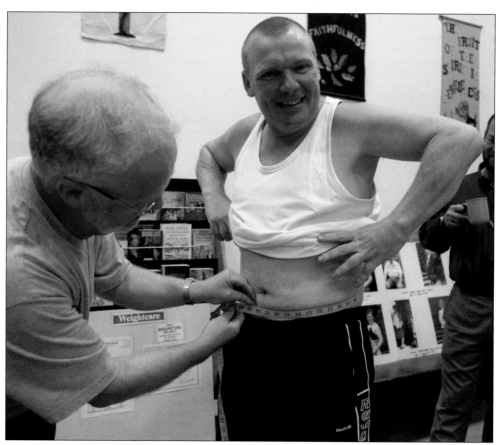

Having support for the health and well-being plan will certainly enable the individual or group to succeed. Support could be in the form of:

- a club, for example, Weight Watchers, or exercise and fitness
- a parent, relative or friend
- professionals, for example, dietician or health promotion officer.

Each of these groups will 'be there' for the individual or group, giving advice and encouraging them to achieve their targets. When working with another person it is far easier to 'keep going'.

Group Activity

Work with another person to think about how the following people could give support to an individual when following a health and well-being plan. Write down your answers for:

- a parent
- a group, for example, Weight Watchers
- a professional.

Share your answers with the whole group.

ASSESSMENT PRACTICE: PREPARATION

Now that you have obtained the information from the chosen individual about their health and well-being, you need to:

1. Explain the features of the individual's lifestyle that have affected their physical health.

2. Identify a range of physical needs to focus on within the health plan and explain why these needs have been selected.

3. Identify **two short-term** targets for the individual and **two long-term** targets for the individual.

4. Draw up a plan for the individual, explaining why the plan is relevant to them.

5. Explain **two** ways in which the individual could be motivated to succeed.

6. Explain **two** ways in which the individual could be supported through the plan.

7. Analyse the difficulties that the individual may have in following the plan.

8. Describe the possible impact of the plan on the health and well-being of the individual, to include P.I.E.S. (physical, intellectual, emotional and social well-being), drawing conclusions.

9. Explain how the targets of the plan meet the individual's needs.

Remember to include the bibliography and to present the information in an appropriate format, using appropriate technical terminology.

4 Health, Social Care and Early Years in Practice

Contents

About this unit

The unit is 'synoptic', that is it links to the previous three units studied within this award. It will include:

- the range of care needs of major client groups
- care values commonly used in practitioner work
- the development of self-concept and personal relationships
- promoting and supporting health improvement.

Evidence required for external assessment will relate to settings and service users. This can be found from any of the following:

- health, for example, doctor's surgery, hospital
- early years, for example, nursery school, workplace crèche
- care of older people, for example, residential home, informal care by relatives
- individuals with specific needs, for example, adults with learning difficulties attending a local centre.

This unit is externally assessed through a 1-hour and 15-minute written examination.

The examination will test knowledge and understanding and the ability to apply that knowledge and understanding to a range of situations. Information will be presented in the form of three short scenarios or case studies and you will be required to analyse and evaluate information given within these. You will also be expected to present conclusions and to draw reasoned judgements from the material presented in the case studies and short scenarios.

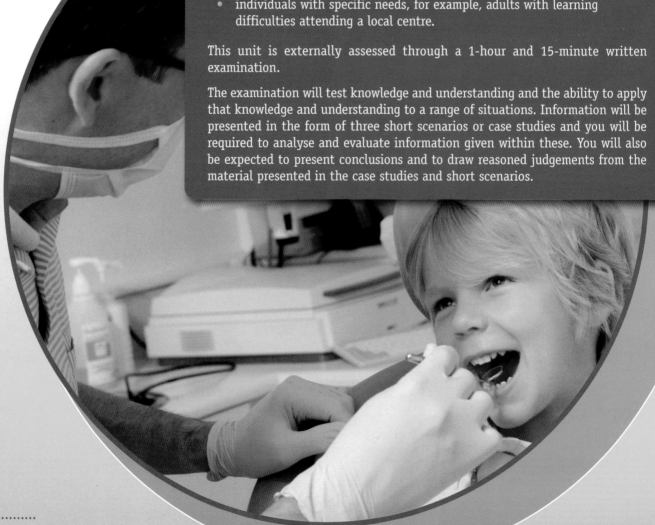

▸ Introducing this unit

A care practitioner such as a doctor or social worker must try and treat each client as an individual by recognizing what their particular needs are. To do this, they must understand all the possible reasons why an individual requires help. These could include unfortunate events in their past or living an unhealthy lifestyle. To provide good care the practitioner must be aware of the care values and put them into practice every time they work with a client. By doing this, he or she will be treated with dignity and respect, and this should promote a positive self-concept. This should also encourage the individual to work hard to improve their own health. To further encourage good health, the care practitioner should use a range of strategies including health promotion campaigns.

This chapter will look at the way care practitioners work with individuals in order to understand what the problem is, why it might have occurred, and what support and advice is needed to promote good long-term health.

The range of care needs of major client groups

▶ Getting started

In this unit you will gain an understanding of:

a the range of care needs of the major client groups

b the basic needs of service users split into the following areas:
   i   physical needs – basic needs of humans such as food, water, shelter and clothing
   ii   intellectual needs – the ability to learn and develop new skills
   iii emotional needs – the expression of feelings, giving and receiving love and security
   iv   social needs – the ability to develop and maintain relationships including friendships, intimate and sexual relationships and work relationships

c the factors which affect human growth and development divided into:
   i   life course events
   ii   lifestyle choices

d how expected and unexpected events impact on individuals during their life course

e how these events affect an individual physically, intellectually, emotionally and socially, focusing on:
   i   lifestyle choices people make – such as diet, exercise, socializing with others and recreational activities undertaken
   ii   expected events – such as starting school, marriage/partnership formation, employment, death/bereavement
   iii unexpected events – such as serious illness, relationship breakdown, financial difficulty, loss of job
   iv   how these factors/events affect human growth and development (physical, intellectual, emotional and social) and how they can lead to new learning.

THE RANGE OF CARE NEEDS OF THE MAJOR CLIENT GROUPS

What are the needs of these different groups of individuals?

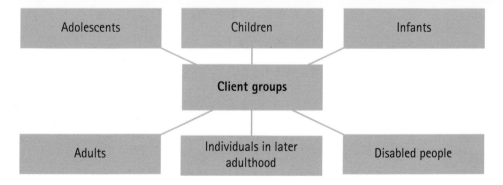

Services in the community provide for the needs of individuals. In areas where there are large numbers of older adults, for example retirement areas such as the south coast of England, there will need to be provision for additional hospital and residential services. Additional specialists who care for people in later adulthood will need to be trained and recruited. On the other hand, inner cities with growing numbers of young adults who will be starting families will require a range of nursery and other early years provision. SureStart provision will need to focus upon these areas, particularly if they are in areas of deprivation.

In this unit you will find out which needs client groups have, which services they use to help meet those needs and how people's basic needs are met.

How do the professional care workers who practice within the settings use care values? How do they apply them when meeting your needs?

Group Activity

Work with another person and write down **three** needs that you or your family have experienced. Now produce a table with the three different types of services and place those that each of you have used to help meet those needs. Why did you use the services?

Compare your table with that of a different pair within your group.

Are they similar or different?

THE BASIC NEEDS OF SERVICE USERS

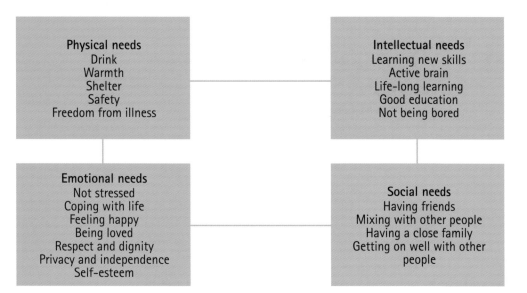

The most important and basic need is physical. If individuals struggle on a daily basis to keep warm and have enough food to eat, the quality of their life is very low. Many individuals in the world struggle to survive at this level, which is why in some countries they never reach the stage of later adulthood, as their average life expectancy is below 40 years. There is, of course, a shortage of care practitioners to help overcome the devastating effects of poverty.

How are the needs of parents, particularly women, met by a workplace crèche?

Group Activity

How could health promotion improve the quality of life for service users who are at different life stages? For example:

- infants
- children
- adolescents
- adults
- older adults.

In Britain most individuals have the opportunity to meet their intellectual needs. Children from a very young age go to a range of early years services and about 40 per cent of 18 year olds go on to study at university. Of course, not everyone takes up the opportunities that are available. Older adults often meet these needs through **The University of the Third Age**.

A growing number of care practitioners now work with people trying to help them meet their emotional needs. This could be marriage guidance counsellors, such as those who work for Relate, or organizations like the Samaritans who deal on a daily basis with individuals who are depressed and suicidal.

Individuals today have high expectations that their social needs will be met. Increasing numbers are using the Internet and websites such as Friends Reunited to keep in touch with old friends or meet new ones, possibly new marriage partners.

Practitioners will try to encourage us all to work towards improving our own health and well-being. Our needs for improvement will be different as we work through the different life stages. For example, as adolescents we will need intellectual stimulation, we will need to eat a balanced diet and to have a supportive group of friends. In later adulthood we will still have these needs but older people will not be able to do things at quite the same speed as an adolescent and also they could have more fragile bones, or suffer from arthritis or hardening of the arteries. Health promotion is helping people who are at different life stages to improve the quality of their lives. It is raising people's awareness of how to prevent ill health, how to improve levels of fitness and how to extend life expectancy.

We all have the same basic needs. Maslow represented these needs in the form of a pyramid showing which needs must be met first before other needs could be satisfied.

Abraham Maslow included five levels of need and arranged them in the form of a pyramid (see page 104).

 What basic needs do you have in order to keep you alive?

Hospital services provide secondary care, which attempts to meet the needs of all individuals. Below is a table that shows the needs of different individuals and gives some examples of the practitioners and services who work in hospitals and how they provide for those needs:

Individuals	How needs are met
Babies	Maternity units – safe childbirth Baby special care units – help with any problems at birth
Children	Paediatrician – specialist child doctor who treats childhood illnesses Vaccinations – to prevent serious illnesses
Adults	Consultants – to advise on best form of treatment General surgery – to carry out operations Radiography x-ray departments – to see what is causing ill health and where the potential problem is
Older people	Geriatricians – specialize in the needs of older adults Terminal illness care – to provide holistic care in the last years of life – this is often provided in hospices
People with disabilities	Physiotherapy – to help movement and mobility Occupational therapy – to provide aids for increased mobility Psychiatric units – to treat a range of mental illnesses

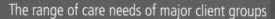

Individuals with disabilities are found in all the client groups. Their needs will differ according to which of the groups they belong. For example, an older adult is more likely to need help from physiotherapists and occupational therapists, whilst an adult might need help accessing education and training and leisure facilities. The help needed will also be influenced by whether the individual acquired the disability at birth or as the result of accident or illness. When a person becomes disabled by accident or illness, it will alter the person's personal relationships and friends; family and work colleagues will need to adjust to take account of the person's disability. Whatever the condition, the disabled person's needs are those that able-bodied people have within whichever age group they fall.

CASE STUDY   Sam

Sam is a 16-year-old girl who lives in a large city in the north of England. At the beginning of Year 11 Sam was involved in a serious road traffic accident and as a result had to have her left leg amputated. She also lost the sight of one eye. She was off school for three months and became worried about her GCSE exams. Partly because of the stress of the accident, her parents began to have relationship problems and Sam is worried about what is going to happen to her in the future. Sam is showing signs of depression and loss of confidence and has told her friends that she is going to leave school and not go to university as planned. Her parents and friends are at a loss as to who to go to for help.

1. Identify five needs Sam has at the moment.
2. Which health and social care services would be able to offer care and support to Sam?
3. Which care practitioners would work with Sam?
4. How would the care services try to work together to help Sam?
5. Assess Sam's needs using Maslow's pyramid of needs (see page 104).

THE FACTORS WHICH AFFECT HUMAN GROWTH AND DEVELOPMENT

Life course events

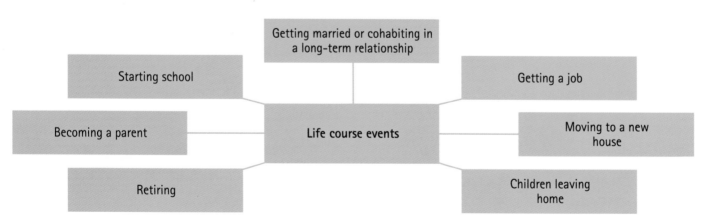

How a person develops is the result of many events throughout life starting immediately after birth. Some of these events are predictable and expected, whilst others are unpredictable and unexpected. It is often the unexpected events that have a bigger impact upon a person's development because they cannot be planned for and they can have a serious impact upon the individual.

Most individuals go through the main events in their life quite happily and predictably. It is likely that you will get through school successfully and many of you will go on to college or university. You will have relationships, most with the opposite sex, and eventually settle down and possibly marry, having one or two children. It is likely, though, that you will live with that person first and probably not marry, unlike your parents and grandparents, until you are about 30 years of age. Unfortunately a growing number of such marriages will end in divorce and the individuals will either remarry or cohabit with another partner. Most will live until retirement and probably live for another 20 years – more likely if you are female than male!

ACTIVITY   Life events

1   Which of the following life events are expected and which are unexpected? Make two lists and add two more predictable and unpredictable events to your list.

- Starting school
- Retirement
- Starting work
- Losing a job
- Physical injury
- Winning the lottery
- Divorce
- Getting married.

Care practitioners often have to deal with individuals who experience unexpected events in their life. Social workers and health workers often have to pick up the pieces after an individual has experienced traumatic unexpected events in their life.

CASE STUDY   Philip

Philip, aged 25, was happily married until recently when his wife told him that she was leaving him to go and live with another man. At the same time Philip lost his job at work because the factory closed down. This made him depressed and he started to drink heavily. He also began to buy more lottery tickets to try to solve his financial situation. He is spending more time at home and losing touch with his friends. He has been trying to get another job but has found it difficult as so many other people are also unemployed. He is now having problems paying the mortgage and the household bills. He would become homeless if his house was repossessed.

1   Identify three needs Philip has at the moment.

2   Identify three care practitioners who could help Philip.

3   Explain how Philip could change his lifestyle to try and overcome his problems.

4   Which events in his life does he have some control over?

5   Discuss the statement: 'Problems in life tend to build up and together make it very difficult to escape from.'

Lifestyle choices

Growth and development is also influenced by the lifestyle choices that we make. To some extent we all have control over such choices and they will affect a range of issues including how long we live, illnesses we might suffer from, our educational achievements, relationships with our peers and family, and job opportunities. However, not everyone is able to make the right decisions. Individuals who are disabled or suffer from mental ill health, stretched for money, out of work, poorly qualified or who live in inadequate housing are likely to have less control over their lives than others.

In society today individuals are increasingly worried about diet and obesity as a result of eating an unbalanced range of foods. Junk food has become a way of life for many, partly because it requires little preparation and partly because of the busy lifestyles we lead today.

▲ Are we becoming a nation of couch potatoes?

One fifth of Britons spend as much time watching television as working. A survey by the Alliance and Leicester Building Society found that 21 per cent of respondents watched 36 hours of television a week – more than five hours a day on average. According to the World Health Organization, the lifestyle of couch potatoes has overtaken smoking as the major cause of ill health in European countries for the first time.

As a result of growing levels of obesity the care needs of children have changed from lack of food in the 1930s and 1940s to obesity in the twenty-first century. Jamie Oliver's healthy school dinners was a high-profile campaign to overcome the growing epidemic by introducing healthy eating in schools.

◄ Jamie Oliver has campaigned to improve school meals.

 Group Activity

Find out about the Jamie Oliver campaign and your school's policy on healthy eating. Is it working? What are the reasons why it might not be as successful as the government hopes?

A useful website is: www.jamieoliver.com

HOW EXPECTED AND UNEXPECTED EVENTS IMPACT ON INDIVIDUALS

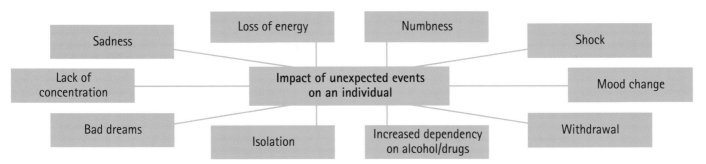

Sadness · Loss of energy · Numbness · Shock · Lack of concentration · **Impact of unexpected events on an individual** · Mood change · Bad dreams · Isolation · Increased dependency on alcohol/drugs · Withdrawal

 Group Activity

Work in small groups and draw up a list of expected and unexpected events which might affect an adult in their fifties. In addition, discuss which of the P.I.E.S. are most affected by the events.

Example: being made redundant – most likely to occur with adults – can lead to loss of income (P), less opportunity to learn new skills and the danger of boredom (I), depression and low self-esteem (E) and relationship problems (S).

One unexpected event that has a serious effect on an individual is the sudden death of a son or daughter. The normal life course is that parents die before their children. Dealing with the death of a son or daughter through a tragic event, such as a car accident, is likely to have a range of physical and emotional effects. Parents are likely to feel guilty that they have outlived their child and this can bring about serious psychological issues. Some parents try to come to terms with the death by possibly helping others in the same position or perhaps doing something to try to stop the cause of the accident repeating itself. They might campaign for safer roads and reduced speeding by motorists.

Others may turn to using alcohol to forget what has happened and never really come to terms with the tragedy. They may keep the child's bedroom as a shrine by which to remember them by.

The fact is that unexpected events can never really be planned for and we never really know how we will cope. The good thing is that there is now a wide range of health and social care services, such as bereavement services, available to help.

CASE STUDY — Janine and Jack

Janine and Jack are engaged and plan to get married as soon as they have saved up enough money for the wedding. They both want to continue working but also want to start a family. They want to have their own house near a good school for their future children.

1. Outline some of the expected events Jack and Janine are likely to face in the next 20 years.

2. What possible unexpected events could affect both Jack and Janine?

3. Assess the changes both Jack and Janine will need to make when they are married, compared to when both were single.

4. How will having children affect Jack and Janine? Will they both be affected in the same way?

5. Analyse the statement: 'Marriage is the biggest life event most people experience because it brings about the greatest changes in their life.'

HOW THESE EVENTS AFFECT AN INDIVIDUAL PHYSICALLY, INTELLECTUALLY, EMOTIONALLY AND SOCIALLY

Lifestyle choices

Lifestyle choices, which have a big impact upon the physical, intellectual, emotional and social aspects of people's lives, include lack of exercise, binge drinking, smoking and using other illegal substances. Young people are to some extent influenced by role models in the media and many adults believe that celebrities such as Amy Winehouse are setting bad examples. In the past it was mainly young men who led unhealthy lifestyles but it is clear today that young women's lifestyles have changed dramatically and this has led to doctors treating more and more women in their thirties with health problems such as liver disease.

Teenage girls are suffering the kind of serious liver damage normally found in women 20 years older because of the growing binge-drinking crisis. Professor Ian Gilmore, liver specialist at the Royal Liverpool University Hospital, warned of a time-bomb among young women caused by soaring levels of alcohol consumption of women in their late teens and early twenties with alcohol induced liver problems.

The fashion for body piercing as a lifestyle choice can have long-term health effects. A study for the British Medical Journal found that some piercings were carried out by friends and relatives. This was leading to complications such as swelling, infection and, in some cases, hepatitis. Dr Angie Bone, one of the authors of the study, found that 46 per cent of 16–24 year olds have a body piercing and if this pattern continues through the generations, it might be a problem for the NHS. The study was jointly carried out by the Health Protection Agency and the London School of Hygiene and Tropical Medicine.

Smoking as a lifestyle choice continues to be popular amongst young people. It is known that smoking is linked to more than 50 different diseases and disorders. Half of people who continue to smoke will be killed by it – losing an average 16 years of life.

Smoking-related disease and illness costs the NHS roughly £1.7 billion each year (Department of Health).

Alcohol is probably the main lifestyle choice that affects human growth and development. It is socially acceptable to drink and it is part of our **culture**. Recently, concern has been shown with regard to binge drinking, particularly amongst young girls.

▲ Amy Winehouse – a role model for young people?

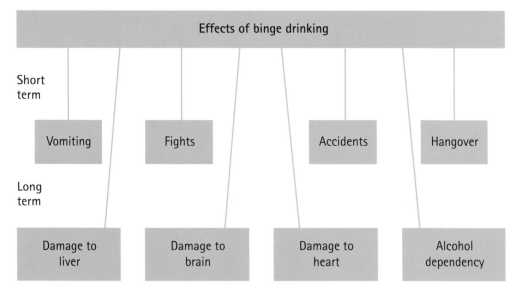

Effects of binge drinking

Short term

| Vomiting | Fights | Accidents | Hangover |

Long term

| Damage to liver | Damage to brain | Damage to heart | Alcohol dependency |

Compared with our great-grandparents most of us do not have to take as much exercise because of improvements in transport, and so on. Walking to school for many young people is no longer required because of the 'school run'.

Exercise is not just important for physical health such as improving blood circulation, building muscle strength and improving mobility. It also develops social and emotional needs such as building confidence, relieving stress, improving self-esteem, meeting new people and giving a feeling of well-being.

Individuals are able to choose their friends and this will have an impact on their physical, intellectual, emotional and social development. If we have no friends and no real opportunities to fulfil our potential, we may suffer social exclusion.

Group Activity

Research, using newspapers and the Internet, the care needs of adults as a result of lifestyle choices such as smoking, drinking and lack of exercise. Find out what professional care workers are trying to do to deal with the problem in both a treatment and preventative way. Some useful websites are:

www.alcoholics-anonymous.org.uk

www.nhs.uk

www.dh.gov.uk

www.ash.org.uk

...WORD CHECK

culture – the way of life of a whole society or particular groups within that society; it would include the norms and values of that group – the way they live.

What factors can lead to social exclusion?

All the client groups at different life stages are at risk of social exclusion. Some older adults may be affected because of:

- lower incomes because of retirement
- lack of friends because of lack of opportunities to socialize
- poor pension provision
- fear of leaving their home because of crime
- no access to transport
- family members having moved away.

Expected events

Expected events such as starting school, getting married and getting a job can have very positive effects on an individual. Physically, they are likely to have health benefits as individuals will feel good about themselves and this should reduce the chances of illness. New learning opportunities will take place and the individual is likely to be happy and content with life. Socially, new friends can be made though work. Being married can produce stability and close intimate relationships. At the end of an individual's long life, death can be understood and relatives will usually be able to understand and cope with their loss. Emotionally, they will be able to grieve and move on, knowing that the bereaved had a long and happy life.

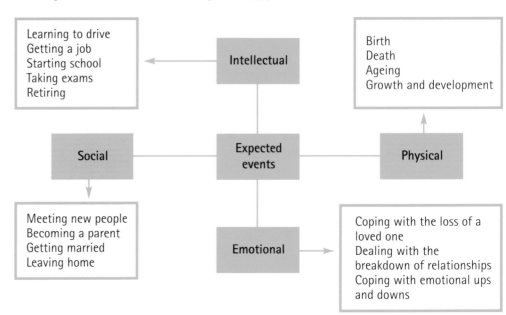

Unexpected events

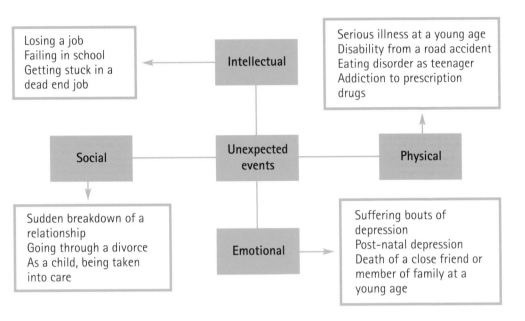

On the other hand, unexpected events such as early death, relationship breakdown, financial insecurity and loss of a job are more likely to have harmful effects on an individual. Adults who become unemployed are more likely to suffer long-term illness both physically and mentally. Many forms of depression are linked to sudden changes in an individual's life. Not being able to interact with colleagues can cause social isolation and reduce the opportunity to learn new skills. This is particularly true for adults in their fifties who lose their job, as they will find it very difficult to get a new position. Divorce is usually a very unhappy life event that will have physical, intellectual, social and emotional consequences, particularly if one partner didn't want the marriage to end. Many divorcees suffer financial loss, low self-esteem and depression, and lose contact with friends gained through the marriage.

Group Activity

Explain the physical, intellectual, emotional and social needs a person requires if they experience the following life events. What support could help them deal with the following situations:

- the break up of a long-term relationship?
- having their house repossessed because they cannot afford the mortgage?
- not getting the exam grades needed to go to university?
- losing their hearing?
- suddenly getting a serious illness?
- finding their son/daughter is addicted to drugs?
- finding their best friend has betrayed their trust?

CASE STUDY   ## Unemployment and suicide

Research suggests that there is a strong link between unemployment and suicide. Becoming unemployed doubles the risk of suicide. There are serious physical, emotional, social and intellectual problems resulting from losing a job, particularly for some individuals.

1. Which individuals are most likely to be unemployed?

2. Identify two physical, emotional, social and intellectual problems a person who is unemployed is likely to suffer from.

3. In what ways can a person plan for the possibility of losing their job?

4. What help is available for people who lose their job?

5. Why is it particularly difficult for people aged over 50 to find a new job after becoming unemployed?

How these factors and events can affect growth and development and lead to new learning

The expected and unexpected events and lifestyle choices can have a positive as well as a negative impact upon growth and development. Being made redundant can encourage a person to learn new skills, a breakdown in a relationship can lead to a new, more fulfilling relationship, losing a loved one can help a person deal with further tragedies and also support people who are experiencing similar traumas.

A number of reformed drug addicts have shared their experiences with young people in order to teach them about the potential risks of such a lifestyle. Reformed prisoners also can help prevent others from making the same mistakes. Such work develops the self-esteem of the drug addict or prisoner.

▶ Simon Weston.

Government ministers in Scotland intend to increase the number of reformed addicts who visit schools to dissuade youngsters from using illegal substances. Minister Cathy Jamieson said that hearing the real-life experiences of people who have been involved in the drug scene is one of the best ways of stopping young people getting involved in drugs.

Simon Weston was a soldier seriously injured in the Falklands War when the ship he was on was hit by an Argentine missile. He escaped alive but suffered 49 per cent burns on his body. This event obviously had serious consequences but Simon was determined to recover, and he tried to overcome the physical and emotional trauma by getting involved in new experiences. He supported a number of charities and set up the Weston Spirit to help disadvantaged young people. He received an OBE in 1992. This is a good example of an individual who used an unexpected event to lead to new learning opportunities.

CASE STUDY   Michelle Dewberry

Michelle Dewberry was the winner of The Apprentice programme in 2006. Her story is one of true grit, determination and achieving success against all the odds. Coming from a deprived background, Michelle ignored school and as a teenager 'went off the rails'. She had few qualifications, a partner in prison, and a social life that consisted of everything she shouldn't have done. At the age of 17 Michelle suffered a devastating blow when she lost her older sister in tragic circumstances. The tragedy spurred Michelle to turn her life around and to be successful. She returned to education and financially supported herself with three jobs each Saturday. At the age of 24 she became a self-employed consultant and went on to win The Apprentice. She is now an Ambassador at the Princes Trust and involved with the NSPCC. In 2007 she ran in the London Marathon and completed her autobiography 'Anything is Possible'.

1   Explain how the unexpected events in Michelle's life led her to new learning and experiences.

▶ ▶ ▶ ▶ ▶   ASSESSMENT PRACTICE

John, aged 34, had been happily married to Anita for 12 years and they had two young children Casey, aged 4, and Madonna, aged 10. Anita was killed in a road accident and shortly afterwards John was made redundant from the job he had been doing for over 14 years. Casey and Madonna have recently started their new primary and secondary schools.

1   Identify the type of events John and his children have experienced.   [3]

2   Identify one physical, social and emotional need John might now face.   [3]

3   What could John do in order to help his situation?   [4]

4   Describe the role of **three** professional care workers who could support the family.   [6]

5   What help could they provide to support their needs?   [4]

6   Explain the lifestyle choices Madonna is likely to be faced with in the next few years.   [8]

Harry is showing the early signs of Parkinson's disease – stiffness, shaking and slowness of movement. Other symptoms likely to occur are: loss of facial expressions such as smiling, difficulty with writing, difficulty with balance, slow monotonous speech, difficulty in swallowing and tiredness with aches and pains.

7   Describe **three** of Harry's needs in the short and long term.   [6]

8   Assess how his lifestyle choices will be affected.   [10]

9   Identify **three** care practitioners Harry would require.   [3]

10   Describe **three** ways those care workers could support Harry and his family.   [6]

11   Discuss the view that Harry would be better looked after in his home rather than going into institutional care.   [10]

Care values commonly used in practitioner work

▶ Getting started

In this unit you will gain an understanding of:

a   how health, social care and early years practitioners promote care values through their work with service users

b   the effects and consequences of these care values not being implemented

c   a range of care values through interaction with service users to include:
   i   promoting anti-discriminatory practice
   ii promoting and supporting individual rights to dignity, independence, health and safety
   iii promoting effective communication and relationships
   iv maintaining confidentiality of information
   v   acknowledging individual personal beliefs and identity

d   how these care values are reflected through practitioner interaction with service users in their attitudes and behaviour, and through professional training and development of care practitioners

e   how these care values are implemented in a care practitioner's work

f   analysis and evaluation of the consequences if service practitioners have not effectively implemented care values, including:
   i   the possibility of discrimination
   ii the possibility of social exclusion

g   the effect of poor care practice on the self-esteem and self-concept of service users, for example, disempowerment and lack of self-worth.

⊘ ...WORD CHECK

empathize – putting yourself in the position of someone else to see what their life is like.

HOW HEALTH, SOCIAL CARE AND EARLY YEARS PRACTITIONERS PROMOTE CARE VALUES

Group Activity

Work with another person and make a list of the care values you would expect a teacher to demonstrate when working with young people. How do they demonstrate these principles?

One of the core principles in health and social care is that all care professionals follow a set of care values with all service users. Having the professional knowledge to deal with the needs that a service user brings to them is only one aspect of care provision. If a GP (doctor) is unable to **empathize**, that is see the problem from the service user's point of view, and communicate, then it is unlikely that the service user will leave the surgery feeling that they have received quality care. If one feels that the GP just wants to give out a prescription and keeps looking at their watch, then the service user would probably feel cheated and not valued.

Similarly, you would expect your tutor/teacher to not only have an understanding of the subject but to also treat you in such a way that you feel valued as an individual.

What are the care values?

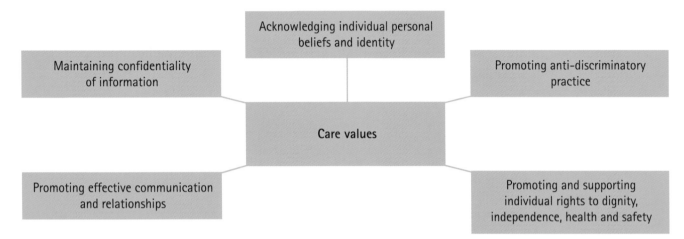

These values together form the care value base and are an essential part of the training of all care workers. The values are based upon ideas about human rights – **minimum** standards by which people should be treated. These rights are often supported by laws passed by parliament, for example, the Race Relations Act, the Sex Discrimination Act and the Children Act. Perhaps the most important influence upon the development of the care values is the Human Rights Act (1998). With this act the rights of service users are **paramount**. This means that health services such as hospitals must not do anything that fails to meet the rights set out in the act. For example, no one should be treated in a **degrading** way or should be discriminated against on the grounds of race, gender, disability and so on. If we value a person, we want the best for them. We should treat people as we would want to be treated ourselves. A care worker should want to act in the best interests of the service user, and will therefore make sure that in everything they do, they show that they 'value' that person. The Children Act says that the interests of children are paramount.

✅ **...WORD CHECK**

minimum – the lowest level of care that should be provided.

paramount – the most important, for example, under the Children Act the child's interests should always come first.

degrading – treating someone in an inhuman way.

What do each of the care values mean?

Care value	Meaning
Acknowledging personal belief and identity	Giving service users choice and the right to be different
Maintaining confidentiality of information	Having secure recording systems and only allowing access to them on a 'need to know' basis
Promoting effective communication and relationships	Making sure that the service user is able to participate in any written or oral discussions regarding their treatment, and so on
Promoting and supporting individual rights to dignity, independence and health and safety	Ensuring that service users are in a safe environment and are treated with respect, for example in relation to personal hygiene issues
Promoting anti-discriminatory practice	Not treating people in a different way because of their gender, race, age, sexuality, disability or class

When working in early years the principles or values that apply to this sector are:

Care value	Meaning
Welfare of the child	The interests of the child must always come first
Safe and healthy environment	Everything must be checked to make sure that children are kept safe and are not at risk
Working in partnership with parents and families	Parents are involved with the school and are encouraged to take part in activities with the children
Providing appropriate opportunities for learning and development	Making sure that children experience a wide range of activities that are suitable for their age and stage of development
Valuing diversity, equal opportunities and anti-discriminatory practice	Recognizing that all children are different and all should be allowed to reach their potential
Maintaining confidentiality	Keeping all records safe and not talking about the children to people who are not directly involved with their care
Working with others	Care practitioners working together as a team to ensure that children are looked after and cared for – sharing information with other care professionals
Being a reflective practitioner	Making sure that teachers, and so on, learn from what they are doing so that they become more skilled in their work – finding new ways of doing things with the children

Care practitioners in all areas of care are trained to promote the care values in their day-to-day work. This would apply if they are helping young children recover from an operation in hospital or dealing with an older adult in the early stages of dementia.

Group Activity

Talk with members of your family and collect together some of their experiences of being on the receiving end of the health and social care system. Were the care values implemented successfully?

CASE STUDY Frank

When Frank was admitted to hospital he had to complete a number of forms when he arrived. He was given a private room to complete them and then they were filed away in a locked cabinet. He was asked if he would prefer a men's ward or a mixed ward. As he had a sight impairment, he was given all the information in large print. At meal times he was given a choice of menus including a vegetarian option. Before he had his operation, the surgeon explained exactly what was involved and answered all the questions Frank asked.

1. Explain which of the care values were being implemented.

2. Explain how this would help Frank and improve the time spent in hospital.

CASE STUDY   Jack and Emma

Jack and Emma were keen for their three-year-old daughter to go to a nursery school and they arranged to visit their local school. When they arrived they were met by the Head of the school who took them to her office. She explained all about the school and gave them a written prospectus. She answered all their questions and then invited them to visit the classrooms. In one classroom the children were dressed in clothes from many different cultures, as they were learning about other religions in the world. Jack and Emma noticed how the children were well behaved and the teachers were trying to involve all the children in the activities, including one boy who none of the children wanted to play with.

1. Identify which of the care values can be found in the above case study.
2. What do you think Jack and Emma felt about the school?
3. Do you think their daughter would be happy there? Why?

CASE STUDY   A case conference

A case conference was called to discuss Michael's deteriorating physical condition. At the moment he lives independently at home with help provided by social services. However, the care workers were getting increasingly worried about his mobility. At the case conference his doctor, social worker, occupational therapist and district nurse were all present. Also, Michael was there with his son and daughter. Michael was involved in all the discussions and his views were paramount. He wanted to remain at home rather than go into residential care. At the end of the meeting it was decided that social services would put in additional support, the occupational therapist would assess Michael's needs and the district nurse would organize weekly visits.

1. Explain how the care values would have influenced the decision made at the case conference.
2. Why might it be better for Michael to stay at home?
3. Do you think this was the right decision?

THE CONSEQUENCES OF NOT APPLYING THE CARE VALUES

The effect of not being cared for successfully can be extremely damaging for the service user in many ways: physically, mentally and **psychologically**. It can do long-term damage so that the service user is unwilling to seek help again in the future. This can be seen in a number of different ways. Service users may:

- feel **devalued**
- have **low self-esteem**
- feel **worthless**
- feel **unimportant**
- feel **resentful** and angry
- feel **rejected**.

...WORD CHECK

psychologically – relating to the mind.

devalued – feeling not very important.

low self-esteem – not valuing yourself.

worthless – feeling that you have nothing to offer other people or society.

unimportant – not having a role to play in society.

resentful – feeling angry towards someone or something.

rejected – left out or not involved in something you feel is important.

Group Activity

Carry out a quick survey of your friends to see if they have suffered from any of the above as a result of a visit to, for example, a doctor, dentist or hospital. How did it make them feel?

CASE STUDY — Julie

Julie is suffering from terminal cancer. She visits her doctor and tells him that she no longer wants to live and has obtained enough tablets to end her life. She tells the doctor that it is her decision and not to interfere.

1. Which of the care values apply in this situation?
2. What is the dilemma facing the doctor?
3. Should Julie be allowed to end her life?

CASE STUDY — Mobility issues

The manager of a care agency that visits service users with mobility problems in their homes has reduced the time the care assistants can spend with each person. The workers have to telephone the company when they arrive at the service user's home and when they leave. This has meant that certain tasks, such as washing and making a cup of tea, have been affected. Also there is no time to talk to the service user and socialize.

1. Which care values might be affected by the reduced time spent with the service user?
2. What long-term damage might be done to the relationship between the care worker and the service user?
3. How would you feel if you were both the care worker and the service user?

CASE STUDY — Yasmin

Yasmin attends her local nursery school and recently she has told her mother that she does not want to go to school. Yasmin has always enjoyed school and her mother is surprised by this situation. Her mother decides to investigate the reason for the problem and talks to some of the other parents and children. It appears that some of the children have been calling Yasmin names in the playground and her teachers are unwilling or unable to do anything about it.

1. Which of Yasmin's rights are not being met?
2. What should the teachers do in this situation?
3. What should Yasmin's mother do?

HOW CARE VALUES ARE APPLIED
Promoting anti-discriminatory practice

Care workers are trained to avoid using language that is discriminatory. Language must not reflect gender bias or racist or **homophobic** assumptions. Also using **complex** words and **technical** jargon to **reinforce** how clever and knowledgeable the care practitioner is should be avoided without appearing to talk down to the service user or appearing to be **condescending**. The key to language is to empower the service user by enabling them to make informed decisions for themselves.

It is important that care workers are aware of the risk of making assumptions about gender, race, age, sexuality, disability and class. This usually means avoiding stereotypes such as girls are good at caring, older adults are not able to learn new skills, or people in wheelchairs need to be talked to very slowly and clearly.

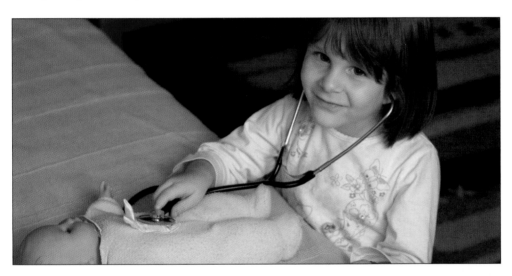

◄ What stereotype is shown here?

⊘ **...WORD CHECK**

homophobic – disliking and being hostile towards same-sex relationships.

complex – involving many parts; complicated; intricate.

technical – specialized and detailed.

reinforce – strengthen and support.

condescending – talking down to someone.

positive discrimination – actions to help the prospects of disadvantaged groups, for example, by employing a person because of their skin colour or gender.

racial diversity – a wide range of ethnic groups.

 Group Activity

Make a list of other stereotypes you have experienced. Do you ever make assumptions about people based upon their appearance and background? How do you think they would feel if they knew your opinions?

When using job titles it is important to avoid terms such as ambulance man by using the term paramedic. Care practitioners should challenge such attitudes when they meet them being used by other service users.

One way the government has tried to change attitudes on prejudice and discrimination is to pass legislation (laws) making such behaviour illegal.

2 Do you think such laws will change people's attitudes towards ethnic minorities and women? Give your reasons.

Sometimes **positive discrimination** is encouraged in order to improve the opportunities for a minority group. For example, preference could be shown towards the recruitment of black doctors to create greater **racial diversity** in the service. This policy is very controversial as it is criticized for not always appointing the most appropriate person for the job irrespective of their background.

 Group Activity

Work with another person to research the Race Relations Acts (1976 and 2000) and the Sex Discrimination Acts (1975 and 1986). Make a handout to show your findings.

Share the information with others.

Practitioners are trained to avoid discriminatory practice by:

- avoiding using language or behaviour that is discriminatory
- avoiding sexist job titles
- taking care when using terms for sexuality
- taking care with language referring to disability
- avoiding physical barriers when working with service users
- ensuring times are convenient and do not create barriers.

Promoting individual rights

It is also important that service users' rights to dignity, independence and health and safety are protected. Hospitals should always provide same sex wards for those individuals who prefer them to mixed wards. In 2007 the government's Chief Nursing Officer said that single sex hospital accommodation should be the norm for all patients pre-booked for treatment. The Deputy Chief Nurse at the Oxford Radcliffe Hospitals, Michael Fanning, said 'Treating older people with dignity and respect must be a priority for anyone working in the NHS. I would like every older person in our hospitals to be treated with the same consideration which I would wish to see for members of my own family.'

The 'National Service Framework', which sets national standards of care for older people, states that:

- All service users should receive quality care and treatment, regardless of age.
- Everyone should be treated as individuals, with respect and dignity.
- Money should be available for conditions which most affect older people.
- Those requiring long-term residential care should be helped financially.

3 ▶ What are the potential difficulties in achieving these aims?

Promoting effective communication and relationships

The extremely important document 'Every Child Matters' states that good communication is central to working with children, young people, their families and carers. This involves listening, questioning, understanding and responding to what is being communicated by children, young people and those caring for them. The skills required for good communication include:

- listening and building empathy
- summarizing and explaining
- consultation and negotiation.

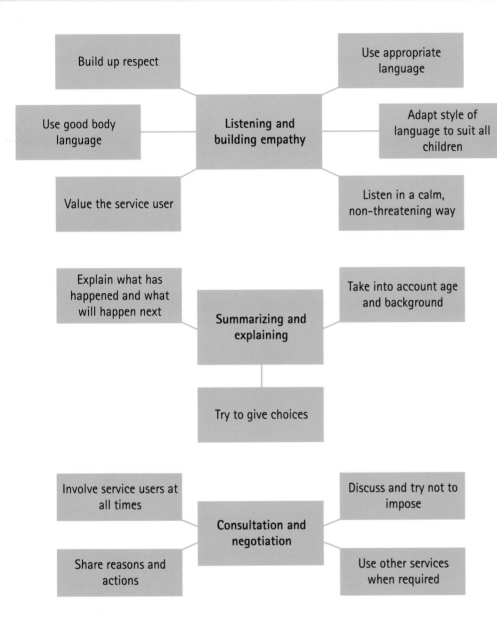

Build up respect

Use appropriate language

Use good body language

Listening and building empathy

Adapt style of language to suit all children

Value the service user

Listen in a calm, non-threatening way

Explain what has happened and what will happen next

Take into account age and background

Summarizing and explaining

Try to give choices

Involve service users at all times

Discuss and try not to impose

Consultation and negotiation

Share reasons and actions

Use other services when required

Group Activity

Try to visit an early years setting and observe the communication taking place between the children and their teachers. Look at the skills being used by the teacher. Get permission from your teacher before you start.

Maintaining confidentiality of information

Care practitioners need to maintain confidentiality of information when working with service users. You would not expect your teacher to talk openly to their friends out of school about something you have trusted them with. Also you would expect your personal files to be locked away and to be only accessible to people who need to have access.

The use of information about patients is partly controlled by legislation (the Data Protection Act 1998 and the Human Rights Act 1998) and by policies set by organizations such as hospitals and schools. Some doctors fear that the computerization of medical records could threaten patient confidentiality. Records are to be stored on a national database, which will allow staff to access information whenever someone is treated. A BMA survey found that 75 per cent of patients surveyed had concerns about the security of their health information. The government has lost a number of files on millions of people that had been kept on computer disks and memory sticks, therefore putting confidential information at risk.

Acknowledging individual personal beliefs and identity

Care practitioners must acknowledge individual personal beliefs and identity. This becomes even more important in a multi-ethnic society. In addition, care workers have their own views and beliefs on a number of moral and ethical issues.

ACTIVITY — Personal beliefs and identity

Discuss in groups the following case studies. Should a doctor be able to refuse to treat the following because of their own beliefs?

1. A lesbian couple wanting fertility treatment.
2. A homosexual wanting a sexual health test.
3. A Jehovah's Witness who has refused a blood transfusion.
4. A 15-year-old girl wanting an abortion.

The General Medical Council says that doctors who are pro-life and anti-abortion must tell patients this and refer them to another medical practitioner. Doctors who wear veils for religious reasons will be told it is good practice to remove them in certain circumstances, for example the treatment of deaf patients who need to lip read, or if the patient is uncomfortable not being able to see a doctor's face.

Group Activity

In groups find out whether your school/college has a uniform policy on the wearing of religious symbols.

CASE STUDY — Excluded!

A 14-year-old girl was excluded from her school for wearing a religious bangle (the Kara) as a sign of her religious faith. The school banned jewellery other than wristwatches and ear studs. She took the case to the High Court and the judge said that the school must allow her to wear the Kara as it was of exceptional importance to her identity and religious belief. After her victory in the court, Sarika Watkins-Sigh described herself as a 'proud Welsh Punjabi Sikh girl'.

1. Do you agree with the decision of the court? Give your reasons. Discuss as a whole group.

CASE STUDY — Helen

Helen is a qualified nurse who is working a day shift. When she arrives in the morning she meets with the other nurses to discuss the care given during the night. She then gives tablets, which have been prescribed by the doctor, to the patients and makes sure they all have a breakfast that meets their dietary needs. She then checks each patient individually and makes sure that they are comfortable and understand what is happening to them. She checks that all the health and safety measures are in place including the fire alarm procedures. One of her duties is to check that the drugs cabinet is locked and that all prescriptions have been recorded.

1. How is Helen putting the care values into practice?

CASE STUDY — Nigel

Nigel is a social worker who has a large caseload of people requiring help. Today he is meeting a young man who has recently been diagnosed as HIV positive. He is homeless and unable to organize his life. Nigel has arranged to meet Graham and offer support. He explains that everything discussed will be in confidence. Nigel respects Graham's beliefs and lifestyle and does not pre-judge him. He keeps a written record of the discussion, which he shows Graham so that they both agree on what they have discussed. During the discussion Nigel tries to assess Graham's needs and offer a range of possible ways forward. He tries to allow Graham to interact and does not impose himself on the discussion. However, he does point out to Graham the health issues linked to his lifestyle.

1 Describe how Nigel is implementing the care values.

CASE STUDY — Janine

When Janine applied for a post as a nursery assistant, she was sent a copy of the job description and a list of the qualities and skills required. The list below illustrates the care values the school feels are important.

1 Good communication skills: promotion of effective communication.

2 Respect for children's different beliefs and values: acknowledging personal beliefs and identity.

3 Basic first aid: promotion of health and safety.

4 Treating all children as individuals: promotion of anti-discriminatory practice.

5 Acting professionally and not discussing the children outside the school: maintaining confidentiality of information.

1 Discuss how these care values should ensure that the children are treated well.

THE PROFESSIONAL TRAINING AND DEVELOPMENT OF CARE PRACTITIONERS

The care values are an essential part in the training of all care practitioners. This can be shown in the training of nursery nurses. CACHE, the Council for Awards in Children's Care and Education identifies the following values and qualities as essential for the training of nursery nurses:

- a warm, caring and patient nature
- good communication skills
- a sense of responsibility
- to be consistent and fair
- a sense of humour
- to be physically fit
- to be creative
- an awareness of safety and hygiene
- to be able to work in a team.

When at work, the nursery nurse would be expected to have all these qualities and would be assessed by the supervisor on a regular basis. The things the supervisor might look for are:

- How does the nursery nurse greet the children when they arrive at school?
- How do they talk to the parents/carers?
- Do they ensure that the classroom is safe and there are no hazards?
- Are they good at working with colleagues?
- Can they show initiative when required, for example, during an emergency such as a fire alarm?
- Do they treat each child as an individual, recognizing their individual needs?

HOW CARE VALUES ARE IMPLEMENTED IN A CARE PRACTITIONER'S WORK

CASE STUDY   Sunita

Sunita works in an inner city surgery and she has a large caseload of patients covering a wide range of different problems and illnesses. Every day before her surgery, if she has time, she reads through the caseload of patients she will be seeing on that day. Her consulting room is arranged in an informal way with chairs and tables in a semi circle. The surgery is open six days a week and she shares evening shifts with her colleagues. All the written material in the waiting room is available in a range of languages, and large print volumes are also available. There is a small play area for young children, supervised by a voluntary assistant. The files for her patients are kept locked in a filing cabinet and Sunita and the other practice doctors are the only key holders. Sometimes she has difficult, rude patients who she tries to deal with in a fair but positive way. She allows patients to bring a family member with them and also an advocate to speak for them. Sunita tries hard to use appropriate language without being condescending. She tries to explain to the patients not only what is wrong with them but also the range of treatments available. She always tries to turn her phone off during consultations and closes the door using an 'engaged' sign.

1 Identify, using examples, the care values applied by Sunita.

CASE STUDY   Jeff

Jeff works in a day care centre in a multi-ethnic community. He has attended training courses to update his awareness of ethnic diversity. He is careful about how he communicates with the adults who use the centre by not appearing to talk down to them. He is also responsible for liaising with the Fire Service to ensure regular inspections are made. The adults often talk to Jeff about personal issues and about other members of the group. Jeff listens but does not comment about their views. A number of the group suffer from a range of health issues including incontinence, and Jeff tries to deal with these problems in a calm and professional way.

1 Make a list of the care values Jeff is applying in the day care centre.
   Give examples of how Jeff implements the care values.

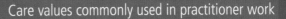

THE CONSEQUENCES IF PRACTITIONERS HAVE NOT EFFECTIVELY IMPLEMENTED THE CARE VALUES

Discrimination

Service users will suffer in a number of ways if care practitioners do not implement the care values. Certain groups might suffer from discrimination in their treatment.

Older adults

The poor

Groups most likely to suffer discrimination in health and social care services

Ethnic minorities

The physically disabled

The mentally disabled

A report by the Healthcare Commission, the Audit Commission and the Commission for Social Inspection '*Living Well in Later Life*' in 2006 found that many of Britain's older people were being neglected and poorly treated by the health system. Older adults were not being treated with dignity, as many were being cared for in mixed-sex wards and were left on trolleys for long periods of time. They were often moved from one ward to another to make way for patients requiring surgery. Often their meals would be taken away from them before they had eaten them. The report also found that many older adults were treated in a patronizing and condescending way.

 Why do you think older adults are particularly likely to suffer from discriminatory treatment?

An investigation into health care given to people with mental health problems and learning disabilities shows they often get worse treatment than others. The Disability Rights Commission found evidence of discrimination and neglect in the checks made on these groups. For example, people with learning disabilities who have diabetes have fewer measurements of their body mass index, while those who have had a stroke have fewer blood pressure checks. More than 50 per cent of the disabled group studied said they had difficulty accessing their GP. They found the attitude of some reception staff inflexible.

Discrimination can also take place if people do not understand the health treatment they are being given. The National Consumer Council found that many patients were unable to make informed choices about their care. They asked 2000 adults about their experiences and found that 20 per cent had difficulty understanding the information they were getting. This was particularly true amongst the poorer sections of society. This means that many people are not empowered and can easily suffer discrimination as a result.

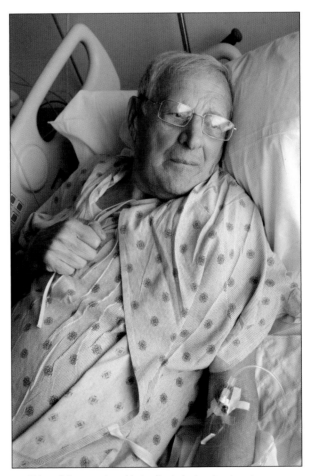

▲ Older adults are vulnerable to discriminatory treatment.

Some of the areas where discrimination occurred were:

- health professionals not always answering questions in a way that could be understood
- written information not always available in plain language
- the lack of bilingual staff and trained interpreters
- some people being embarrassed to ask questions to their GP
- doctors sometimes appearing to be too busy to answer questions
- some patients not having a say over when and where they are treated.

5 According to this research which care values are not being delivered for significant numbers of the population?

Social exclusion

Some groups of people in society can suffer from social exclusion partly as a result of the care values not being implemented.

> **Social exclusion:** excluding people from opportunities to have a healthy and economically comfortable life.

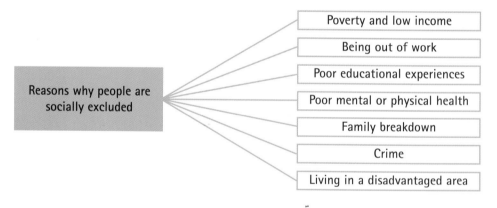

Reasons why people are socially excluded
- Poverty and low income
- Being out of work
- Poor educational experiences
- Poor mental or physical health
- Family breakdown
- Crime
- Living in a disadvantaged area

Group Activity

Discuss in groups the possible reasons for the big differences between teenage pregnancy rates in different parts of the country.

The government believes that 140,000 families are at risk of social exclusion. Hilary Armstrong, the Minister for Social Exclusion, believes that health and social services workers need to work closely with such vulnerable individuals.

Quite often the socially excluded live in areas where the health services are stretched and it is difficult for care practitioners to provide the service they would like to. A study in Scotland by researchers at Glasgow University found that the poorest parts of Scotland's towns and cities had 11 per cent fewer GPs and less access to health programmes than the more affluent areas. Partly as a result, ill health was found to be twice as high in the most deprived group compared with the most affluent.

An investigation by London TravelWatch found that nine London hospitals lacked good transport facilities, making it very hard for patients to access services, thus increasing social exclusion.

Teenage pregnancies are higher amongst the socially excluded and poorer parts of the country. The highest rate of teenage pregnancy is found in the relatively poor area of Southwark, which has five times the number of the lowest area, the relatively affluent Chiltern.

Premature babies are put at risk by a lack of intensive care facilities in hospitals according to a report by the National Audit Office. Many of the poorest facilities were found in areas with the highest number of socially excluded families.

 6 In what ways might individuals living in such areas suffer from social exclusion?

▸ People who live in disadvantaged areas may have less access to health programmes than more affluent areas.

THE EFFECT OF POOR CARE PRACTICE ON THE SELF-ESTEEM AND SELF-CONCEPT OF SERVICE USERS

When the care services provide poor care practice it will inevitably influence the self-esteem and self-concept of service users.

An example of how **disempowerment** and low self-worth can result from a lack of quality care can be seen from some research by MIND into 148 women suffering from post-natal depression. They found that many new mothers suffering from post-natal depression were given medication instead of counselling. One in ten of the women had to wait over one year for treatment. Also four-fifths of the women admitted to psychiatric wards were separated from their babies. Another problem was the lack of mother and baby units. There are only 17 in England and Wales, two in Scotland and none in Northern Ireland.

Lack of self-esteem is a major problem for women suffering from premenstrual syndrome. At this time women often feel worthless and inadequate, which leads to confidence issues. One woman in the survey 'felt worthless and inadequate and thought she looked fat and ugly'.

A report by the mental health charities Rethink and Sane, and the Royal College of Nursing, found that people with severe mental illness were still receiving **sub-standard levels** of physical care, which was having a negative effect upon their confidence and self-worth. The report recommends a more holistic approach to treating mental health.

 7 What is meant by an holistic approach to care?

…WORD CHECK

disempowerment – not being in control because someone else is making decisions for you.

sub-standard levels – unacceptable ways of treating people in care practice.

 Group Activity

Carry out research to find out about the work of MIND on www.mind.org.uk. Share your findings with others.

 Group Activity

Carry out research into premenstrual syndrome. Share your findings with others.

Bandura's theory

A psychologist called Bandura argued that children copy behaviour they see in other people, particularly adults. A child might be taught by a teacher who ignores the care values when working in the school. This could result in the child learning that this behaviour is normal and when they become an adult, they behave like their teacher towards other people.

8 Take each of the care values and explain how Bandura might explain why this child might grow up to treat other adults in unacceptable ways because of bad experiences at school.

ASSESSMENT PRACTICE

Phoday, a four-year-old child of African descent, has just started at his local nursery school. One of his teachers has noticed some of the white children refusing to play with Phoday and also making unpleasant comments to him about his skin colour. Phoday has become increasingly withdrawn and quiet and is refusing to join in group activities in class. Phoday has also missed several days from school and is unwilling to talk to his teacher.

1. Identify and explain **two** care values the teachers could use to improve Phoday's self-esteem. [4]

2. Describe how the school could promote greater tolerance by the white children towards Phoday. [6]

3. Explain what professional training could be provided to help teachers recognize and deal with prejudice and discrimination in the school. [6]

4. Assess the possible consequences for Phoday if the situation in school does not change. [10]

The government are keen to help people who retire by giving them the opportunity to learn new skills and interests. Many older adults suffer a culture shock when they retire. Evidence suggests that people live longer and more healthily if they remain active in later life.

5. Describe **two** ways an older adult's self-esteem might be improved if they remain active and involved after retiring from work. [4]

6. Explain how this might reduce the discrimination and social exclusion of the older adult. [5]

7. Explain which care values the government is trying to promote through plans to develop new skills and interests with retired adults. [6]

8. Describe **two** ways in which practitioners could help promote self-esteem amongst older adults. [4]

9. Assess the reasons why there is going to be a greater need to encourage older adults to remain active in the future. [10]

The development of self-concept and personal relationships

▶ Getting started

To be successful in the examination you need to show a good understanding of the following:

a the factors affecting self-concept and how self-concept is linked to personal relationships

b how self-esteem, self-image and self-concept are formed

c factors that affect an individual's self-concept, including:
- i age
- ii appearance
- iii gender
- iv social class
- v ethnicity/culture
- vi emotional development
- vii education
- viii relationships with others
- ix sexual orientation
- x life experiences, for example, employment status

d how care practitioners can build self-esteem and influence the self-concept of service users through care practice including:
- i relationship building with service users
- ii empowerment of service users
- iii promoting positive relationships with family, partners, work colleagues and friends.

THE FACTORS AFFECTING SELF-CONCEPT AND HOW SELF-CONCEPT IS LINKED TO PERSONAL RELATIONSHIPS

Self–esteem: the view that an individual has of themselves, their own worth and their own identity.

Self–image: how a person sees themselves based upon people's reactions to them.

Self–concept: a combination of self-esteem and self-image.

Self-concept will be very closely linked to the range of individuals a person has contact with and the life stage they are in. The following table illustrates how self-concept develops throughout one's life and is constantly changing.

Life stage	How self-concept is linked to personal relationships
Infancy	Self-concept is almost entirely based upon the parent/carer and child relationship. A child is likely to have a positive self-concept if bonding has taken place. The child's world will almost entirely revolve around the family.
Childhood	Relationships made at school will become important. A child will develop a view of themselves based upon how teachers treat them. Teachers will try to give praise and encouragement, which should help the child to gain in confidence. Also they will begin to have more contact with other children and will learn about who they are based upon these relationships.
Adolescence	Relationships with peers will become important for an individual's self-concept, particularly with the opposite sex. Successful relationships will help individuals get through this particularly difficult stage of life.
Adulthood	Many individuals will establish a positive self-concept based around a long-term relationship and good experiences at work. A person may develop new friends through the workplace, which will provide further identity as to who they are.
Later adulthood	This can be a difficult stage for some individuals as they may have to look at themselves differently. It is possible that they may become more isolated, especially if they suffer a close bereavement. New hobbies may develop, which will provide new relationships enabling a positive self-concept to be reformed.

Who are the important people individuals have contact with who play a part in influencing self-concept?

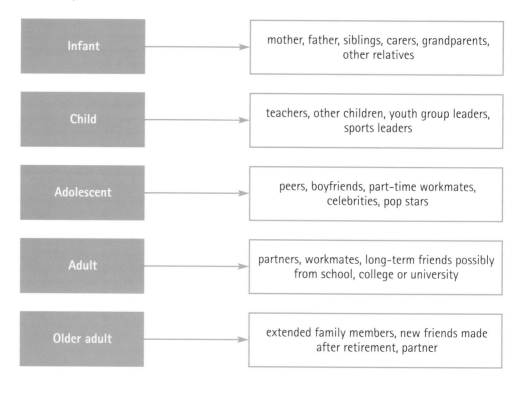

Infant	→	mother, father, siblings, carers, grandparents, other relatives
Child	→	teachers, other children, youth group leaders, sports leaders
Adolescent	→	peers, boyfriends, part-time workmates, celebrities, pop stars
Adult	→	partners, workmates, long-term friends possibly from school, college or university
Older adult	→	extended family members, new friends made after retirement, partner

9 ▷ Describe how the self-concept of each of the individuals above might be influenced by the relationship they have with those groups identified. Draw up two lists: positive and negative self-concept influences.

HOW SELF-ESTEEM, SELF-IMAGE AND SELF-CONCEPT ARE FORMED

An individual's self-concept describes the complete way a person thinks about themselves. There are two aspects to self-concept: first, self-esteem, which means how highly an individual thinks about their abilities and self-worth. The second aspect is self-image, which a person gains from how people react to them. Self-image combines with self-esteem to make up the self-concept an individual may have.

How self-concept is formed

Self-image + Self-esteem = Self-concept

▲ Being in a successful sports team can contribute to positive self-esteem.

Positive self-esteem is formed from a number of factors. These include physical factors such as:
- being good looking
- being fit and having a good body
- being a member of a successful sports team.

Social and emotional factors that are linked to positive self-esteem include:
- having a strong, close-knit family
- having a number of close, reliable friends
- being in a close, long-term relationship.

Economic factors that are linked to positive self-esteem include:
- having enough money to buy the essential goods
- being able to afford the occasional luxury
- not always being in debt.

Environmental factors linked to positive self-esteem include:
- having a comfortable home to live in
- living in a pleasant safe area
- not having to live in a highly polluted area.

Few individuals are fortunate enough to have all the advantages shown above. What affects our self-esteem is the balance between **positive** and **negative factors**. Many individuals have low self-esteem because they struggle to survive and cannot cope with the life they have to lead. Children gain self-esteem from the way they are treated by their parents or carers when they are small. A child who is loved and valued when young will have high self-esteem.

Self-image is formed by looking at yourself in a mirror and creating a picture in your mind of the '**essential you**'. The individual will be influenced by what they see in relation to their height, gender, skin colour, personality and the way other people see them.

A person's self-concept develops and changes as a result of lifetime experiences. At a young age self-awareness begins when a child recognizes their own face in a mirror. From then onwards children begin to form ideas about who they are. This develops through their use of language

> **✓ ...WORD CHECK**
>
> **positive factors** – factors which create high self-concept.
>
> **negative factors** – aspects of life which can cause health problems for an individual.
>
> **essential you** – what sort of person you really are.

and relationships with parents or carers. Early experiences at school will play a part. An individual's self-concept usually begins to settle down when they start work and take on responsibilities. This is the stage when the individual often feels confident in a work role and in social and sexual relationships. When an individual retires, their self-concept can be damaged as they no longer have a real purpose in life since work was a very important part of how they valued themselves.

Group Activity

How do you feel about yourself as a person at the moment? Build up a picture of yourself to include what you like about yourself, what you would like to change, what you are good at and what your weaknesses are.

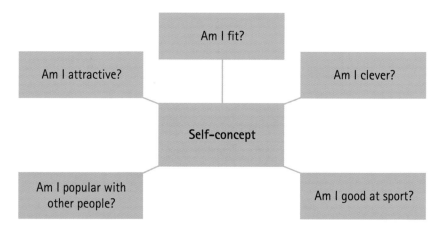

THE FACTORS AFFECTING AN INDIVIDUAL'S SELF-CONCEPT

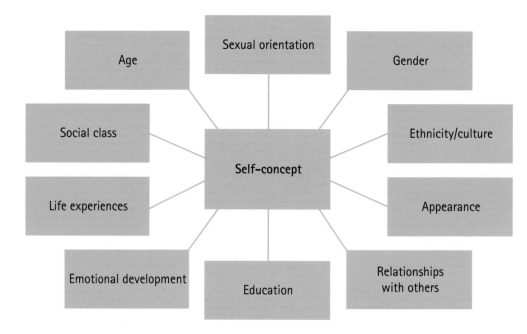

...WORD CHECK

persistent – an illness that won't clear up.

value – to hold dear; to show respect.

Individuals who sometimes show signs of physical illness, for example they cannot shake off a **persistent** cold, and go to the doctor for treatment, are sometimes suffering from issues relating to low self-concept that is the real cause of their illness. For example, they may feel ill because their boss at work does not **value** them, or they have recently had a relationship breakdown, or they may be unsure of their sexual orientation and are worried about how other people might react to them.

Age

In society today there is increasing pressure to remain looking young and hence the huge increase in the use of cosmetic surgery by both men and women. Everyone seems to want the perfect body and the media increasingly seems to make us feel inadequate if we have any physical imperfections. This can have devastating effects upon some individuals who are driven to extreme measures to overcome their low self-esteem and sense of inadequacy. In our society getting old is seen in a negative way and many individuals do all they can to delay the ageing process. More and more medical practitioners are devoting increasing amounts of their time to making the body beautiful rather than curing real illnesses and diseases.

CASE STUDY — Ageing

John is approaching retirement and he is worried about how he is going to cope financially and socially once he stops work. He is beginning to show signs of anxiety and his wife is worried about his health.

1. What could John and his wife do to try and ensure his self-esteem is maintained once he retires?

Appearance

Appearance is increasingly important to how some individuals feel about themselves. Think about the way young people are concerned about having the right designer label clothes and trainers, and how those children who are unable to afford the high costs of such items are made to feel inadequate and suffer low self-worth. This is again partly a result of 'celebrity culture' and the way it is portrayed in the media. Body shape is particularly important to the way young girls see themselves and can lead to extreme feelings of low self-worth with all the health-related consequences such as anorexia and bulimia. As individuals get older, appearance seems to have less impact on our self-concept and we value people for what they are rather than the way they present themselves.

▲ Is this the image all girls would like to have?

Gender

Gender is the way society expects individuals of each sex to behave. They learn their roles from the culture and society they live in. From birth, expectations of behaviour are set and this is reinforced by the way parents dress their children (blue for boys and pink for girls) and the toys they buy for them.

CASE STUDY — Gender roles

Two sociologists, Murphy and Elwood, argue that children arrive in school with attitudes and behaviour already learnt from their parents. For example, boys will play with construction toys and girls with dolls and prams. The sociologists believe that this will influence what boys and girls do at school and in their future jobs. This will mean boys and girls will have different opportunities and girls might be at a disadvantage.

1. In what ways could boys and girls be affected by their early childhood upbringing?
2. How might girls be disadvantaged and suffer low self-esteem?

Group Activity

Compare the way boys' and girls' toys are advertised in a typical catalogue, for example, Toys R Us. Are they stereotypical?

Group Activity

Look up the UNICEF Report and see how British young people compare with children across the rest of Europe (www.unicef.org.uk).

Group Activity

Carry out some research using books and the Internet to compare male and female earnings and the number of women in top jobs in business, politics and industry.

If a child is brought up in a way that **deviates** from the norm their self-concept may be lowered because society will see them as odd or unusual. The child may be unhappy and this can lead to physical, social, intellectual and emotional health problems which health practitioners will have to deal with. Recent research found that British children were amongst the least happy in the whole of Europe despite having one of the highest standards of living (UNICEF Report 2007). One fifth of British young people rated their physical and mental health as poor – the worst among the rich countries surveyed. Girls reported lower levels of well-being than boys.

Gender stereotypes

In modern society there is much less adult gender stereotyping but it still exists. Women still find it difficult to fulfil their potential because of the glass ceiling effect at work and assumptions that they will be the primary carers for children. Emotional ill health is often greater amongst women who do not have fulfilling jobs in which they can develop a positive self-concept. Mental ill health is often higher amongst women who do not work but stay at home looking after their children than women who work.

▶ Is this still the image we have?

> A glass ceiling is the invisible barrier that prevents women from achieving equality with men in the workplace.

10 ▶ Why do you think this glass ceiling has not been completely shattered?

Social class

...WORD CHECK

deviates – behaviour that is seen as different from the norm and is often seen in a negative way.

squalid – really bad living conditions which have a negative effect on health.

Social class is usually defined by looking at the type of job a person does, their earnings, level of education, the type of house they live in and where they live. It can affect a person's life expectancy and their chances of leading a healthy, fulfilling life. Although the division between the classes is narrower today than in the past, class does still influence our view of ourselves. Middle-class children still do better in the education system than working-class children and the top universities, such as Oxford and Cambridge, are still dominated by the middle classes.

Poverty linked to social class continues to be a significant influence upon the value we place upon ourselves. Low self-esteem can be inevitable for children who see opportunities around them, which they are unable to participate in.

CASE STUDY   Tube posters reveal child poverty

Shocking images of children brought up in overcrowded housing are being shown on the London Underground to raise commuters' awareness of child poverty. The homeless charity Shelter said it wanted to show what life is like for some 400,000 children in the city. Digital poster screens of youngsters trapped in **squalid** conditions will appear at three tube stations.

1   In what ways does living in these conditions affect a child's self-concept and their personal relationships?

Ethnicity/culture

Ethnicity and culture affect self-concept in both positive and negative ways. Individuals now live in a multicultural society and are used to seeing people from a wide range of backgrounds in towns and cities. A person who belongs to an ethnic minority, for example, an Indian or Pakistani boy or girl, can gain a sense of belonging and support from the other members of their community. However, this self-concept can be undermined if the host community (White Britain) treats them differently and discriminates or shows prejudice towards them. Although as a society we are more welcoming towards minority groups, it is clear that some white people still find it hard to accept people from different cultures with different values, religions and styles of dress from their own. Care practitioners are trained to be aware of cultural differences and respect individual rights and diversity. For example, Asian women would expect to be treated by a female doctor.

Group Activity

Find out about the culture and background of one ethnic minority that lives in our society.

Prejudice is usually a negative attitude, based upon a stereotype, towards individuals or groups.

Discrimination is treating a person unfairly usually because of their age, gender, ethnicity, sexuality or disability.

CASE STUDY   Barack Obama

In November 2008 the Americans elected a new president, Barack Obama, the first black president in the USA. Millions of Americans queued for hours to vote and thousands attended the meetings held by Obama. In the same month, Lewis Hamilton became the first black Formula One racing champion.

1 In what ways could these events raise the self-esteem of black children in the UK?

▶ A new role model for black children.

Emotional development

Emotional development has a key influence on self-concept. Very young children are unable to describe their self-concept and this often leads to difficulties for parents in understanding their child's behaviour, for example, temper tantrums. As the child grows older they can express their feelings but they tend to be unable to understand other people's feelings fully. By their late teens young people can begin to compare themselves with other teenagers, and by adulthood, people are usually able to see who they are and be able to use language to express their self-concept.

I now know who I am with my role as a parent, worker and husband. I wish I'd known this when I was younger and confused.

11 ▶ Why are teenagers often confused about who they are, which can lead to bad behaviour and rebelling against their parents and teachers?

Education

Group Activity

What courses are available for 14–19 year olds in your centre? Do they meet the needs of all students?

Education is now compulsory up to the age of 16, which is going to rise to 18. The reason for this is that the government believe that everyone should have the opportunity to fulfil their potential, which will make children feel good about themselves and have a sense of achievement. Doing well in exams or performing well at sport makes people, including adults, feel good about themselves. On the other hand, school can be a very frustrating place for some children if they are unable to cope and succeed. Poor behaviour by some children at school is the direct result of finding education difficult and unrewarding. This is why schools now try to provide a range of courses to meet all children's needs.

Schools also try to develop self-concept. Young people meet new adults and children and lasting friendships are often made. Think about how many individuals use Facebook and MySpace to keep in touch with their friends. This can boost self-esteem because it shows that they continue to want to be your friend. Teachers are expected to encourage all children to succeed and develop the wide range of talents the children in their classroom have. As a young person you learn a great deal about yourself, including your strengths and weaknesses, from education and from interacting with a wide range of people at school.

CASE STUDY — Daniel

Daniel teaches in a primary school and he is concerned about his students' negative approach to learning. A lot of the students come from disadvantaged backgrounds with limited opportunities to develop fully. He has been asked by the head teacher to come up with some ideas to improve the self-esteem of the children.

 1 What would you do if you were Daniel?

Relationships with others

All individuals need to develop relationships with other people. Strong, close relationships with family and friends will provide emotional security and a sense of happiness. This will lead to individuals having a positive view of who they are and an opinion of what other people think about them. A number of writers are concerned that today, because of the

▲ Strong family relationships provide emotional security.

increase in relationship breakdowns through divorce, and so on, more individuals are unhappy and isolated and this can lead to problems for society. The increase in anti-social behaviour orders may be a sign of such problems. The decline of the extended family may also lead to children having less contact with their grandparents and all the benefits this once provided.

Group Activity

Research into the extended family and discuss in groups what the advantages and disadvantages are to children who live in close-knit extended families.

An extended family is a large close family group, for example, grandparents, parents and children living together or brothers and sisters living together with their partners and children.

CASE STUDY   David

David, aged seven, enjoys the company of his grandparents who live nearby and they pop in to see him and his sister several times a week. David's parents both work full time and find it difficult to meet all of his needs. As a result David is showing signs of withdrawal and isolation.

1. How could David's grandparents help him to become happier and more secure?

2. Why might a child who has experienced a difficult family relationship have a poor self-concept?

Sexual orientation

Sexual orientation refers to our choice of sexual partner. Individuals live in a broadly **heterosexual society** where they have relationships with the opposite sex. Some, however, are attracted to their own sex (homosexual or lesbian) and a smaller number are bisexual (attracted to both sexes). Our self-concept is strongly influenced by who our sexual partner is. Heterosexuality is positively viewed by society because it is seen as the norm. As teenagers boys and girls begin to develop close intimate relations with the opposite sex and this gives them a feeling of self-worth.

Until the 1960s homosexuality was illegal and, although there is much greater tolerance to same sex couples today, it can still be a traumatic experience for a young person to cope with. Admitting your homosexuality to your friends and parents takes a lot of courage, because you may anticipate shock, disappointment and humiliation. Some members of society still express homophobic attitudes (an intense dislike of homosexual people) and homosexuals may experience prejudice at work and in laws relating to pensions and adoption. It may be difficult for homosexuals to have a positive view of themselves as a result of the negative symbols they see around them. Fortunately, as a result of more gay role models in the media, such low self-esteem is less likely than in the past, when homosexual men had to hide their sexual orientation and often married a woman as a cover for their sexuality.

▲ Campaigning for equality of rights and equal treatment.

 Group Activity

Do a small survey of young people's views on homosexuality.

Life experiences

As a person gets older, they go through a range of life experiences (the day-to-day things that happen to all of us). These will influence our self-concept, as we will begin to learn a lot about who and what we are.

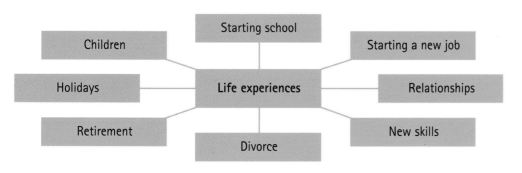

Children — Starting school — Starting a new job — Holidays — Life experiences — Relationships — Retirement — Divorce — New skills

✓ **...WORD CHECK**

sexual orientation – your sexual preference.

heterosexual society – a society where male/female relationships are the norm.

Learning to cope with new experiences is important. As young children all our decisions were made for us by our parents. As individuals get older and gain more independence they increasingly have to make choices: which friends to have, whether to smoke, at what age to drink, what job to try and get, whether or not to marry. All these decisions will influence our self-concept and how other members of society see us. Being exposed to difficult experiences, such as the death of a close friend, can teach individuals how to cope in the future, if faced with a similar situation.

 12 Make a list of the life experiences you have had so far in your life. How did you cope with them and what did you learn about yourself as a result of each experience?

CASE STUDY   Osama going to university

Osama has just received his A level results and is now able to go away to university. He is the first member of his family to go to university and he is worried about how he will cope. His parents support his decision but they are also concerned about losing him and what might happen to him when he is away. They are not sure what to do and how often they should visit him. Osama wants to be more independent but he has relied almost entirely on his parents so far in his life.

1 What are the best ways for Osama and his parents to cope with this new experience?

HOW CARE PRACTITIONERS CAN BUILD SELF-ESTEEM AND INFLUENCE THE SELF-CONCEPT OF SERVICE USERS
Relationship building with service users

 Group Activity

Discuss with other members of the group the way you have been treated by a care practitioner, for example, doctor, dentist or social worker. Did you feel valued?

Care practitioners need to try and build self-esteem and influence the self-concept of service users through good care practice. Good practice should follow the care values discussed earlier. One example of how good relationships are built with service users can be seen from the Nursing and Midwifery Council Code of Conduct, which identifies the following values:

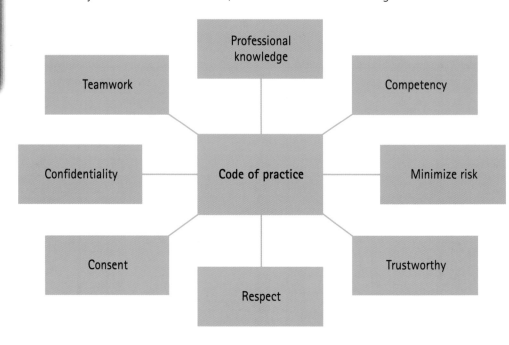

These are the shared values of all the UK health care regulatory bodies:

- General Chiropractic Council
- General Medical Council
- General Osteopathic Council
- Nursing and Midwifery Council

- General Dental Council
- General Optical Council
- Health Professions Council
- Royal Pharmaceutical Society of Great Britain.

Group Activity

Look up one of the councils on the Internet and find out how they treat service users and promote their self-esteem.

Empowerment of service users

One of the most important skills used by care workers is empowerment. This means encouraging a service user to make decisions and take control of their own life. The care worker should involve the person being treated at all stages of their care, giving them the opportunity to reply and respond to any points made by the professional. This should build a service user's self-esteem and confidence in their ability to make decisions. The World Health Organization (1978) states that 'people have a right and a duty to participate in the planning of their health care. This is clearly a basic **human right**'.

...WORD CHECK

human right – basic rights that all people should have, which formed the basis of the Human Rights Act 1998.

CASE STUDY   Julie

Julie is a resident in a nursing home. She did not want to leave her own home but it became increasingly difficult for her to manage daily tasks. In the nursing home she has to follow the rules of the home including times to get up and go to bed, what to eat and when. Julie's health begins to deteriorate and she withdraws into herself and does not want to leave her room.

1. In what way is Julie being disempowered?
2. What could the nursing home do to empower their residents?
3. Do you feel empowered in your school/college?

Promoting positive relationships

Care workers are involved in building positive relationships with partners who may be going through a difficulty in their relationship. A good example of this in practice can be seen from the work of Relate. They try to rebuild self-esteem when it is often at its lowest following a breakdown in relationships.

Group Activity

Research into Relate (www.relate.org.uk) and find out more about the work the organization does.

Ways that Relate rebuilds self-esteem and family relationships

- counselling partners
- rebuilding parent–child relationships
- helping children cope with family breakdown
- mediation services.

Most schools and colleges today have a trained counsellor to deal with relationship problems such as bullying, which clearly have negative effects on a child's self-esteem.

Occasions when a counsellor can be helpful:

Parents divorcing	Death in the family	Suspicion of abuse

Bullying or teasing	Difficulty settling into a new school	Child has extreme mood swings	Drug problems

Alcohol problems	Eating problems	Sexual orientation issues

Many schools now use students as counsellors because some students would prefer to talk to someone of a similar age to themselves. Bullying UK is a voluntary group who work with the victims of bullying.

Group Activity

Find out about what support is available to promote positive relationships in your school.

Group Activity

Look up Bullying UK (www.bullyinguk.co.uk) and see what help they provide to try and restore self-esteem in the victims of bullying.

Adults at work may also suffer relationship difficulties with their colleagues. Workplace bullying is more widespread than many people believe. Research undertaken by the University of Manchester Institute of Science and Technology found that 47 per cent of employees witnessed bullying over a five-year period. This could be in the form of:

Group Activity

Look up the work of this charity:
www.andreaadamstrust.org.

- being given unrealistic tasks to do
- being shouted at in front of colleagues
- being given very simple trivial tasks to do
- being forced to leave your job.

Most companies have a Human Resources Department with people trained to deal with incidents of bullying. The Andrea Adams Trust is a charity working with victims of workplace bullying.

ASSESSMENT PRACTICE

Julie is aged 14 and attends her local comprehensive school. She used to enjoy school but recently she has become withdrawn, and her teachers are finding it difficult to get her to concentrate and work. She was upset by her recent SATS results. They have also noticed marks on Julie that could be the first signs of self-harm. Her friends have noticed that Julie is becoming more secretive and she rarely goes out with them into town to eat at MacDonald's. They have also noticed that Julie has been buying a lot of fashion and celebrity magazines rather than spending her money on school lunches. Julie has also stopped attending the dance classes after school, which she used to enjoy. Julie's parents have recently split up following a long period of arguments.

1 Identify two possible factors that might link to Julie's self-esteem. [2]

2 Explain how Julie's friends could support her. [6]

3 Identify which care workers could help Julie. [3]

4 Discuss the type of help they could provide and how they would carry out that help. [10]

The psychologist John Bowlby carried out many experiments with babies and their parents. This enabled him to describe the importance of a strong bond developing between a baby and a parent. A good close relationship is very important for the child and a poor relationship can create problems for the child's development.

5 Identify and explain the positive effects of a close parent (carer)/child relationship for a child's self-esteem. [6]

6 Describe the possible negative effects for a child if a close bond is not established between a child and a parent/carer. [8]

Judith is 79 years old and she has lived alone in a small village since the death of her husband five years ago. She is lonely and finding it difficult to carry out basic household tasks. Her daughter, Jane, wants her to move and live with her in a large city 90 miles away. Judith is worried about leaving the area she has lived in all her life.

7 Describe **five** factors that may affect the development of Judith's self-concept. [10]

8 Discuss how care practitioners could try to build her self-esteem. [8]

Promoting and supporting health improvement

▸ Getting started

You will gain an understanding of:

a factors affecting health and well-being throughout the life course and the effects of these factors on the individual's health and well-being

b the different ways health professionals can support service users to change their lifestyles in order to improve health, including considering the importance of:
  i   diet
  ii regular exercise
  iii supportive relationships
  iv work
  v   rest and sleep
  vi stress
  vii recreational activities
  viii financial resources

c how these factors can influence health in both a positive (health improvement, longevity, reduced morbidity rates) or negative (increase in sickness rates, premature death, poor mental health) way

d health promotion, including:
  i   the aims of health promotion – to include raising awareness, preventing ill health, improving fitness levels and improving life expectancy
  ii the approaches used in health promotion to improve health and well-being – to include disease prevention, the adoption of healthier lifestyles and actions taken at national level to improve the nation's health
  iii how health professionals support individuals to change health-related behaviour – to include diagnosis, monitoring progress, health planning, advice and counselling, and evaluating progress against targets

e how effective promotion and support for health improvement is built upon through the careful implementation of care values, including:
  i   promotion of choice
  ii respecting identity and culture
  iii empowerment
  iv promoting independence
  v   respecting individual right to choice.

FACTORS AFFECTING HEALTH AND WELL-BEING THROUGHOUT THE LIFE COURSE

Even before a baby is born, the health and well-being of that boy or girl has started to be affected by a wide range of factors. The health of the mother will already be playing a part in influencing the health of the baby. She may smoke, drink alcohol and not have a healthy diet. These factors may continue to influence the health of that baby throughout their life. The individual will have some control over some of these factors; others will be more difficult to influence because of their own circumstances. For example, the individual may find it difficult to lead a healthy lifestyle, despite wanting to do so, because of poverty and **deprivation**.

> ⊘ **...WORD CHECK**
> **deprivation** – lacking the basic essentials such as food and shelter.

The main factors influencing an individual's health are:

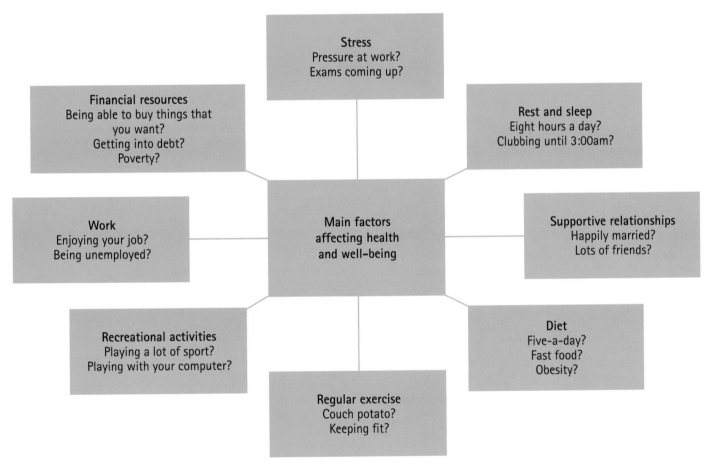

At each stage of life some of these factors become more important than others. For example, an adult may be most influenced by work factors, stress and financial resources. They are likely to have a family including children and will be under pressure to provide for their physical needs, for example, food and a home. This can then result in pressures at work that can then lead to stress. This could put a strain on their relationships with family and friends, resulting in being unable to relax and sleep. This can then make the problem worse by creating more difficulties at work because of time taken off due to physical or mental illness. Each problem links together to become a circle that is very difficult to break away from.

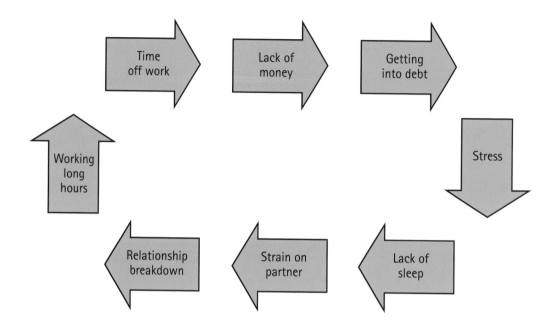

CASE STUDY — Jack and Hilda

Hilda and Jack have recently retired and are having to live on their state pensions. They were unable to save money throughout their life because they were both in low-paid jobs without pension schemes. They live in rented accommodation on the fifth floor in a block of flats. They have problems meeting their day-to-day living costs and they are starting to argue about how their money should be spent. Their two daughters have both married and emigrated to Australia.

1. Describe the factors affecting their health and well-being, and the possible effects this will have on their physical, social and emotional health.

CASE STUDY — Sunny

Sunny is doing her AS levels in her local college. She did quite well in her GCSEs but is finding the work at AS difficult. Her parents are very keen for her to succeed and they want her to go to university. Sunny is unsure about going away and really wants to leave college and get a job. She has also started to go out drinking at weekends with her friends and staying in bed for most of Sunday. She used to belong to a gym but she rarely goes there now. Her parents are concerned and there are constant arguments.

1. What are the main factors affecting Sunny's health and well-being?

2. How might these affect her physically, emotionally and intellectually in the longer term?

When an individual is trapped by the factors discussed above, they are likely to require professional help in order to try and break out of the vicious circle.

The information on the following page gives an idea of the scale of the problem facing health practitioners in Britain today.

Unhealthy Britain

- One in five adults is obese.
- Twenty-one per cent of boys aged six to ten and 14 per cent of girls will be obese in 2025. In 2004 the figure was ten per cent for both boys and girls.
- One million children will be obese by 2012.
- One in four men and one in six women drink more alcohol than the recommended levels.
- Most adults do not exercise enough.
- Just one in four people eat the recommended five portions of fruit and vegetables a day.

Promoting health should be an important aspect of our lives, particularly after considering the facts given above. The government is trying to persuade individuals to take more responsibility for their own health and well-being so that fewer people become obese, experience mobility problems or are prone to illness and disease.

In recent years there has been a definite move away from concentrating just on treating people who are ill, to trying to prevent illness in the first place. 'Prevention is better than cure' is a phrase that clearly makes sense. It means that long-term savings could be made by the health services and many beds, which at the moment are taken up with people who have led unhealthy lives, such as smokers and excessive alcohol drinkers, could be released for people suffering from the normal effects of ageing. This would reduce the burden of health care costs.

Expenditure on the National Health Service:
1997 £34 billion
2007 £84 billion
2010 (estimated) £100 billion

Source: *Managing not to Manage: Management in the NHS*, by Harriet Sargeant, Centre for Policy Studies, 2003

The government tries to promote healthy living in a number of ways, for example, by running health campaigns, and using the media and celebrities such as Jamie Oliver to get their message across.

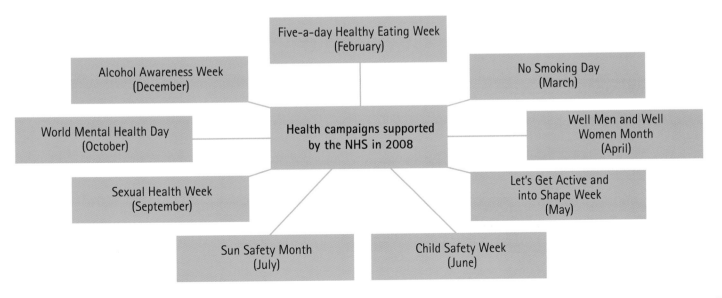

Five-a-day Healthy Eating Week (February)

Alcohol Awareness Week (December)

No Smoking Day (March)

World Mental Health Day (October)

Health campaigns supported by the NHS in 2008

Well Men and Well Women Month (April)

Sexual Health Week (September)

Let's Get Active and into Shape Week (May)

Sun Safety Month (July)

Child Safety Week (June)

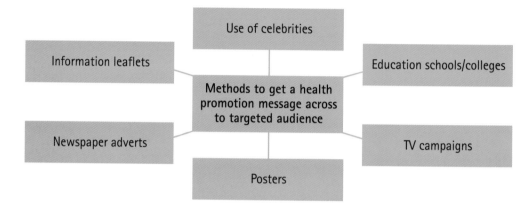

Use of celebrities

Information leaflets

Education schools/colleges

Methods to get a health promotion message across to targeted audience

Newspaper adverts

TV campaigns

Posters

Group Activity

Research **four** of the following health promotion websites and produce a handout on them:

- www.5aday.nhs.uk
- www.liverpoolactivecity.net
- www.sunsmart.org.uk
- www.wfmh.org
- www.nosmokingday.org.uk
- www.capt.org.uk
- www.fpa.org.uk
- www.drinkaware.co.uk

CASE STUDY — Dr Alice Roberts

There is a lot of publicity in the media promoting healthy living. A very popular BBC programme, 'Don't Die Young' presented by Dr Alice Roberts, covered many aspects of health, including one of the growing health epidemics: liver disease. Women in their thirties are becoming the first generation of women of that age experiencing growing levels of cirrhosis of the liver.

1. Why do you think liver damage is affecting more and more young women?
2. What other lifestyle factors might put women's health at risk in the future?
3. Do you think this way of promoting health (on television) will be successful?

Group Activity

Carry out research into 'Health Action Zones'. What do you think these areas have in common?

...WORD CHECK

inequalities – the things that divide people such as money, housing and social class.

Look back to pages 233–234 and remind yourself of the way lifestyle choices and unexpected events can influence the health of an individual. Different groups of people from different backgrounds are affected in different ways by such factors. The government has tried to reduce these **inequalities** by campaigning in areas of the country that have above average levels of poor health. One way they

▲ Girls' lifestyles can put the next generation at risk.

did this was by launching 15 Health Action Zones in 1999. The aim of these zones was to reduce health inequalities between rich and poor. This was to be achieved by close **partnership** between all the care practitioners in the social care and health agencies. The zones were in both rural and inner city areas. Some of these zones are shown below:

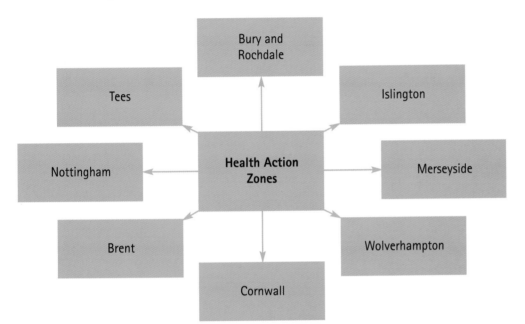

- Bury and Rochdale
- Tees
- Islington
- Nottingham
- **Health Action Zones**
- Merseyside
- Brent
- Wolverhampton
- Cornwall

> ✅ **...WORD CHECK**
>
> partnership – working together as a team and sharing ideas about care.

CASE STUDY   Lifestyle gurus

Another way the government has tried to promote and support health improvements is by the introduction of 'lifestyle gurus'. People who want to give up smoking, lose weight and live more healthy lives are given expert health advice funded by the NHS. Family doctors and other health services can refer patients to personal lifestyle coaches who will create fitness programmes for them. Fitness trainers and nutritionists are two care practitioners involved in this scheme. The health trainers will try to identify the possible barriers to individuals making healthy choices and help them to find solutions.

1. Do you think people will use these gurus?
2. Will they appeal to the least healthy in society?

CASE STUDY   County Durham

One example of health trainers at work is shown by the County Durham Primary Care Trust Health Trainers Programme. They work with people who want to improve their health but have little contact with the health services. The trainers meet with individuals to:

- talk about how they want to improve their health
- provide accurate information to help them decide the most appropriate course of action (empowerment)
- agree an action plan to achieve personal goals
- build confidence to make the changes they want to make.

1. In what ways might people in Durham benefit from this programme in terms of health?
2. What barriers might make the scheme less effective?

THE DIFFERENT WAYS HEALTH PROFESSIONALS CAN SUPPORT SERVICE USERS TO CHANGE THEIR LIFESTYLES IN ORDER TO IMPROVE HEALTH

Group Activity

Find out about the health promotion work of environmental health officers.

...WORD CHECK

monitor – to check up on something, such as an individual's progress after an operation.

Health professionals try to support service users in a number of ways in order to improve their health and lifestyle. Such care practitioners include:

- health visitors
- social workers
- doctors
- occupational therapists
- practice nurses
- school nurses
- community midwives
- environmental health officers.

Community midwives **monitor** and support expectant mothers pre and post-birth; in some cases carrying out home deliveries. A health visitor's primary role is to monitor child development from the first week of birth. They carry out regular assessment tests and advise on parenting. School nurses carry out screening of school-age children and support vaccination programmes. Occupational health nurses provide support on site for larger employers, which can include health-promoting activity, such as health check-ups and anti-smoking advice.

The care practitioners encourage healthy living through the following strategies:

Screening, to help individuals with a high risk of diseases such as breast cancer

Tertiary prevention, to control diseases such as Parkinson's and heart disease

Health education, giving advice about smoking, safe drinking and safe sex

Strategies used in health education and promotion

Primary prevention of illness, for example, immunization, cervical cancer injections for Year 8 girls

Secondary prevention in early stages of illness to reduce blood pressure and high cholesterol

Group Activity

Find out what your school/college nurse does with different age groups to promote and support healthy living.

Diet

Health professionals concentrate on trying to encourage individuals to change their lifestyle in a number of practical ways.

Eating the correct diet is a major aspect of health promotion. It is estimated that obesity could cost the NHS £6.3 billion by 2015 (Source: Department of Health 2008). The British Dietetic Association represents care practitioners who work with dietary problems amongst a wide range of service users.

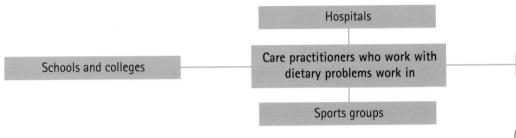

A range of care practitioners work with service users to try and promote healthier living. These include:

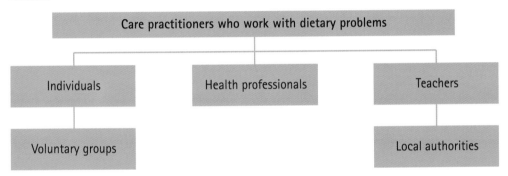

The problem with **obesity** is reaching such a high level that social services may have to **intervene** more and more and treat obese children as victims of 'parental neglect', in the same way as **malnourished** children. Also, social service practitioners are having to deal more and more with **housebound** people suffering from conditions caused by obesity, such as arthritis, heart disease and diabetes.

Group Activity

Carry out research into the work of the British Diabetic Association – a voluntary group campaigning on behalf of diabetics.

How could the work they do improve the health of individuals?

Regular exercise

One in three people are at risk of having a heart attack because they are failing to do enough exercise according to research carried out at Queen's University Belfast and Glasgow University.

CASE STUDY   Health promotion through exercise

'Trying to do 30 minutes of physical activity on most days of the week will have major health benefits' (Health Promotion Agency NI 2004).

Each year, the Department of Transport supports a 'Bike Week', which attracts over 250,000 participants in an attempt to make all age groups more active and fitter.

Improving physical fitness is one of the key challenges being tackled by St Xavier Catholic Primary School in Oldbury, Birmingham. They have successfully used less traditional pursuits like ballroom dancing.

A number of care workers encourage people to use stepometers to measure the amount of exercise they take each day. For most adults it is estimated that 7,500 to 10,000 steps per day are required to burn off the calories consumed by the average diet.

1   Which of the above schemes do you think is most effective? Why?

2   What other ideas might encourage people to take more exercise?

Supportive relationships

▲ Supportive relationships can improve health.

In addition to physical support, health professionals also feel it is important to help build supportive relationships as part of their health improvement work.

This is the **holistic** approach to care and is best shown by the government's launch of a scheme to support the most disadvantaged families in society in January 2008. The 'Think Family' report will try to ensure whole families are supported, not just individuals. This should lead to health improvements across generations and involve the P.I.E.S. aspect of care.

The plans for the scheme are:

- all services working together – joined-up thinking
- whole family support, for example, alcohol treatment would combine with parenting classes and supervised childcare
- to build on family strengths – empowering families to build good relationships.

It is, in fact, extending the 'Every Child Matters' idea to 'Every Family' so that 'Every Individual Matters'.

As society includes more divorce, more single-parent families and more people living on their own, the need for more support for relationships will increase. More and more people will be left on their own and not have the strong support that existed in the past.

Work

...WORD CHECK

holistic – looking at the whole (person).

status – a person's position within a society or organization.

sedentary – a lifestyle which is largely inactive.

Work is a very important part of a healthy life. Having a job which provides not just money but also **status** and self-esteem helps meet both intellectual and social needs. Many people find it very hard when they have to retire and for many their health begins to deteriorate after stopping work.

13 ▶ Why is a satisfying job so important and why does unemployment link to poorer health?

On the other hand, the workplace can be an unhealthy place. More and more people lead **sedentary** lives at work. Employers are being encouraged to promote the health of their employees. One example of this is the 'Working for Health' Scheme run by County Durham and Darlington. They award companies bronze, silver and gold awards if they provide a healthy work place. A gold award is awarded if a company has a three-year strategy and a one-year action plan that promotes health in at least one of the following areas:

- smoking
- alcohol/drugs
- healthy eating
- physical activity
- HIV/AIDS/sexual health
- stress/mental health
- dental/oral health.

The county provides a health promotion specialist to support companies in achieving the award.

Rest and sleep

There is a lot of research that shows the importance of rest and sleep for good health. Sleep deprivation is bad for individuals but the average night's sleep in the UK is now about 90 minutes less than it was in the 1920s when it was nine hours a night. Some interesting research by Dr Elizabeth Susman of Pennsylvania State University appeared to show that staying up late and lack of sleep are linked to anti-social behaviour amongst teenagers.

Stress

Health workers are reporting growing levels of stress in society and the link this has with physical illness. Stress is pressure that makes you feel tense, nervous, anxious or upset. Sometimes stress can be positive. Getting a little anxious before taking part in an important event, for example, an interview or a sporting event, can make you perform at a higher level. However, most stress is harmful and can have long-term effects. Your teachers often suffer high levels of stress because of the pressure they are under to produce good exam results.

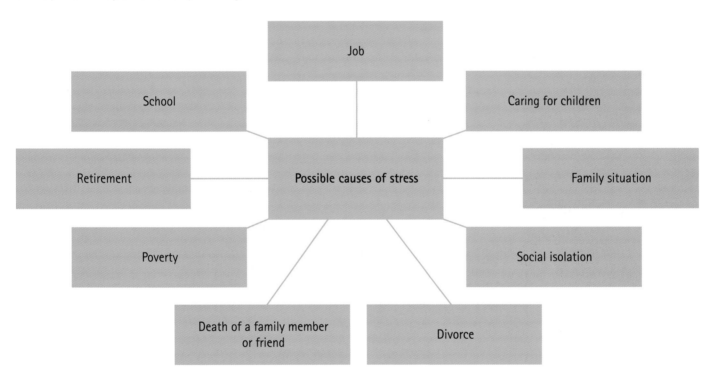

Over time, stress can lead to a range of serious emotional and physical health problems such as:

- depression
- alcoholism
- substance abuse
- heart disease
- cancer
- hypertension.

Care practitioners try to encourage service users to reduce the risks of stress through some of these health promotion strategies:

- knowing the warning signs of stress
- trying to find out what the real cause of the stress is
- eating a healthy diet
- drinking plenty of water
- practising relaxation exercises
- taking regular physical activity
- expressing feelings
- considering taking a stress management course.

14 Why do you think there seem to be higher levels of stress in society today?

15 When do you feel under stress? Share your views with the rest of the group.

Recreational activities

▲ Rebecca Adlington's success at the 2008 Olympics might inspire young people to take up swimming.

There is growing concern amongst health practitioners about the lack of involvement in recreational activities by young people today. More and more young people spend long periods in front of a computer or television. British children aged 11–15 now spend 55 per cent of their waking lives in front of televisions and computers. Health practitioners hope that the fantastic successes by Team GB at the 2008 Olympic Games will lead to more young people taking up activities such as swimming and cycling. This should also be helped by the fact that the 2012 Olympics are being held in London.

Health promotion in Ealing, London, tries a number of strategies to develop recreational activities. These include:

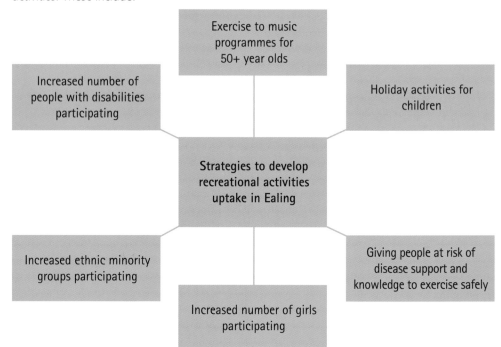

Financial resources

Financial resources available both for the individual and health practitioners influence the opportunities for overall health improvement.

The 'postcode lottery' refers to the big variations in health care in different parts of the country. You may get better health care depending upon where you live. This includes health promotion aspects such as:

- waiting times for NHS treatment
- access to cancer screening programmes
- availability of the multiple sclerosis drug
- assessment of children on social services 'at risk' registers.

Oral health promotion is also suffering as a result of the decline in NHS dentists. There is some evidence that many patients now go without treatment or even try pulling their own teeth out. Of those questioned in a survey, 19 per cent said that they had missed out on dental work they needed because of cost (research by England's Patient and Public Involvement Forum, 2007). This is particularly worrying as a lot of dental work helps to detect early signs of other potential illnesses. There is one dentist for every 5000 people in some parts of Britain!

HOW THESE FACTORS CAN INFLUENCE HEALTH IN BOTH POSITIVE AND NEGATIVE WAYS

The above factors can influence health in both a positive way (health improvement, increased **longevity**, reduced **morbidity rates**) or negative way (increase in sickness rates, premature deaths, poor mental health).

Greater health awareness has clearly led to overall improvements in health, even if this improvement is not at the same rate for all social groups. Improvements in hygiene, water supplies and immunization, along with the introduction of the NHS and Welfare State, have all contributed to health improvements in a number of areas. The Health Profile of England 2007 showed improvements in:

- declining mortality rates in cancers, circulatory diseases and suicides
- increasing life expectancy
- reducing infant mortality.

...WORD CHECK

longevity – the average number of years a person can be expected to live; life expectancy.

morbidity rates – the rates of illness in a population which often vary between different social groups.

infant mortality – the number of deaths of infants under one year of age per thousand live births.

Life expectancy (longevity) has improved dramatically in recent years, partly as a result of health-improvement programmes.

Table of life expectancy at birth: England

1901: Boys 45 Girls 49
1941: Boys 59 Girls 63
1971: Boys 69 Girls 71
2004: Boys 77 Girls 81
2021: Boys 79 Girls 83

(Source: Office for National Statistics)

It is interesting that the biggest increase in life expectancy happened before many of the health promotion schemes were started. This was because of general improvements in hygiene and health awareness.

The present health promotion programmes need to target the wide gap in life expectancies between the rich and poor in Britain. Official statistics suggest that your teacher is likely to live over six years longer than the person who collects your rubbish each week. Middle-class men could expect to live to 80 years of age by 2005, compared to working-class men's life expectancy of 74. In the poorest parts of Glasgow, men can only 'expect' to live to 63 years of age.

16 What might be the possible reasons for this different life expectancy?

One real success of some health promotion campaigns is the reduction in morbidity rates (the amount of disease in the population). This can be shown by the 45 per cent decline in lung cancer amongst men in the last 25 years. This must be linked to the many smoking-related campaigns involving warnings on cigarette packets, and the banning of cigarette adverts on television and of sponsorship of major sports events such as snooker. The law passed in 2007 banning smoking in all public places will probably reduce smoking-related cancers even further.

▲ Smoking is now banned in all public places.

A second area where health promotion has helped to lead to significant health improvements is circulatory-related illnesses, which remains the most common cause of death in Britain. The biggest improvement is amongst male deaths.

Other areas of improvement include:

- children getting measles
- children contracting rubella
- deaths from suicide.

17 Why do you think the number of children suffering from measles and rubella has fallen in the last 40 years but recently we have seen a slight increase in the number of children with measles?

18 Why has there been a recent increase in children getting mumps? (Think about vaccination programmes.)

The negative impact of lifestyle on health can be seen by the growing concerns about:

- obesity
- alcohol-related illnesses
- skin cancers
- diabetes
- sexually transmitted infections
- poor mental health.

HEALTH PROMOTION

Many of the current health promotion campaigns target the areas shown below:

All campaigns try to increase our understanding of the potential problems that could occur if we do not change our behaviour. This can be seen through the Health Promotion Agency in Northern Ireland. Their main aim is to 'make health a top priority for all people in Northern Ireland'. One of the areas they have tried to raise awareness in is sexual health amongst 16–25 year olds by showing the risks of sexually transmitted infections such as chlamydia, HIV and AIDS. They also want to raise awareness of the risks and consequences of unplanned pregnancy.

Campaigns must also concentrate upon preventing ill health in the first place. SunSmart, the UK's national skin cancer prevention campaign, sends out the following message:

> Spend time in the shade between 11:00am and 3:00pm
> Make sure to never burn
> Aim to cover up with a tee shirt and sunglasses
> Remember to take extra care with children
> Then use factor 15+ suncream

They also recommend that people should check moles on the skin and take extra care when using sunbeds.

The five portions of fruit and vegetables a day campaign aims to prevent many consequences resulting from a poor diet.

CASE STUDY **Wayne Rooney**

Improvements in fitness levels, resulting in longer life expectancy, are inevitable aims of health campaigns. A DVD produced in 2005 involves Wayne Rooney and his teammates targeting growing levels of obesity amongst children in Manchester. They swap football for cycling, basketball and even yoga in an attempt to get children to take more exercise. In addition, schools were given advice on how to build exercise into their lessons.

 In groups, discuss whether you think Rooney's message can help turn the tide of obesity.

Cancer Research UK campaign for people to take more exercise. They argue that keeping active can prevent 9000 cases of cancer each year. Just 30 minutes of moderate activity a day, five days a week, can have a positive effect on a person's health.

Organizations working in health promotion have to decide what approaches they should use to encourage people to adopt healthier lifestyles. The use of celebrities is widespread, as already shown. Young men may be influenced by role models such as footballers. Portsmouth footballer, John Utaka, backed a major police campaign against booze-fuelled violence and its consequences. He unveiled a banner 'How much is too much?' at a home Premier League match.

Other organizations have used a longer campaign, such as breast cancer awareness 'Wear it pink'.

CASE STUDY   Breast cancer awareness

Some of the awareness and fund-raising ideas suggested by the 'Wear it pink' campaign include:

- have a pink dress day at work where everyone pays £1 to wear something pink
- organize a girls' night in at home with pink food, pink drink and so on
- organize a pink quiz.

  1   Find out more about the breast cancer care campaigns.

  2   Do you think this is a good way to make women more aware of breast cancer?

A very different approach to health campaigning is the use of shock tactics.

CASE STUDY   Shock tactics

In 2005 the British Heart Foundation produced posters featuring the gristle and bone found in fast food, such as burgers and chicken nuggets. The full gory detail of what some fast food manufacturers put in their products is censored in the posters but children could see the full detail on the charity's website. Similar tactics have been used in the government's campaign on binge drinking. Adverts show young people deliberately injuring themselves and smearing vomit in their hair. 'You wouldn't start a night like this, so why end it that way?' is the message, designed to show the consequences of drinking too much.

  1   Discuss, in groups, whether you think shock tactics are likely to work?

  2   What other campaigns could use similar approaches?

Health professionals work with individuals to support them in trying to change their behaviour and make them healthier. This will start with the diagnosis of the person's health.

As part of health improvement, the government runs Well Women and Well Men clinics. The idea of these is to try and have an early diagnosis of possible health problems by:

- checking weight and body mass index
- checking cholesterol levels
- checking blood pressure.

▲ Getting an MOT of your health.

Such diagnosis might pick up early signs of various cancers and heart disease, and if detected the health professionals can offer advice about the lifestyle changes that are needed.

Monitoring progress is then required. This can be achieved by regular visits to a GP or using modern technology as an alternative. Italian researchers have developed short questionnaires that can be sent to patients' mobile phones and completed using their phone keypad. The questions ask people to rate symptoms such as weight loss, shortness of breath and sleep loss. The results are gathered and presented on a secure web page which gives the doctors a quick overview of how their symptoms are progressing. Any serious change in symptoms causes a flashing light to appear by their name to help doctors prioritize those in most need of help.

...WORD CHECK

monitoring – to check up on something such as an individual's progress after an operation.

19 What do you think are the advantages and disadvantages of this system?

It is important that targets are set so that health improvements can be evaluated in terms of how successful they have been. Most of us work better if we set a realistic target, for example, what exam grades we think we should achieve.

The NHS Cancer Plan drawn up in 2000 proposed that by 2005 no patient would wait longer than 62 days for urgent GP referral to first treatment or longer than 31 days from diagnosis to first treatment. By 2006, 93 per cent of patients were treated within the 31-day target and 76 per cent within the 62-day target. Without these targets we would be unable to measure the success of the government's health programme.

The government has had to abandon its target to halt childhood obesity by 2010; instead it has now set a target of reducing it by 2020.

 20 Why do you think it seems so difficult to tackle childhood obesity?

...WORD CHECK

legislation – laws passed by Parliament which become acts, for example, the Children Act.

HOW HEALTH PROMOTION AND SUPPORT FOR HEALTH IMPROVEMENT IS BUILT UPON BY THE CAREFUL IMPLEMENTATION OF CARE VALUES

All health improvement campaigns must avoid trying to make people change their lifestyles but concentrate upon using the care values as the basis for change. Most of us do not like being told what to do – we need to be persuaded that it is in our interests to make the necessary changes to our way of life. Telling a young person not to smoke is likely to make them want to try cigarettes. Pointing out how much smoking costs and the anti-social aspect of smoking alongside the health risks might make the young person think twice about starting to smoke.

It is important to remember what the care values are and how they affect the way care practitioners work. When trying to promote healthy living and make improvements to people's lives, health workers must follow the guidelines of the care values. They cannot impose what they think is the right way to live, without considering the individual's own circumstances and values.

Group Activity

Look back at the care values on page 243. Remind yourself of what they are and how they influence the way care practitioners work with service users.

Promotion of choice

People need to be encouraged to make healthy choices. This can be done by taxation and **legislation**. Increasing the tax on cigarettes might help people choose a healthier lifestyle, as might the recent law on banning smoking in public places. Better food labelling would help us make informed choices about the food we eat. Educating young people about sexual health should help them choose a safe sex lifestyle. If a person chooses to take drugs, smoke and drink excessively, the decision should be one based upon information not ignorance. In the same way, no teenage girl should choose to become pregnant because of poor health promotion.

Group Activity

Find out about the health curriculum in your school.

Respecting identity and culture

...WORD CHECK

advocacy – procedure where a person can speak or act on a service user's behalf.

Group Activity

Research into Makaton and braille.

Health promotion must also respect identity and culture. One obvious way is to ensure that health information is available in a number of different languages and in formats needed by people who have eyesight or hearing problems.

Many Asian women would prefer to get the support they need to improve their health from female care workers and, if the campaign is to be effective, this option needs to be in place.

When promoting safe sex, it must be recognized that the targeted group is likely to contain people with a range of values. Sex education involving discussions on contraception and abortion would need to be handled differently in Catholic schools compared with non-Catholic schools.

21 Why is this?

▲ Some Asian women may prefer to get support from female care workers.

People with language difficulties will require extra help and a form of **advocacy** may be required.

Empowerment

When deciding what is best for a person's health, care practitioners must avoid making all the decisions and telling the service user what is best for them. The individual should be allowed to choose freely for themselves based upon accurate and unbiased information. Care practitioners should try to avoid making judgements about the lifestyles of the individuals they work with. They should not compare their own lifestyle with that of the service user.

CASE STUDY — Susan and Demmi

Susan is a midwife and she is meeting Demmi, who is eight weeks pregnant. Demmi has been smoking for five years and is continuing to do so. Susan discusses the potential damage to the unborn child with Demmi and further health damage to herself if she continues to smoke during pregnancy and after birth. However, Susan must respect Demmi's right to choose whether to continue smoking, and not allow this decision (should she continue smoking) to affect or change their relationship.

1 In what ways is Susan empowering Demmi?

Promoting independence

Effective health promotion must try to give individuals the confidence to feel able to look after themselves instead of expecting health professionals to look after them. In the long term, encouraging self-help in individuals will benefit them more than improving medical treatment will. More people will improve their own health by giving up smoking than will ever be helped by the medical profession once they have become ill with a smoking-related disorder, such as lung cancer or emphysema. Individuals need to be motivated to improve their health. This means that they want to make the necessary changes and improvements to their lifestyle and are prepared to put up with short-term difficulties for long-term gain.

Respecting individual right to choice

This can cause difficulties for some individuals. When promoting health care, practitioners must recognize that service users have a choice as to whether to accept the advice or not. However, individuals must also recognize that no one has the right to damage the quality of other people's lives. This problem can be highlighted through the issue of passive smoking. Despite all the health campaigns on smoking, millions of people continue to smoke. This is their choice. However, they must also respect the choice of other people not to smoke. Only recently has the government banned smoking in public places, thus giving non-smokers the right not to inhale other individuals' smoke.

Group Activity

In small groups, develop a health promotion campaign to improve the level of exercise done by older people. Present your campaign to other groups.

1. Choose an appropriate logo/message.
2. Decide the most appropriate methods that you could use and explain why you think they would work.
3. Which health professionals would you use?
4. How could these professionals support older people to take more exercise and at the same time implement the care values?
5. How would you evaluate the success of the campaign?

▶ ▶ ▶ ▶ ASSESSMENT PRACTICE

Martin, aged 54, lives on his own and works in IT for a local engineering company. His body mass index indicates that he is obese and this is clearly linked to an unhealthy lifestyle. As he lives alone, he tends not to cook meals but relies on takeaway and frozen foods. He drives the short distance to his work. He tends to go out most evenings to his local pub and he never keeps a tally of his alcohol intake.

1. Identify **two** of Martin's health needs. [2]
2. Describe **two** aspects of Martin's lifestyle that might affect his well-being. [6]
3. Describe **two** ways that health practitioners could help Martin adopt a healthier lifestyle. [6]
4. Explain how these care workers could use the care values to ensure Martin is receiving appropriate help to adopt a healthy lifestyle. [8]

The Right Honourable Sir Alan Johnson, the Health Secretary, raised the prospect of life expectancy falling for the first time in hundreds of years unless young people begin to eat healthier diets. They also run the risk of developing diabetes and heart trouble, with increased numbers likely to experience ill health for far longer than previous generations. One in three children under the age of 16 is considered to be overweight or obese.

5. Identify **four** aims of a health promotion campaign designed to reduce obesity in children. [4]
6. Describe what the government could do to tackle this problem. How could it promote a healthier diet for children? [8]
7. Describe **two** ways that health professionals can support children to lead a healthier lifestyle. [6]
8. Discuss the potential factors that might stop the government achieving its aim of reducing obesity. [10]

Appendix 1 – Calorie counter

Food	Measure	Calories	Food	Measure	Calories
All bran	1/3 cup	113	Dried apricots	5–6	80
Almonds	25–30	170	Eggs (large)	67g	100
Apple (medium)	1	65	Fanta	375ml	195
Apricots (medium)	1	15	Fillet steak	100g	196
Asparagus spears (medium)	3	10	Fish (white fish, low fat)	100g	100
Bacon (grilled)	1 rasher	112	Flake	30g	177
Baked beans	220g	205	Grapefruit (medium)	1/2	20
Banana (medium)	1	87	Grapes (medium)	125g	125
Banana chips	1/4 cup	155	Hazelnuts	30g	185
Bean sprouts	100g	30	Ice cream single flavour	1 scoop	90
Beans	1/2	13	Kit Kat	2 wafers	104
Biscuit (chocolate)	1	98	Kiwifruit (medium)	1	40
Biscuit (chocolate chip cookie)	1	35	Leg of roast lamb	2 slices	170
Biscuit (ginger nut)	1	42	Lemon	1	23
Bread (wholemeal)	1 slice	62	Lemonade	375ml	160
Bread (white plain)	1 slice	66	Lentils (cooked)	100g	260
Broccoli	2 florets	11	Lettuce	3 leaves	2
Butter	1 tsp	36	M&Ms	1 pkt	238
Cabbage	1/2	7	Mango	1	102
Carrots	1 small	23	Margarine	1 tsp	36
Cashews	12–16	180	Mars bar	60g	265
Cauliflower	1/2 cup	20	Melon (medium)	1/2	135
Cheese	30g	120	Milk (full cream)	1 cup	167
Chicken (roasted breast)	100g	110	Milk (skim)	1 cup	88
Chicken (leg/thigh)	100g	210	Milk (soy)	1 cup	160
Chocolate (plain/nuts/fruit)	5–6 rows	160	Mince (beef)	100g	210
Cola	375ml can	154	Mushrooms	1/2 cup	15
Coco pops	3/4 cup	115	Oil (vegetable)	1 tbsp	176
Corn flakes	1 and 1/3 cups	113	Onions	medium	30
Corned beef	100g	210	Oranges (medium)	1	80
Cream soda	375ml	170	Peach	1	40
Crunchie	80g	413	Peanuts (raw)	30g	120
Cucumber	150g	12	Pear	1	69
Dates	4–5	83	Peas	1/4 cup	20
Diet coke/Pepsi	375ml can	1.5	Picnic	55g	290
Dr Pepper	375ml	157	Pineapple	1 slice	33
Dried apple rings	10 rings	75	Plums	1	33

Continued on next page

Food	Measure	Calories	Food	Measure	Calories
Potatoes	medium	105	Sultanas	2 tbsp	92
Prunes (moist)	2–3	70	T-bone steak	100g	135
Rice (white, cooked)	1/2 cup	92	Tomato (medium)	1	20
Rice (brown, cooked)	1/2 cup	93	Tonic water	375	135
Rump steak	100g	190	Walnuts	15–20	185
Shredded Wheat	1/2 cup	240	Yogurt (flavoured)	200g	190
Smarties	25g	116	Yogurt (low fat)	200g	120
Snickers	60g	283	Yogurt (natural)	200g	160
Strawberries (medium)	6	10			

Appendix 2 – Exercise planner (for a person weighing 160 pounds)

Activity	Exercise time	Calories used	Activity	Exercise time	Calories used
Aerobics	30	214	Playing piano	30	89
Basketball	30	286	Reading	30	64
Biking (leisurely)	30	214	Riding	30	143
Boating	30	89	Rock climbing	30	393
Bowling	30	107	Running (5mph)	30	286
Canoeing	30	143	Running on the spot	30	286
Cooking	30	89	Running up stairs	30	537
Cross country	30	322	Shopping	30	82
Dancing	30	161	Skiing	30	250
Driving	30	71	Sleeping	30	32
Exercise bike	30	214	Squash	30	358
Fishing	30	143	Swimming	30	286
Football	30	250	Talking on the phone	30	35
Gardening	30	179	Tennis	30	250
Golf	30	161	Volleyball	30	107
Hiking	30	214	Walking (4mph)	30	125
House cleaning	30	89	Watching TV	30	35
Jogging	30	250	Weightlifting	30	107
Mountain biking	30	125	Writing	30	35
Playing guitar	30	107	Yoga	30	143

Index